AKWESASNE NOTES is an international newspaper by, for, and about native peoples. It is published by a multi-media communications group from the Mohawk Nation at Akwesasne, via Rooseveltown, N.Y. 13683.

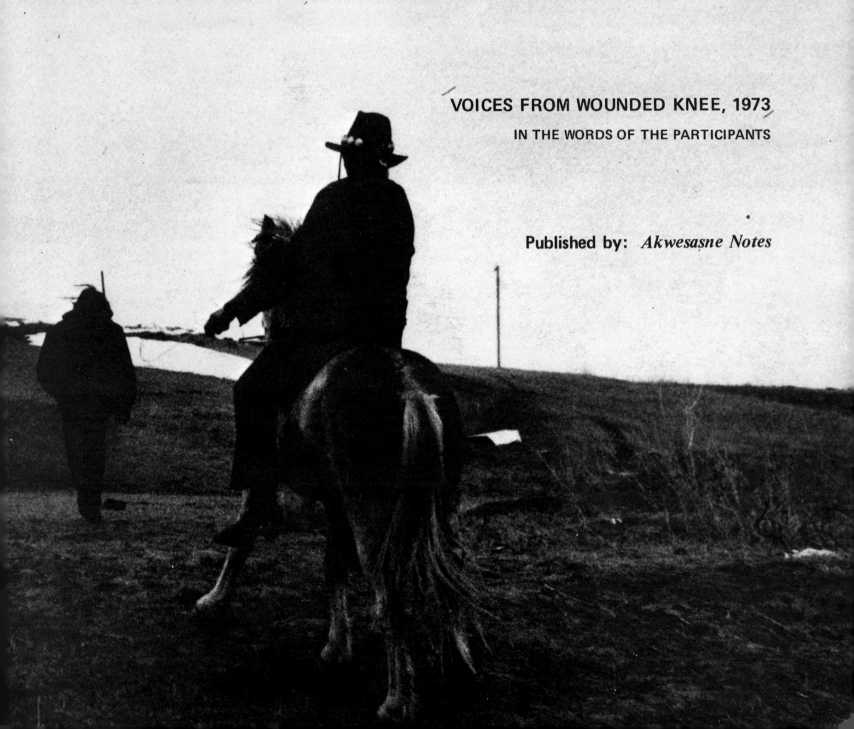

VOICES FROM WOUNDED KNEE, 1973

IN THE WORDS OF THE PARTICIPANTS

Published by: *Akwesasne Notes*

AKWESASNE NOTES is grateful to all the people who helped to make this book possible. To those who transcribed tapes, printed photographs, and gave of their time to proofread, criticize, and sustain us along the way, we give thanks.

We thank the people from *The Rest of the News* and *Unicorn News* and the others who worked in the Wounded Knee Information Collective — who recorded and distributed audio material throughout the siege. Four of them transcribed the tape recordings, edited them, set the type, and did the design and layout for the book.

We thank the many photographers who sent us their fine work to be included in this book.

Most of all, thanks to the many people who are in this book. We hope you like it.

Third Printing: June, 1975

Glad Day Press
UNION SHOP · I.U. 450
308 Stewart Ave., Ithaca, N.Y. 14850

THIS BOOK IS DEDICATED TO
FRANK CLEARWATER, BUDDY LAMONT, PEDRO BISSONETTE,
AND ALL THE OTHERS WHO GAVE THEIR LIVES IN THE STRUGGLE

CONTENTS

PUBLISHER'S INTRODUCTION

Likely in most "American History" books, one of the largest uprisings against the Government of the United States on its own turf will be briefly mentioned in an inconsequential paragraph. The occupation of Wounded Knee/1973 is important history, not only for native peoples, but for all who care about this land and life — yet even now few people know why it happened, or even what happened there.

The problem is that Wounded Knee doesn't seem to fit what United States people have been taught about Indians — how in the late 1800s they were finally subdued, how happy they are on the reservations, how successfully they are integrating into American life. Wounded Knee doesn't fit the taught concepts of how democracy was brought to this land under the Bill of Rights, how people obtain perfect justice in the courts, how benevolent government agencies are to Indians. Wounded Knee, people say, must be a bad dream — probably done by "bad Indians," influenced by "outside agitators," and unrepresentative of "responsible native people."

These distortions of history are not accidental. The people of the United States, by and large, would rule strongly in favor of native demands at Wounded Knee if they could only find out what happened there. But with the press and television personnel moving along to bigger and better and more violent headlines, with the U.S. Government managing the news emerging from the Pine Ridge Reservation, and with even the reports on the resulting trials of the participants absent from the media, the people of the United States will not have the information on which to base an intelligent judgment.

That's why this book is so important. It tells the story by the participants themselves. It contains just what the U.S. representatives said in the negotiations. And gradually, the human drama of a suppressed and oppressed people getting themselves together to restore some dignity to their lives emerges.

It is unfortunate that of the hundreds of millions of people in North America, there are so few who are willing to dedicate their lives to something they believe strongly about. Those who occupied Wounded Knee bet their lives that there would be change — and that the change would restore to them their humanity — and would restore humanity to the United States of America at the same time.

AKWESASNE NOTES is proud to publish this book. The courageous persons of the alternate media who collected the tapes and photos and who have edited this book have spent a year of their lives on the tedious details of writing, typing, snipping, measuring, pasting to make it possible. It is accurate and honest.

We hope it will be carefully studied and understood. We hope it will be seen as American History, not as a document for those who "like to read about Indians." But most of all, we hope that those who read it will somehow catch the spirit of those who put their lives on the line. We hope readers will become a part of the growing movement that Wounded Knee/1973 brought back to life — a struggle to ensure that our unborn generations will have a good life on the land which our Creator has given to us.

— AKWESASNE NOTES

EDITORS' INTRODUCTION

In the winter of 1890, U.S. Government forces massacred nearly 300 Indian people, mainly women and children, after they had surrendered all but one of their weapons. The site of the massacre was Wounded Knee on the Pine Ridge Reservation. In the winter of 1973, several hundred Oglala Sioux and their supporters from other tribes returned to Wounded Knee to make a stand. They did so at the request of the Oglala traditional leaders, after all other means of changing conditions on the reservation had been exhausted.

This stand on Indian land for Indian rights was met by the U.S. Government with armored personnel carriers, helicopters, automatic rifles, and other Viet Nam era weapons. But for 71 days no Federal law enforcement personnel or Bureau of Indian Affairs officials had any authority in Wounded Knee. For 71 days, through countless battles and negotiating sessions, and despite the Government's blockade of food, fuel, and medical supplies, a self-governing community was built.

This book is a documentary about the occupation. It came out of our own experiences at and around Wounded Knee, as part of an alternative media collective set up at the time. The story is told mainly in the words of the participants, both Indian and U.S. Government.

We, like many other people in the country, were moved by the armed takeover of Wounded Knee, by the strength of the people we saw on our televisions, and by the risks they were taking. We felt immediately that Wounded Knee was important. The U.S. Government's military response to a grass-roots stand for justice, seemed to repeat the lessons of Viet Nam, and to bring back to light the long history of U.S. mistreatment of Indian people. All of us were involved in the anti-war movement; one of us is a Vietnam veteran. Our work in alternative media is an outgrowth of that experience. As with Viet Nam, we felt that our Government should not be permitted to secretely conduct an undeclared war.

Two of us had been working with *The Rest of the News,* an alternative radio network in Ithaca, N.Y. We found it im-

possible to get first-hand reports for our programs, so we finally went to South Dakota ourselves. The other two of us also made our way there from New Mexico and Chicago, one to do support work and one to cover the confrontation for a newspaper. In South Dakota we joined others in an information collective which continued throughout the occupation to provide news for anyone who wanted it, including 80 radio stations and various newspapers across the country. Most of the information was distributed through *The Rest of the News* on the East Coast and *Unicorn News* based in San Francisco.

When we arrived in South Dakota in mid-March, the Government was allowing some of the press into the village after thorough FBI checks. But within several days, the press was restricted and finally barred altogether from Wounded Knee. We stayed. After the press pulled out an assault became more possible than ever, and we felt that it was important that lines of communication be kept open between the people inside and their supporters around the country.

We spent much of our time talking at length with the people who had made Wounded Knee happen — the local grassroots leaders, the people involved in the running of the community, and the American Indian Movement spokesmen. People wanted to talk. They felt, as we did, that what was happening had an historic significance and a depth to it far beyond what could be conveyed on a three-minute news blip.

It turned out that instead of attempting to retake the village by a military assault, the Government tried the old tactics of siege warfare, trying to starve the people into negotiating a surrender while keeping up the pressure by continually shooting into the village from the surrounding hills. The siege dragged on, as supporters brought food in at night over the hills, and meals were cut down to one a day.

Three of us were inside until the end, participating in the community as well as doing our work of sending tapes out to the media collective in Rapid City, where our fourth member worked. One of us was "processed" out through Government

lines on the last day with the rest of the people. Two of us hiked out just before the end, were arrested by U.S. marshals, and spent two days in Pine Ridge jail.

When we left South Dakota in June, 1973, we had a wealth of tape recordings of people talking, meetings, negotiations, battles, and press conferences. We had made several long programs for radio, and began thinking of other ways to reach people. Over the summer the people at *Akwesasne Notes* suggested the tapes be made into a book, and offered to publish it. We liked the idea of publishing with *Notes* because we believe it is important to build alternatives to the mass media, and because this way any profits could remain with the Indian movement, instead of large publishers. All profits from this book return to *Akwesasne Notes,* and to the Wounded Knee Legal Defense/Offense Committee.

So in October, 1973, we began the long process of transcribing tapes, editing, and writing narratives. In a sense this book put itself together, as interviews fell into place to make a complete story. We have tried to be accurate with our facts, checking and rechecking dates and events, though these are not the most important aspect of the book. More important to the accuracy of the book is that everything besides our narratives were taken directly from taped conversations made at the time, recordings of actual events, or documents. We have tried, as much as possible, to let the people and the events speak for themselves.

— The Editorial Collective

OGLALA INTRODUCTION — statement made at the signing of the May 5 agreement by Vern Long, president of the Oglala Sioux Civil Rights Organization.

Right from the beginning
a dictator took over our reservation —
pushed us traditional Indians to one side
and took over our reservation.
No laws to protect us
couldn't turn to nobody.
We tried everything
we've made complaints
gone to court
instead they throw us in jail.
They turn around when we walk out
and put some kind of trumped up charge on us.

So the ones that start out fighting,
they got the goon squad out intimidating.
The ones that are really fighting
get shot at — so they quiet down.
So trying to figure out a way to fight them back
we organized this Interdistrict Council
of which Eugene White Hawk is President.

And they start in petitioning
to get Dick Wilson out.
But he's pretty well organized —
all opposed to him, he knows which ones to pick on.
They're scared to sign the petition.
We tried everything.

Then we formed the Civil Rights Organization —
maybe we can stand on that.
So they made me a President out of that deal,
and Pedro a Vice-President.
We started having meetings, standing on our civil rights.
We start in at first — just meeting —
in three, four days, we got the *people* together
and they decide what to do
to get our reservation back.
Some of them — their homes burned down
they couldn't do nothing
they couldn't get loans
nothing.

Who's helping us?
Chief Fools Crow, from the beginning
he was with us.

They decide to abolish the Tribal Constitution,
the Tribal Government,
cause it's not helping us, from the beginning.

I was born about that time
when the Tribal Government started.
I don't know too much back in the treaty days.
But from history, the way I heard,
people were alive
the real Oglala Sioux
they got something to live for.
But since this New Deal started
they're going down
losing our land
white ranchers coming on this reservation
and us Indians – pushed out.
And there was no enrollment up to that time, 1935.
From then on, people just coming in registered –
groups that relinquished their rights
they didn't want to be Indians no more.
Them's the ones that's coming back in,
just registering. Taking over.
They know what they done.
But us fullbloods own this land.
They worked us over
with the help of the BIA and
the United States Government.
They want to get rid of us –
slow death,
our land,
losing everything.

We're not benefitting by the Tribal Council.
Then Dick Wilson got to be Tribal President.
That's the worst Tribal Council I ever seen.
He got in with this bunch
and they took over our reservation.
Money coming in from Washington,
we don't know – no treasury report.
They only had three meetings.
So we had a meeting in Calico,
decided to abolish that Tribal Constitution,
get away from BIA

and go back to the 1868 Treaty.
And the ones that came – four, five hundred – they agreed.
We had to get attention from the United States,
cause we tried everything.

Then this Wounded Knee started up
and we knew there were going to be some lives sacrificed
in order to get attention from the President.
So that's what's happened.
True warriors were sacrificed.
And it hurt my heart.
Yet I know
we are all fighting for our treaty rights.
This is not ordinary politics,
running for office –
This is something else,
that we're fighting the United States Government.

Today, everybody knows why
Wounded Knee –
and they're all facing this way every day.
They want to help.
I hope all our problems are solved
with the help of our brothers and sisters
across the United States and Canada.
Things have turned over and
Wilson's all by himself
today.

1. THE HISTORY

"One does not sell the earth upon which the people walk."
— Tashunka Witko (Crazy Horse)

BRIEF HISTORICAL INTRODUCTION

The Oglala Sioux of the Pine Ridge Reservation are one of the seven bands of the Teton Sioux, who, in turn, are one of the seven divisions of the Sioux nation which at one time made its home on the great northern plains. In their language the Sioux call themselves the *Ocheti Shakoy,* the Seven Council Fires.

In the mid-nineteenth century the craving for gold and western homesteads led European Americans in great numbers with their wagon trains, railroads, and cavalry along the Bozeman Trail through the heart of the plains Indians' lands. The Sioux, along with their neighbors the Cheyenne and Arapaho, fought the invaders. At first their close touch with the land was a strength and they beat the U.S. cavalry time after time. Eventually the U.S. suffered defeat and sued for peace in 1866. Finally a treaty was signed at Fort Laramie in 1868 between the Sioux and the U.S. Government, with each nation speaking as equals. In the treaty the U.S. agreed to abandon its forts along the Bozeman Trail and to close the trail permanently; the Indians for the first time agreed to boundaries on their lands. The treaty provided for an "unceded Indian territory" from which whites were to be excluded, stretching from the Missouri River west through the Powder River hunting grounds into the Big Horn Mountains in Wyoming, and from the Canadian border south into Nebraska. The treaty designated part of this territory, the western half of what later became South Dakota, and a bit of North Dakota,

to be the "Great Sioux Reservation." Although not stated in the treaty, it was intended by the Government that the Sioux would come into the reservation from the hunting grounds during the winter months. As the years went on, the Government attempted to confine the Sioux to the reservation areas.

But the settlers and fortune hunters kept coming. In 1874 General Custer led an expedition which confirmed that there was gold in the Black Hills, the heart of the reservation and sacred land of the Sioux. The U.S. Government sent a delegation west with authority to buy the mountains. But for the Indians, the earth is the Mother and is not owned, much less bought or sold. Crazy Horse, a leader of the Oglalas, and Sitting Bull, a Hunkpapa Sioux, refused to even attend the council. More than twenty thousand Sioux, Arapaho, and Cheyenne came to advise their chiefs who did meet the commission. The U.S. delegation's offer was refused, and they returned to Washington.

The Government then claimed the Black Hills and the "unceded Indian territory," in violation of the 1868 Treaty, which required approval by three-quarters of the adult Sioux males for any changes to be made in the document. Later, in the winter of 1875-76, the Secretary of Interior issued an ultimatum that any Sioux found off the now reduced reservation would be considered "hostile," and the Army was sent to force them into the agencies. That summer, the Sioux, Cheyenne, and Arapaho gathered for their yearly Sun Dance in the Big Horn Mountains, in what is said to have been the largest gathering of native people ever to take place. There, Sitting Bull, the Hunkpapa Sioux medicine man, had a vision. He heard a voice saying, "I give you these because they have no ears." When he looked at the sun, he saw soldiers falling like grasshoppers into his camp. Soon after that, the 7th Cavalry, under Custer, came upon the great camp. It was then that Sitting Bull's vision was fulfilled and Custer met his famous defeat. After the battles that summer, the Indians broke camp and moved on, hoping to avoid any more fighting.

But the people from the east kept coming and coming. Hunters and sportsmen rode west on the new railroads and slaughtered the buffalo with their new repeating rifles — often leaving the hides and meat to rot on the prairie. By 1883, the great herds that 30 years earlier had numbered 40 million were gone. At the same time, Christian missionaries were flocking to the agencies to erect churches and schools, to teach their culture to the native people. Many sacred Indian ceremonies, such as the Sun Dance and the sweat

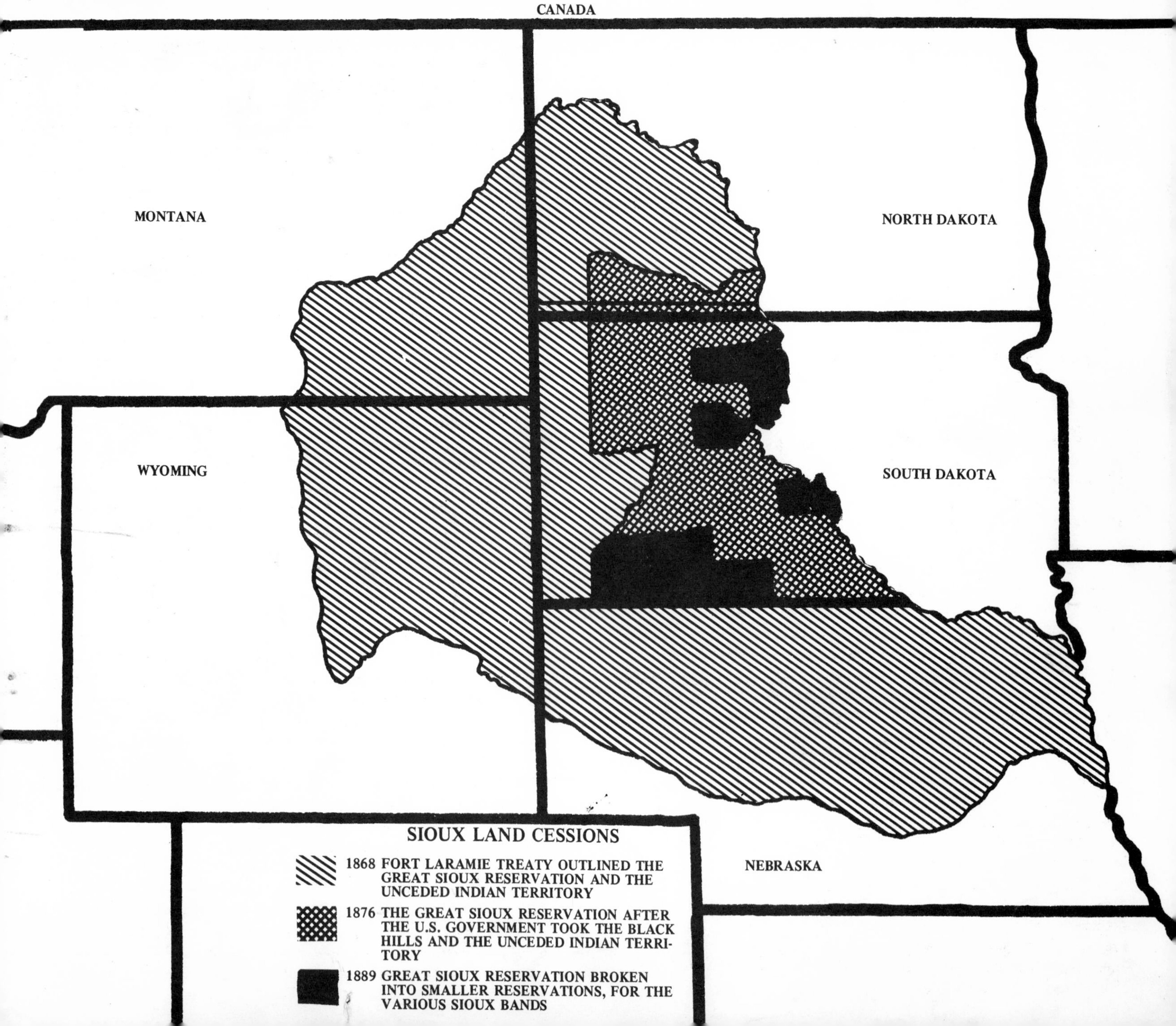

CANADA

MONTANA

NORTH DAKOTA

WYOMING

SOUTH DAKOTA

NEBRASKA

SIOUX LAND CESSIONS

1868 FORT LARAMIE TREATY OUTLINED THE GREAT SIOUX RESERVATION AND THE UNCEDED INDIAN TERRITORY

1876 THE GREAT SIOUX RESERVATION AFTER THE U.S. GOVERNMENT TOOK THE BLACK HILLS AND THE UNCEDED INDIAN TERRITORY

1889 GREAT SIOUX RESERVATION BROKEN INTO SMALLER RESERVATIONS, FOR THE VARIOUS SIOUX BANDS

Photo above: massacre site in Wounded Knee, during the occupation.

"The Indian must conform to the white man's ways, peaceably if they will, forcibly if they must. This civilization may not be the best possible, but it is the best the Indians can get. They can not escape and must either conform to it or be crushed by it."
— Report of the Commissioner on Indian Affairs, Department of the Interior
58th Annual Report, October 1, 1889

lodge, were made punishable "Indian offenses." Then in 1889, under pressure from politicians in the newly established state of South Dakota, the Great Sioux Reservation was reduced once again and split into five separate tracts allocated to the various Teton bands. The Oglalas found themselves penned to the desolate stretch of plains between the Great Sand Hills and the Badlands, just to the east of the stolen Black Hills.

With their source of life disappearing, and soldiers chasing them, bands gradually began to come in to the reservation agencies, like Red Cloud and his Oglalas who made their camp at Pine Ridge. There they received annual rations of clothing and "commodity foods" — mostly flour and lard — and lived in a state of antagonism with the Indian Agents sent from Washington, who controlled the food and ammunition supplies, and played chiefs off against one another.

But some of the Indians refused to give in. Sitting Bull and his people had gone north to Canada for a time, and Crazy Horse and his Oglala band fought to stay free in their last good hunting ground, the Powder River Country. Finally, these too had no choice but to come in.

Others chose still a third route, working for the U.S. Government as Indian Scouts and BIA police in return for food and protection. From the beginning, scouts had helped the cavalry to find resistant bands which had fled. And it was Indian people working for the U.S. who killed Crazy Horse, and later Sitting Bull.

By 1890, the Sioux were in a desperate condition. Their first crops, planted at the urging of the Indian Agents that summer, had failed. At the same time, Congress had cut appropriations for the food and clothing guaranteed in the treaty. That same year, the Ghost Dance, a spiritual movement then sweeping the tribes of the West and the Great Plains, reached them. It prophesied a coming purification in which the whites would disappear and the earth would be made new again, with the Indian dead and the slaughtered buffalo coming back to life. The Ghost Dance took rapid hold.

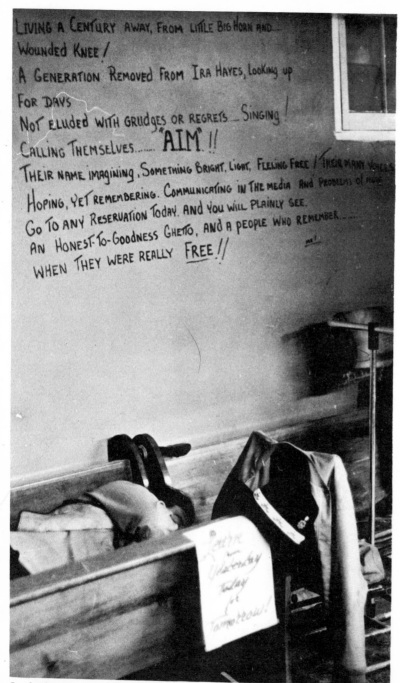

LIVING A CENTURY AWAY, FROM LITTLE BIG HORN AND
WOUNDED KNEE/
A GENERATION REMOVED FROM IRA HAYES, LOOKING UP
FOR DAYS
NOT ELUDED WITH GRUDGES OR REGRETS _ SINGING!
CALLING THEMSELVES ...... "AIM" !!
THEIR NAME IMAGINING , SOMETHING BRIGHT, LIGHT, FEELING FREE / THEIR MANY VOICES
HOPING, YET REMEMBERING. COMMUNICATING IN THE MEDIA AND PROBLEMS OF MINE
GO TO ANY RESERVATION TODAY. AND YOU WILL PLAINLY SEE.
AN HONEST-TO-GOODNESS GHETTO, AND A PEOPLE WHO REMEMBER ......
WHEN THEY WERE REALLY FREE !!

In the basement of the Catholic Church in Wounded Knee.

One center of the dancing was at Sitting Bull's camp on the Standing Rock Reservation. There, the Indian Agent saw the movement as the beginning of an uprising, and sent out a force of Indian police who killed Sitting Bull. But the assassination of their medicine man did little to quiet the fervor of the Ghost Dancing Indians, and eventually the Agents called the U.S. Army onto the five reservations, in yet another violation of the treaty.

Two months later, in December 1890, some of Sitting Bull's people who had fled their camp reached that of Big Foot's Minneconjou Sioux. Together they went south to council with their Oglala relatives at Pine Ridge and seek protection under Red Cloud there. They were intercepted by the Army near Wounded Knee Creek, 18 miles from the Pine Ridge Agency. During the night they were surrounded by the 7th Cavalry, re-formed since Custer's defeat in the 1876 campaign. The next morning, December 29, after seizing the warriors' arms, the troops opened up with their rifles and Hotchkiss guns, killing nearly 300 people. Wounded Knee became known as the last "battle" in the Indian Wars.

Even after the reservation boundaries had been reduced in 1889, and the Indian Wars had come to their bloody end, the Government continued to break up and claim reservation lands. The Dawes Allotment Act of 1886, applied at Pine Ridge in 1902, provided that the land be divided into plots assigned to each family. The intention was to transform the traditionally nomadic Sioux into settled farmers, and open the "leftover" land for homesteaders.

At first the allotments were held "in trust" by the Government. The Indians did not have legal title to their plots and thus could not sell them. But under pressure from the increasing white settler population, a system was introduced by which Indian landholders could be judged "competent" and given deeds, or "patents" to their land. Now they had to pay taxes on it. Some mortgages and subsequently lost it through foreclosure. And many simply sold it in time of need.

Through this and various later policies, Oglala land was soon whittled away. By the 1970's, Pine Ridge Reservation had become a patchwork of white- and Indian-owned property. Of its three million acres, one-half million are owned and controlled by the Tribal Government, one million are owned by whites, and only one-and-a-half million acres, or half the total — remain in Indian hands. Of those Oglalas who do own land, 83% have been forced by their poverty to lease all or part of their holdings. And it is the ranchers, most of whom are

whit́e — who are in a position to rent it. This they do at lease prices fixed by the Bureau of Indian Affairs.

Just as Indian land has been taken away in stages, the native government and social organization has gradually been undermined. Since 1871, the U.S. has administered the native people through the Bureau of Indian Affairs [BIA], originally a part of the War Department and now an agency of the Department of Interior. In the early days, an "Indian Agent" sent from Washington held near-dictatorial power over his reservation. But despite the Agent's presence, the people's respect for their traditional leaders survived.

Then, in 1934, the Wheeler-Howard Indian Reorganization Act was passed. The bureaucracy was expanded, and its grip on reservation life grew tighter. Elected Tribal Councils, supervised by and answerable to the BIA, were established to replace the white Indian Agents as the local authorities carrying out Federal policy. This "Indian New Deal" was thought of in Washington as a progressive move to give the tribes "self-government." Interior Department lawyers wrote Tribal

"Pretty soon they seen some good farm-lands so they start opening up land sale. They call it 'forced patent,' and that's how a lot of non-Indians are buying Indian land. The Government says, 'You have five hundred acres and you don't need two hundred acres. Why don't you sell it? We'll fill out your application.' A lot of old people didn't realize that this was forced patent, and you didn't have to do it. They got around one dollar an acre, then it went up to five, ten — now it's $33 an acre. The BIA sends the appraiser out from the Area office. He walks around the land and he looks around and says, 'Well, it's worth $17 an acre.' That's how we lost quite a bit of our reservation."

— Severt Young Bear, Porcupine District Chairman

"Indian people didn't have any type of government that set down a law that was enforced by one guy like a chief. They were free. They made special rules, maybe, for an occasion like a hunt. They would have one of the societies within the tribe enforce those rules for as long as that hunt was going on. But no one was obligated to follow any of the leaders, and that's the way it should be now for our people.

"Indian leaders were chosen by their deeds, the manner in which they acted towards their people, their generosity, and their willingness to serve their people above all else. They were there to guide their people but they weren't there to rule their people. A chief might have a large band one summer, and if they suffered a really hard winter, the next summer he wouldn't have very many. Someone else would have a large band. Our people didn't understand the theory of dictatorship, and the idea that all people aren't individually free and responsible for their own acts. So in order to try to explain this to our people, they made the Indian Reorganization Act.

"Under the Reorganization Act, the U.S. recognizes a Tribal Government supposedly patterned after the U.S. Government — a Tribal Business Committee, or a Tribal Council that has no relationship to the people. Its relationship is to the Bureau of Indian Affairs, hence to the Federal Government.

"On the Pine Ridge Reservation it's a group of people who live in Pine Ridge village, are dependent upon the BIA school there and the BIA hospital, and the bureaucracy of the BIA. They all work in there, and they'll elect one of their number to perpetuate that type of system. The Indians that live out in the districts — here in Wounded Knee, in Wanblee, Porcupine, or Oglala — they have no input into that government. That government doesn't represent them at all, it doesn't work for their own interest. In fact, it works against their interest in almost everything that it does."

— Carter Camp, AIM leader

Constitutions patterned simplistically on the "democratic" model of U.S. government, and mailed them out from the capital to nearly every reservation. Not surprisingly, they contained little of traditional ways.

Over the years, BIA policies have been oriented towards assimilating Indian people into the "American way of life." To that end, for many years, welfare and other benefit checks were withheld if parents refused to send their children to BIA or mission schools, where native dress, customs, and language were forbidden. While the practice of traditional religious ceremonies was outlawed, Christian missionaries were encouraged, often with grants of free land, to work among the Indians. On the Pine Ridge Reservation they have built 137 churches, more than one for every hundred residents.

The poverty at Pine Ridge has grown steadily worse, as the land, on which the Oglalas had first hunted and then raised cattle, has been lost to them. By the 1970's, unemployment on the reservation had reached 54%, not counting the many who have been forced into the cities to look for work. One-half of those who do work are employed in the Tribal Government/BIA bureaucracy. There is almost no industry on the reservation, and even the tourists who come to view the Wounded Knee massacre site and "see how the Indians live" leave little money there, returning to Rapid City and other off-reservation towns at night to find accomodations.

One-third of the people on the reservation are dependent on welfare or other pensions for their survival. A comparison of the Indians' economic level with that of neighboring whites can be found in state welfare statistics. For example, while only 7.1 per cent of those under 18 in South Dakota are Indian, native people receive nearly half the state's aid to dependent children. Most businesses, like the "trading post" general store-gas stations in the outlying reservation districts, and the Sioux Nation supermarket in Pine Ridge village, are owned by whites and charge prices significantly higher than stores off the reservation.

The combination of these factors have led to the inevitable symptoms of life under colonial rule. Oglala life expectancy is 46 years. Alcoholism and suicide are severe problems. Against this increasingly desperate backdrop, the events which led to Wounded Knee played themselves out.

PINE RIDGE RESERVATION

The settler class that invaded Sioux country in the mid-nineteenth cen-
tury still inhabits the border towns surrounding the Pine Ridge Reservation.
They own the stores, restaurants, banks, and small businesses, of which
there are virtually none on the reservation. They also own the bars where
Indian people go to drink, as liquor is outlawed on the reservation. Vio-
lence by whites towards Indians is common in these communities. In
February, 1972, Raymond Yellow Thunder, from the reservation communi-
ty of Porcupine, was beaten in Gordon, Nebraska by two white men,
thrown naked into an American Legion dance, beaten again, and locked in
an auto trunk. His bruised body was found two days later. His attackers
were released without paying bail, and charged with second degree man-
slaughter. Incidents like this had happened many times before, but this
time the people decided to do something about it. Severt Young Bear,
District Chairman from Porcupine, and a local American Indian Movement
leader, described what happened:

Map of Pine Ridge Reservation showing Rapid City, Custer, Scenic, Buffalo Gap, Pine Ridge Reservation, Wanblee, Kyle, Potato Creek, Manderson, Porcupine, Oglala, Wounded Knee, Pine Ridge, Denby, Bennett County, White Clay, South Dakota, Nebraska, Gordon, Rushville.

KEY
- Reservation border
- Roads
- Black Hills
- Badlands

SCALE: 1 inch = 23.5 miles

Raymond Yellow Thunder was an uncle of mine, and his sisters all live in Porcupine. When that happened, they went to the BIA for help, they went to the Tribal Government for help, they went to some private attorneys for help, because they wouldn't let them see the body, they wouldn't let them see the autopsy report, and they sealed the coffin when they brought it back. This is what really hurt his sisters.

So after they ran into all these brick walls, they had no place else to go. That Friday evening, I came back from work and I was sitting and watching TV and a car pulled up and there's my three aunts, all three of them. They came in crying and said, "Sonny, we don't have no place to turn. So we came over — maybe you could help us." They said, "You have some friends that are with AIM. I wonder if you could go to them, ask them that we want something to be done to the people that killed our brother, and we want a full investigation."

So that same night I left. I went and talked to the storekeeper, he gave me gas, and I packed up and drove all the way to Omaha. That same night I talked with the leaders [who were at at conference there] — must have been 3-4 o'clock in the morning. The next day they passed a resolution that everybody was coming into Gordon. So I came back and we got the Billy Mills Hall [in Pine Ridge] ready and people were there waiting when they came. They held a rally that Monday and that Tuesday night they went to Gordon.

They forced a full investigation. And the Government promised to have a full Congressional investigation on all towns in western Nebraska. But we're still waiting for that to come about.

People here still talk about Yellow Thunder and what happened in Gordon. When AIM came in and helped the family look into the death, that made the older people that are living out on the reservation, out in the country — they kind of lifted up their heads, and were speaking out then. And they been talking against BIA, Tribal Government, law and order system on the reservation, plus some of the non-Indian ranchers that are living on the reservation and been abusing Indians. It was brewing and it finally happened in Wounded Knee.

THE FIGHT AGAINST WILSON

Ellen Moves Camp, an Oglala from the community of Wanblee, was fired from the Public Health Service along with Geraldine Janis and four other Community Health Representatives, for her opposition to Wilson. Making home visits, they came to know most of the families on the reservation. Inside Wounded Knee, Ellen spoke about the situation under Wilson's administration:

Ever since Wilson's been in office it's just been a one-man council. He's just some kind of a dictator that got in there. It's really bad to say but our people did go for the money and all the promises he made when he was campaigning. Different men went out to these districts and told what Dick Wilson promised. They'd take a cow, butcher it, and feed the people. Our people must have been pretty hungry to elect him.

Then a few months after he was in there he got his goon squad with guns and billy clubs and gas bombs, plus the policemen on the reservation — they were helping him. They would go around and anybody that stated anything against Dick Wilson, why, they were automatically beaten up or threatened. And this is what people got tired of.

We all wonder why it is that the Government is backing him up so much, because none of our other Tribal Councilmen were ever backed up like this. Nothing like this has ever happened before, where we have guns all over the reservation, threatening people, hitting people, putting them in the hospital. You don't have no protection at all on the reservation. You have to carry a gun on this reservation now, ever since he's been in there.

There's been homes burned in Pine Ridge. One of them goons came up to me and asked me what I would feel if something happened to my children. So I told him nothing better happen to my children, because I know every one of them and one way or another, they would get back what they done to my children.

And with our brothers and sisters of the American Indian Movement, we feel stronger. We're not scared of them. This is what we needed — a little more push. Most of the reservation believes in the AIM, and we're proud to have them with us. And now that we've done it, my feeling is, "What did I get them into?" I hope that they don't get punished as severely as we do — I don't care how *I* get punished — because our people need these men. That's why we invited them in here.

"The past administrations all along have been pretty sly and crooked with Indian funds, but they weren't quite as hard on us as this drunken fool we got now, who hasn't got the backbone to stand up and protect his Indians. We know this is what the Federal Government wants — the bigger crook you are, the better liar and the better thief you are — is what the Government hires to mistreat the Indians. We've been intimidated and harassed, but this is something we couldn't bear any longer."

— Gladys Bissonette

Richard Wilson, Tribal Chairman

The main road in Pine Ridge village.

During the siege at Wounded Knee, Severt Young Bear was interviewed at his home in Porcupine about Richard Wilson's administration:

When did the resentment against Richard Wilson first begin?

Right from the start, people resented him. Right from the day he took office, the 10th of April, 1972, people constantly been fighting him.

Why were they fighting him?

Because of some of the under-the-table dealings that he done when he was a Tribal Council member before, and when he was with the Housing Authority. He was one of those guys setting up [illegal] liquor on the reservation a couple of years ago. People just know him.

And if you look at it, two rich white guys are behind him. During the campaign, he told these two guys from Rapid City that if he gets in as Tribal Chairman, he promised them a housing contract of $13 million, and a liquor contract that runs into millions of dollars. These two white men put a little over $10,000 into his campaign. So he was throwing money around, used wine to buy votes, and that's the kind of dealing that he done.

When people first started opposing Wilson, what did he do to stop them?

What he done was, any resolution going in saying that they want him to be impeached or suspended — like from Porcupine District we sent in resolutions — and our Tribal Councilmen wouldn't even support our resolutions.

Why was that?

Because he bought them off, giving one guy money, and he promised a high salary job to the other one. So even during that impeachment, a little over a month ago, the Porcupine District unanimously voted in favor of the impeachment of Mr. Wilson. When the Councilmen took the resolution to the meeting, they said, "We have civil rights, and we're going to vote individually. We're not going to support that District resolution." And they voted for Wilson.

So the Councilmen refused to vote as their districts directed them to. That's why he got fourteen votes, because of threats and money and promise of high-paying jobs. Wilson gives them money from liquor dealing and from housing. Like the housing contract he promised those guys in Rapid City. That housing money is coming out of HUD [Housing and Urban

"That's why they have this cluster housing, this instant ghetto jazz — to get the Indian off his land so they can take the rest of it. I know there's got to be gas and oil there and that big money's getting ready to go after it."
— Hobart Keith

Development] in Washington.

Was that housing ever built?

Yes, they started building houses in Wanblee, but during Gerald One Feather's administration [the Tribal Chairman just before Wilson] they built some houses and we started our own Oglala Sioux construction company. One of our own members was the manager of that. And they proved they could build their own houses. But once Wilson got in they fired all the people that was working under this Oglala Sioux construction company, and he fired the board. Then he awarded the contract to outside.

Now they want to give us 65 houses in Porcupine. We voted 13 times on this, and each time we defeated this cluster housing. So back in September, Wilson sat down with his Executive Board and said, "Whether they like it or not, they're going to get those houses. So they've been constructing houses in Porcupine, cluster housing. What we're asking for is some individual homes on our own land, but they're forcing that on us. We sent a delegation and we told them to stop the construction or they're going to have trouble.

SANITATION FACILITIES
MANDERSON & WOUNDED KNEE COMMUNITIES
A COOPERATIVE PROJECT
OF THE
OGLALA SIOUX TRIBE
AND THE
OGLALA SIOUX HOUSING AUTHORITY
AND THE
DEPARTMENT OF HEALTH, EDUCATION AND WELFARE
INDIAN HEALTH SERVICE
UNDER
PUBLIC LAW 86-121
DAY CO., INC.

Severt Young Bear (center) with Vernona Crow Dog (Oglala) and Leonard Crow Dog (Brule Sioux).

Why do they want to build that kind of housing?

I don't know — just to get people off their land. They gave us from the Missouri River up to Little Big Horn. They keep cutting that down. Now they're going to cut us down to one 80-acre tract, 65 houses. They're going to pull all the people off their own land. Next thing they're going to do is sell it. And the non-Indian is the only one with the money to buy it.

Has Wilson done anything for the people on the reservation?

No, not so far. There's nothing we can see that's going to benefit our Indian people. We had OEO [Office of Economic Opportunity] monies that are funded to go out in the districts to promote more jobs or more help to people, and it's all used up in Pine Ridge [village] before it gets into the districts. They got some new positions created. There's more high-paid salary right in Pine Ridge village and very little of that money is going out into the districts where the people really need it.

When did people first start talking about impeachment?

Back in October, that's when I first got wind of it. People started circulating some petitions and things got worse when

this Trail of Broken Treaties was in Washington, D.C. and they took over the BIA building there. Wilson used this as a scare, saying that when AIM people came back to Pine Ridge, they were going to take over our BIA building and destroy it. So with that, BIA Superintendent Lyman and Area Director Babby got $62,000 and that's when this goon squad started. This was November 15th. They were all local drunks and guys that didn't have jobs. He just paid them a good salary so they were on his goon squad.

Have you ever been threatened by the "goon squad?"

I'm on their list.

Why is your name on the list?

Because I campaigned against him when he was running for Tribal Chairman, and the Porcupine District's against Wilson, the majority are against Wilson. Very few are supporting him. Three quarters of the people are against him and I'm the Porcupine District Chairman. I knew they were after me and they even had a Court Order against me and Russell Means not to go to any assembly or hold any assembly for 30 days. It's not legal. It's a dictatorship of government. Once somebody speaks out a little bit and stands for what's right, they get those kind of harassment.

One Oglala described, in an affidavit, how he was recruited for the "goon squad."

I am employed by the Tribe in water works and well repair. George Wilson, Richard Wilson's brother, is my boss. Richard Wilson asked me and my co-workers to stand guard at the BIA building and at the Tribal office. There were training sessions for this riot squad . . . for defending the buildings, hand-to-hand combat, using riot sticks, and so on . . . I found out that it was Indian people being trained against Indian people so I didn't want to do it . . . The reason I and my co-workers first went to the training sessions was because we were afraid of losing our jobs. I believe that most of the people on Dick Wilson's goon squad . . . are there because they are afraid of losing their jobs. A lot of people acting as goons now are unemployed and are doing it because they need the money. The commander, Glen Three Stars, has never held a permanent job. As long as this keeps up, he'll have one.

Geraldine Janis, an Oglala from Pine Ridge, was the Director of the Community Health Program on the reservation. She was fired from her job in early April, 1973, for demonstrating against Wilson. On the day she was fired, she was interviewed at her home in Pine Ridge:

Can you tell us about how the Oglala Sioux Civil Rights Organization was formed?

We had a group of people that didn't like how the present administration was running things, how they were misusing funds. A lot of funds that come in are not meeting the needs of the people in the districts. As a Community Health Coordinator, I have aides in every community that know and work with the people, know their needs, and are usually the voice for the people.

Where does most of the money on the reservation come from?

It's Federal money that comes in for programs. We have our Community Health Program, that is funded by HEW [Department of Health, Education, and Welfare], and our grantee is the Tribe. Then we have an Emergency Medical Program. That money should be going to the people that are on special diets, low income, and maybe special formulas that some of the babies are on, that the parents can't afford. But they're buying milk cows, and just a chosen few are getting them — mostly political people that are friends of the Tribal Chairman. We also have a Head Start Program, and the director is Dick Wilson's wife. The whole program has been at a standstill for weeks — I think on account of not keeping up with her books and not being able to give a financial statement. There again, that program is all political appointees. They even brought in a white lady that owns a bar in a nearby town to be a secretary, when we have a lot of secretaries on the reservation.

Why did they give her that job?

Because her husband furnishes Dick Wilson with booze, cases of whiskey, and beer for his goon squad. And that Personnel Director in the Tribal office is Wilson's nephew. That job wasn't even advertised. He was just put in there as a Personnel Director. And Wilson's goon squad people — the majority of them have jobs with the BIA — some of them are ex-convicts and dope addicts and everything else.

Were they working for the BIA before this?

Those are the people that Wilson went around with, so those were the first to get jobs. If there's an opening, he'll tell the director of that program who to hire, and if he refuses, then Wilson will try to get at him some way — give him a hard go. The people who are hired are not really qualified for their job. And sometimes you never see them for a month, yet they are getting a regular salary check every two weeks.

Is there a lot of money coming into these programs?

There is. Our program brings in about $143,000. I think there's about $4.3 million that comes into the reservation yearly.

Does all this go through the Tribal Government?

It does. The Tribal Government has the power to rule all programs, even State grants that come into the reservation.

"BIA police — that's who killed Crazy Horse and Sitting Bull — Indian people dressed in the uniform of the U.S. Government."
— Oren Lyons, Onondaga chief

There have been a lot of charges of corruption with this money — do you think they're true?

Yes. My office was right next door to the Tribal Accounts. He spent most of that money last year in the OEO account. They didn't have enough money last year to pay their bills. Some of Wilson's friends got $500 a piece for doing surveys — we never have seen the surveys that they've done. We also know that he gave his brother Jim Wilson $15,000 for consultant fees — his brother has never come down. Wilson raised his own wages by Council resolution, by $10,000 a year, which is illegal. He's now getting about

---

"Sure we need a lot of jobs here. We're trying to put these things together to get 'em. And make these people more respectable, if that's what you want to call it. I think everybody feels more useful if he's earning something."
— Richard Wilson

$20,000 because he's dipping into all programs, taking trips, and saying he's a consultant.

He keeps getting away with it because people are afraid for their jobs. See, he has the power as Tribal Chairman. We never knew until we start fighting him how much power a Tribal Chairman has. We never really cared about the Tribal elections, or how we voted. We just thought they couldn't hurt us. We didn't pay much attention to politics. That's how most of the people feel on the reservation, so a lot of people don't vote. So this time he paid them off with wine, money, and beer. That's why there were more voters than there usually is — about 4,000. But now, it's really been an education to the Indian people, and now they're going to think, in later years. If we do continue to have a Tribal Council, they're going to think before they vote . . .

We know they're keeping the money and we seen the checks that went through, but we can't get the facts. Everything that he's doing is illegal, but only the Interior Department can come down here and check the books. And the Interior Department is backing him up. When our BIA auditors come in, they don't even finish a job that they start — they're always covering up for the Tribe.

ON TO WOUNDED KNEE

"At the time it was something we had to do and we had to do it real quick-like, because they beat people up. They were always constantly harassing us. They broke the windows out of the car, they cut our tires, they chased my kids home from school, they call my kids all kinds of dirty names, when I go down town they follow me in the grocery store. And that cop, it got so he sat outside across the street watching the house all night long. It just went from bad to worse. And that's why I just keep fighting. And I think what we're doing is right, I really do. Because I ain't the only one that's suffered. In fact, I think there's a lot of people in Pine Ridge that's suffered, that's still suffering."
— Lou Bean, Oglala

Lou and Billy Bean

In February, 1973, three Oglala Sioux Tribal Councilmen filed impeachment proceedings against Richard Wilson for the fourth time in his ten-month old administration. The move against him had gathered much popular support, and in response, Wilson called on the U.S. Marshals and the Federal Bureau of Investigation for help. He told them that the American Indian Movement, in Rapid City organizing civil rights hearings after the Custer demonstrations, was planning to come to Pine Ridge and take over the BIA building.

The Federal Government, whose various agencies had been keeping close surveillance on AIM since the occupation of the BIA building in Washington in November, was more than willing to step in and support the Tribal President. On February 11, a contingent of 65-75 U.S. Marshals began to arrive and established a command post in the BIA building in Pine Ridge. Shortly afterward, an FBI contingent arrived and established a separate command post.

Wilson then postponed his own impeachment hearing, scheduled for February 14, so that the marshals could train the local BIA police in riot control. He cited "road and weather conditions" as the reason for the postponement although over 300 people showed up for the hearing. The Oglala Sioux Civil Rights Organization, angered by the postponement and by the marshals' arrival, demonstrated in front of the BIA building. They demanded the removal of Wilson, BIA Superintendent Stanley Lyman, and the marshals. Gladys Bissonette, Ellen Moves Camp, and Lou Bean are three women active in the Civil Rights Organization. Later, inside Wounded Knee, they spoke about the demonstration:

Gladys: They let our kids out of school so Dick Wilson and Stan Lyman could use the buses and vans to go up to Rapid City, or somewhere, and pick up all these Federal Marshals and haul them down on our reservation in our school buses. And they unloaded them at the Billy Mills Hall, because they thought the Civil Rights Organization might just move up there to the Billy Mills Hall and take over and start meetings. This is what they were afraid of . . . The morning of February 14 we marched on the Billy Mills Hall. We surrounded it. We had our plaques, we had our signs taped to our cars — all about Dick Wilson and Stan Lyman and how corrupt and — we marched on the Billy Mills Hall, and then we were trying to bring that impeachment to the Billy Mills Hall. We demanded a speedy trial — and we couldn't get it. So then we marched on the Superintendent. And when we marched there were nothing but us women. We had a drum, and the girls had to beat the drum and sing, because the men were afraid of being arrested, which they would have done if the men got out there.

Ellen: We had people from all over the reservation, all eight districts. We called and we told them what we were going to do so they all came in to help us. We demanded the removal of Dick Wilson and Stanley Lyman, and the removal

Ellen Moves Camp (left) and Gladys Bissonette (right).

of the United States Marshals that were here, that were sent for by Mr. Lyman and Dick Wilson.

Lyman called Dick Wilson and told him to come over and talk to us. Wilson told Stanley Lyman that he did not have to come over and talk to us — he didn't have to face nobody. And he told Stanley Lyman, "And I told you that before, so why in the hell are you calling me?" That's just what he said to him.

Lou: You know, that one day too, when we were all at the Billy Mills Hall — it was around noon and we were all standing out there. Goodness, there was about 300 of us, all out there. And those marshals, they were all standing there eating those little lunch buckets. And one marshal, he had a Southern accent, he said, "Us marshals, us 75 marshals could whip you 300 Indians very easily." Well, that's all it took! Cause we told them to go ahead and come over — we was all fired up — we even went over there! But they wouldn't lay a hand on us. But if they tried it I think we would've fought back. We were pretty well teed off, boy. We were willing to fight. If that's what it comes to, that's what it's going to be. We're not scared of the U.S. Marshals. All they have to do is lay down their guns and come in and I think us women could whip 'em.

What the Justice Department did at Pine Ridge, in an unprecedented act, was to create an illegal Federal army by turning the normal law enforcement agencies of the FBI, the U.S. Marshals, the BIA and State police into a para-military force equipped by the Pentagon. This was done to avoid the public attention that would have been drawn if the National Guard or the Army's 82nd Air Borne had been used. Sending the Army onto the reservation would have made it clear to the world that the U.S. Government was forcibly putting down a popular revolt. So instead, the Government tried to make it appear that it was merely helping out local authorities. At Pine Ridge, the BIA police were incorporated into the Justice Department's army under Federal command, but it was made to appear as though the Federal agencies were merely supporting the local police in a neutral fashion as they protected Wilson and the BIA building during the impeachment process.

While the marshals may have come to Pine Ridge partly to protect Wilson and the BIA building, it is clear that they were sent by the Government to coordinate some kind of attack on the American Indian Movement, which was effectively leading Indian people in revolt against the whole BIA system. High-level officials of the U.S. Marshal Service, the U.S. Attorney's office, the FBI, and the BIA were on the scene in Pine Ridge from February 20 on, days before Wilson's impeachment hearing. The Director of the Marshal Service flew in from Washington on a plane provided by the Pentagon. An elaborate radio communications system was installed to connect the command posts in Pine Ridge with the police radio network and the wire-fenced motel compounds in Rushville and Chadron, Nebraska, where many of the marshals and FBI agents stayed.

Additional BIA policemen arrived from other reservations as the marshals set up programs to instruct the Indian police in how to manage "civil dis-

orders." With the help of State and Rapid City police, the FBI and the marshals began an extensive surveillance of the Oglala Sioux Civil Rights Organization and the American Indian Movement members.

It seems that the marshals who came to be a "neutral element . . . to protect life and property . . . and not interfere with local problems" were no ordinary agency of the Government, interested in serving warrants and arresting felons. The first group of marshals to arrive were members of a 110-man elite volunteer unit called the Special Operations Group (SOG). This unit came into existence as a response to an early American Indian Movement protest over Indian lands in Minnesota and it was the branch of the Justice Department responsible for ending the eighteen-month Indian occupation of Alcatraz Island, plus several non-Indian demonstrations involving anti-war issues.

SOG

According to the Director of the U.S. Marshals, Wayne Colburn, "SOG is a strike force deployed only at the request of the President or the U.S. Attorney General." Colburn has said that SOG is "striving to become a completely self-sustaining unit able to handle most situations without dependence on other organizations." One of the marshals described their agency as a Federal strike force, going anywhere, anytime, without having to worry about local and state jurisdictions.

The members of the Special Operations Group are professionals with military careers or training. Colburn, the Director, is an ex-Marine and an ex-policeman; many others are former Green Berets. One of the SOG groups that came to Pine Ridge was a four-man "anti-sniper" team, headed by Wayne McMurtrey, a former Mississippi state trooper. An anti-sniper team is itself a sniper-team, supported by a squad of men with automatic weapons and two-way radios.

U.S. Marshals in Pine Ridge village

During their operations at Pine Ridge, the marshals' command post kept detailed notes of events and radio transmissions. These are excerpts from the U.S. Marshals' Log.

February 14, 1973

0930   Command Post [CP] established.

1145   Advised by Grider that there was a party making a speech in the lobby of the BIA building. SOG 1 [Special Operations Group leader] advised. SOG personnel standing security on second floor at stair wells.

February 15, 1973

0801   FBI agent Bruce Erickson arrived relieving Jim Dix.

0905   SOG Group 1 arrived at BIA building.

1005   U.S. Attorney [William] Clayton and U.S. Marshal [for South Dakota] Tennyson arrived at Command Post.

1030   SOG Group 2 training exercise, BIA police — riot formation, gas training and etc.

February 16, 1973

1130   Group 1 training BIA police. Group 2 secure BIA building.

1330   Training session with BIA police. Classroom lecture and firearms demo. (Basic firearms) followed by dry fire practice in classroom. .38 cal. pistol and 12-gauge shotgun.

1720   Mr. Lyman [BIA Superintendent] reported that Vern Bellecourt went on radio and TV in the city of Rapid City requesting that all Indians report to Pine Ridge / state of siege.

1845   Informed by FBI that Vern Bellecourt on the above made no, repeat no, comment as to Indian movement towards PR area.

February 17, 1973

1545   No incidents to report. Group 1 and 2 remain on alert. Support group members and command post personnel remain on the range with members of BIA police force, training exercise.

1820   Tac 11 Alarm Monitor (RF System) installation completed by Charles Burrows, 10th circuit coordinator. Body Warn devices not assigned.

February 18, 1973

1045   SOG alert.

1143   Mr. Kash [official of U.S. Marshal Service] advised of above status. Total time elapsed between alert and arrival — 56 minutes (Gordon, Nebraska, to this 10-20 [location]).

1345   Group 1 and 2 released to return to motel.

1346   Mr. Kash advises he is en route to Calico to attend a meeting of the organizations (AIM), wanted Mr. Eastman [BIA police chief] advised.

1511   Deputy McKinney advised that five shot guns were taken to the

range by the BIA police and only 4 were returned.

1730 FBI radio technicians Howard McPherson and Chuck Bobcowski installed FBI base station.

February 19, 1973

1010 Mr. Kash and Dick Wilson, president of the tribal council, arrived at the Command Post.

1400 Confidential informant has indicated . . . AIM was going to seize the BIA building on the reservation and lock up the superintendent and his pigs. He further states [AIM] is going to establish an Independent Indian state on the Pine Ridge reservation. A second source that tends to verify the above information is the local office of the FBI.

1445 Local contractor from Rapid City installed Motorola radio unit to allow capacity to reach the Hacienda Motel and the Standby units located there. This unit also gives this command post the capability to contact direct the State Police.

February 20, 1973

0850 Reese Kash departed for meeting with Dick Wilson.

0925 Local FBI received radio communication from SAC [Special Agent in Charge] Trimbach who indicated his ETA [expected time of arrival] at 9:25 a.m. at the Oglala Sioux Airport in Pine Ridge.

0945 Associate Director, United States Marshal Service, Mr. William Hall, called CP from DC for an Up-Date on the situation at PRR.

1344 Mr. Kash was advised by the Director's Office that 50 additional (SOG) men will be departing for Rapid City as soon as possible.

1910 Carr and Romancuzk out to check POW WOW.

February 21, 1973

0835 FBI advised that on the night of 20-21 Feb. 73 at Rapid City, S.D. city police evicted AIM members from the Imperial 400 Motel, seizing one shotgun, a .357 magnum pistol, and one Ruger automatic pistol. Rapid City police were cordoning off the Mother Butler Center, Rapid City, intending this AM to evict AIM from that building.

0905 Rushville Police Department advises, No arrest was made last night by Rushville P.D. of AIM personnel.

1120 Jess Grider advised that there was approximately 75 AIM members holed up in a church in Rapid City, S. Dak. The Bishop has refused police permission to move them out. They are conducting a meeting [while attending civil rights hearings].

1235 Incoming deputies are holding up at the Highway Patrol office.

1445 Mr. Kash reports that the 75 AIM members are still in the Rapid City location, expected to be in Pine Ridge 2/22/73.

1645 Rapid City Highway Patrol reports 19 individuals East bound on Hwy 40 in 5 vehicles between 3:45 pm and 4:15 pm.

2040 Del Eastman brought his local Pine Ridge PD for a tour of CP.

South Dakota State Police in Pine Ridge in February, 1973.

IMPEACHMENT

During the siege at Wounded Knee, Pedro Bissonette, Vice President of the Oglala Sioux Civil Rights Organization, and Gladys Bissonette, looked back on the impeachment proceedings and described their frustration at Richard Wilson's manipulation of his own hearing and trial, on February 22 and 23.

Pedro: So then we, the Civil Rights group, were gathering a pow-wow at Calico Community Hall six miles north of Pine Ridge. We left Calico that morning of the 22nd at 9 o'clock — the impeachment was scheduled for 10 o'clock. We had a caravan of 150 cars, 350 members, at the Billy Mills Hall. We circled the Billy Mills Hall three times, we parked there and then we walked in. We had our drummers and singers with us, and we were singing. We had our peace pipe and our

spiritual leaders with us. I was notified that the impeachment was going to be held under closed doors, and piped out through TV to the public. But I told them that the Civil Rights group members were demanding a public hearing. So they voted on it and gave it to us because there were so many of us. (Six hundred and fifty were seated on our side.)
In the meantime they postponed the impeachment until 2:00 and they showed a movie [*Anarchy, USA,* produced by the John Birch Society] about the colored people rioting and burning houses down. The only ones that were interested were the Council members. We were singing and doing our thing.

Gladys: Well, the Council members had to vote on whether Wilson should be impeached, after which the Tribal President should be suspended for a length of ten to twenty days [until a trial was held]. / So what happened is the Council voted on having an impeachment trial on Wilson. [But he went ahead and demanded the trial right away — which nobody was ready for.]

So the next day [February 23rd] we went back for the trial. The Civil Rights group covered one whole wall of the building and about one quarter of the other side. There were quite a few of us and it was a pretty big hall. [We weren't allowed to say *anything* in this impeachment trial. We all had to sit there mum. But Wilson sneaks three or four members over in our corner and they started making a racket, so we ran them out of there.] They're dirty. They're tricky. They're sly. They're — I don't know — I'd hug a rattlesnake before I'd kiss one of that outfit.

Well, this impeachment proceeding started and they were looking for a judge, you see. /A judge would have to be acting Chairman, in Dick Wilson's place./ [They searched all over in the hall for a judge, and everybody refused the chair. Dick Wilson gets up and says, "Well, god damn it — nobody wants this hot seat of mine? I'd like to see them sit down in this hot seat of mine." — which *is* correct, it is pretty darn hot.]

(Well, they had this judge — they called him a referee. They bought him off the night before, is our understanding.) Now *there* was a puppet if there ever was one. Dick Wilson stood behind him and he did everything Dick Wilson told him to. Dick Wilson acted as Chairman of the Tribal Council, and his own attorney, and his own prosecutor.)

There was three Council members that were impeaching him, for misuse of Tribal funds, and so forth, so many Tribal

Pedro Bissonette

laws that he's broken. These three Council members knew that he wasn't acting on behalf of his people, which he was supposed to have done./ That's the first ... . broke. Because he was for Dick and his .... and his friends. He wasn't for the C .... e, these Council members have beei .... to know what's going on. They we .... hard Wilson when he was elected as Pi .... w that he didn't keep any books and die .... ssions like he was supposed to.

Now these complaining witne .... their speech and this judge would jump .... n three minutes and take the mike a .... .nd it to some of the members that we .... side — some of the bought-off mem| .... off by Dick Wilson — you could see .... they just cut them three Council mei .... finally Hobart Keith jumps up — he .... he jumps up and says, "I'll take this ....

Pedro: |So they walked off the floor .... it to Federal Court and our 650 jump .... lering and screaming. Then we went t ..... Calico and we talked it over| Every time you approach the Tribe, the BIA, in the normal way they always shut the door on us.

February 22, 1973

0130 Bus arrived from Rapid City. Personnel billeted.

0630 All SOG Units on station: Group 1, BIA building, Group 2, located in roads building. BIA Police all on station.

0945 Reservations made for 47 SOG members at Harold Motel, Martin, South Dakota.

0945 Reese Kash departed Command Post for Billy Mills Hall.

1030 Kash advises . . . approximately 300 spectators there now and that a quorum of the Council has arrived. They are ready to go now. All quiet and respectful. Council meeting beginning. Mr. Wilson is starting to show his movie "Anarchy, U.S.A."

1045 Kash reports movie half over. No problem as yet. Approximately 400 people in attendance. Happy!!! No problems. Singing and dancing. Mood of crowd happy.

1205 Associate Director, William Hall, advised telephonically of the events of the last hour. [Washington, D.C.]

1600 Call Mr. Hall advise him of the operation during the preceeding hour.

1735 Kash advised that Tribal Council meeting adjourned until 10:00 Friday, Feb. 23, 1972. Further advise a group of approximately 10 AIM members from Minnesota are congregating around one doorway of BMH. Bystander advises that some of the people in this group were at Custer.

1805 Special Agent of the FBI returned Poloroid camera and accessories to the Command Post.

1820 All riot equipment secured from BIA building roof and placed in Command Center.

1910 Mr. Kash issued the following standing order that should Mr. Toranes of the Community Relations Service [of the Justice Department] request to see any of our personnel he is to be escorted to the office adjacent to Mr. Lyman's office. He is not to be admitted to the command post.

February 23, 1973

0815 FBI reports AIM group still in Rapid City at this time.

1045 Kash advised . . . there were approximately 150 people in the BM Hall and that Russell Means along with approximately 25 others were congregating in one end of the hall.

1046 Cottman and Burrows assigned to Command Post. Markham and Colosanto on roof detail. Tatum assigned to Reese Kash on photograph mission at BMH.

1300 Purple Pontiac seen in area was reported by Indian Police to have weapons loaded into the vehicle, and would be checked by Indian Police, if a traffic violation was committed by the driver of the same.

1422 Received information from BIA Police source that Dick Wilson was voted back into office, 4-0 vote.

1500 Dick Wilson and family in lobby for protective reasons.

1516 Markham reports gathering to the south side of the building.

Women and children looking at BIA building. Extremely heavy traffic. 5 or 6 kids approaching the building. Crowd appears to be waiting for something.

1516 Markham, on roof post, reports that he has observed signs among crowd he previously observed. Appears to be a demonstration in the making. . . Reports demonstrators request permission to talk with Mr. Lyman. Reese Kash has gone to the site . . . to talk to demonstrators as they appeared peaceable. Grider reports that there are approximately 75 demonstrators at the east door. Mostly women and children.

1532 Approximately 100 cars came into town prior to the above cited buildup . . . Few sticks visible and a few bean shooters. Vernon Long is among the crowd. Slack spotted sack. Cannot identify what is in same. Balloon filled with water also spotted. Emergency radio to Hacienda Motel to be activated.

1547 Grider reiterates that demonstrators appear quiet and friendly. Kash advised the demonstrators that we are here to protect life and property in general and no one in particular.

1550 . . . All of crowd has dispersed with the exception of 6 or 8 kids approximately 12 or 13 years old.

1600 Demonstration over. Kash called conference of all staff personnel.

1705 Taubel advises that there are approximately 40 to 45 cars at Calico. He is in the company of a BIA policeman.

1840 Kash 10-8 [en route] to Calico Meeting House. Dick Wilson departed Command Post.

February 24

0740 Reese Kash in automobile. Surveillance of area of Pine Ridge.

0750 Kash requests License check of the following tag numbers: Gray Chevy – Montana Tags 222916 and Mercury (yellow) Montana tags 221529 and Ford LTD Montana tag 221406. Contacted BIA Police ref: this subject.

0815 Jessie Grider held briefing of all day-shift personnel. He indicated hard intelligence from informant that AIM leadership had discussed killing a marshal in order to save face. Grider advised that all personnel should maintain a low profile and to be extra alert.

1220 Superintendent [Lyman] has departed, has secured building, and is taking back road home.

1610 1) Banks in Pierre today. 2) Clyde Bellecourt was in Rosebud last night – had memorial service for Black Elk. 3) Vern Bellecourt in Rapid City today. 4) Means enroute to Pine Ridge for wake (with new people). 5) Will have dance at Calico tonight. 7) Pow-wow in Pine Ridge tomorrow. 8) About 60 AIM members back at Mother Butler's now. Above information from Community Relations Service to Mr. Clayton [U.S. Attorney].

1630 Call from Mr. Martinez (CRS) who advised that people at Calico had seen group of Mr. Wilson's following drinking heavily.

2135 . . . Community Relations officer Martinez said that Banks

would come to Pine Ridge to confront the BIA and the U.S. Marshals with the information that the U.S. Marshals have orders to shoot to kill. Confrontation is set for tomorrow.

215? Called by police chief, Verdell Veo, from Eagle Butte. Means spotted by Hwy Patrol making phone call from Faith, S.D. . . . Police will keep us posted on a as-happen basis.

February 25, 1973

0120 Received call from Mr. Grider and cancelled the deputies leaving South Dakota . . . Called Don Herman in Rapid City to facilitate in location of deputies still in Rapid City.

0915 Mr. Kash called Director Colburn ref: current status. Advised to cut out bugle calls over air.

1001 Mr. Kash advised Calico meeting hall has been checked and reports no weapons are in the building.

1310 BIA PD advises green-over-black Cadillac believed owned by Hobart Keith and driven by Pedro Bissonette crossed state line headed toward Rushville, occupied by Indian and other unknown as to name.

1655 Col. Simmons, Pentagon, called ref: Director [Head Marshal Colburn] will arrive at 1830 at Rapid City airport and requests transportation.

1731 At present there are 40 vehicles at Calico Community Center. There is nothing unusual at this time. A list of license plate nos. has been filed with this station.

1735 Mr. Colburn [Director, U.S. Marshals] . . . will arrive at Rapid City regional airport at approx. 1905 on military U.S. twin engine propeller aircraft. Piloted by [Army] CWO Stevenson. Have Mr. Colburn confirm his arrival at Rapid City with Col. Simmons [Pentagon].

1805 State Police Pierre [S.D.] report following: Texas van has left Faith believed returning to Red Scalpel and in addition three carloads of Indians travelling east on I-90 from Kadoka. [lists

Ellen: /And from that time on [February 24] we went on down to Calico to have our meetings and decide what we were going to do next. We had our dances. We were told that nobody could have dances or meetings on the reservation. This was Dick Wilson's word, but we said that this was *our* reservation, that the reservation belonged to the *people* and we were still going to have our meetings and continue dancing if we wanted to./ And he couldn't stop us . . .

/Twenty-four hours, round the clock, we were being watched — all the time we were at Calico./ We had U.S. Marshals all around the place. Some of the goon squad would come in there drunk — we would ask them to leave because we weren't drinking there and we didn't want no drunks coming in there. We wanted a peaceful meeting.

Ellen Moves Camp

car licenses]

1950   Gartner drew up new defense plans for the BIA building and disseminated the information to the men.

1950   BIA reports there are 60 cars at Calico for a meeting at this time.

2100   BIA advises that the following new cars are in Pine Ridge . . .

February 26, 1973

0049   McPherson reported that Banks was in Manderson with the Bellecourts.

0050   Gary Thomas from Legal Aid called for Del Eastman. He registered complaint against the BIA police for intimidating people around wake of Ben Black Elk. Gartner then called BIA police and passed on the information with the explanation to both parties that we are a neutral element and that we do not interfere with local problems. He wanted Kash's number, did not get it.

0115   Lt. Brewer of BIA police called and reported that they missed the Bellecourts and did not serve the restraining order on them.

0747   Col. Dunn would like the Director to call him at the Pentagon, 202-695-0441, Ext. 215.

1020   An informant of established reliability in a position to know advises that he was informed by AIM leadership that there would be a meeting at Calico at 1530 this date and that this is where the action will be.

1033   Rapid City detectives advise Marshal Tennyson that Means and 30 carloads of people in Rapid City at Mother Butler's Center.

1042   R. Kash requested Mr. White of the Rosebud Agency to furnish additional personnel at Pine Ridge. He will send 5 men.

1142   SAC [special agent in charge] Trimbach, FBI, arrived Command Post.

1150   Director Colburn, Marshal Tennyson, and agent Jim Dick, Special Agent FBI, arrived at Command Post.

1255 State Radio indicates 8 car caravan heading south on State Highway 79.

1255 CRS [Community Relations Service of the Department of Justice] representative Toranes advised that as of 1235 there were 16 cars at Madona Hall, Mother Butler Center, containing an estimated 100 people. The AIM members are reportedly moving out of the building permanently . . . CRS advised that they had seen no weapons, no gas masks.

1335 20-man strike team formed out of existing squads to handle problems that might arise around perimeter of building.

1340 Caravan of 11 or 12 units . . . passing through Hot Springs area approximately 50 or 60 miles from Pine Ridge Reservation. Caravan composed of AIM members from Mother Butler Center . . .

1420 Caravan 2 miles east of Oglala, 17 miles from this command post.

1447 Reactionary squad (Ray Gartner) on scene at BIA building.

1600 Kash reports from Calico that there are approximately 150 people at that location. Mostly young people, obviously AIM but also some older people. All is quiet and no disturbances at this time. Kash describes them as peaceful.

2015 Martinez, Department of Justice, called for Reis Kash. Kash not at command post. Unable to raise on air. Martinez claimed Kash had a meeting scheduled at the Sacred Heart Church across street from Command post at 9 pm. When I informed him that I could not raise Kash and that he was probably at dinner he stated, "Oh! That's bad news."

2110 BIA police advised USM personnel that Russell Means, Pedro Bissonette and David Long were at Sacred Heart Church on Pine Ridge Reservation.

2115 Mr. Terrones [CRS] advised proposed meeting still on.

2138 Two representatives of Community Relations at main entrance to BIA to see Mr. Kash. He is still unavailable at this time.

2145 Approximately 20 people leave Calico heading for Pine Ridge.

2155 Bart Schmidt called Mr. Kash re: Terrones efforts to reach him relative to a meeting at Sacred Heart Church. Mr. Kash advised Mr. Schmidt to inform Mr. Terrones that CP was unable to contact.

2156 Mr. Terrones called CP and was advised that Mr. Kash could not be contacted.

Calico Community Hall

2245 John Terrones, Dept. of Justice [CRS] called to inform CP that the people were leaving (Sacred Heart Church). They got tired of waiting.

2330 All quiet. No incidents to report.

February 27, 1973

0100 Received information from BIA that there are several hundred people at Calico, there are 8 AIM guards with helmets and night-sticks, and are checking all vehicles and personnel entering area.

0250 Propotnick returned with following information: He was approached by a Mr. Janis of AIM while on patrol with BIA near near the Calico meeting hall. Janis stated that, "We want to meet with Mr. Kash tomorrow, any time is ok."

1030 Information provided by Special Officer Price is as follows: At the meetings in Calico yesterday the theme was the inability to conduct business as usual at the BIA building in Pine Ridge. It was suggested that the old people carry this message to the people.

1223 Information from FBI that eight (8) AIM vehicles with one (1) U-Haul van are moving west from Martin, S.D. The eight vehicles are on Rt. 18 and show one Colo. tag, two S.D. tags, five

"These BIA police and marshals and FBIs, they don't have a brain of their own. Like they told me, 'They're the ones that formulate and I'm just merely a sworn-in officer. And my job is to enforce them laws with guns.' They have to go by what is written in the book. They have to go back to Washington and ask, 'Is it in the book? Is it okay Mr. Nixon? Shall we let him have it or shall we shoot him?' 'Oh, go shoot him.' "

— Wallace Black Elk

Ellen: We decided that we did need the American Indian Movement in here because our men were scared, they hung to the back. It was mostly the women that went forward and spoke out. This way we knew we had backing, and we would have more strength to do what we wanted to do against the BIA and Dick Wilson. All the people wanted it. This was a meeting of people from all over the reservation. All eight districts were represented. All of our older people from the reservation helped us make the decision. Practically all the chiefs on the reservation — just one medicine man wasn't there, but he's real old and he's sickly and he couldn't make it.

The place was jam packed. The figures that we counted when we voted to invite them was 300, but there was more people than that standing outside that wanted to get in but couldn't fit in the hall. I figured that it should be done because it was people from all over the reservation and the people are the ones that are supposed to have the voice on the reservation and not Dick Wilson himself.

There were only two members from AIM that was with us when we had that meeting, and that was our brother Russell Means and about an hour later Dennis Banks came in and set by the door and listened to us. And when we kept talking about it then the chiefs said, "Go ahead and do it, go

to Wounded Knee. You can't get in the BIA office and the Tribal office, so take your brothers from the American Indian Movement and go to Wounded Knee and make your stand there. Throw them off and don't announce that you're going to Wounded Knee. Say you're going to Porcupine for a meeting." So this is what we did.

Lou: There was 54 cars when we counted them — that left Calico to come up here that night — 54 cars and they were all packed. All the cars were just packed.

Gladys: It was late at night, some of us come in a little later than others, we moved right up in that church up there. And that's where we sat till morning. We didn't sleep, none of us, 'cause we was afraid of the goon squad coming in or somebody pulling in on us, because they already had those Federal Marshals with their sand bags on top of the BIA building and machine guns pointed at us Indians for at least ten days before we had come to Wounded Knee.

You know, this is the first time a lot of us been on something like this — a takeover of a building or a takeover of a piece of land. And most of us figured that we'd be here overnight or maybe a couple of nights at the most. And we'll be here now a month in four days.

Neb. tags. The U-Haul van is on Rt. 40 between Interior and Scenic moving west.

1305 Caravan of cars to the Calico meeting passed by CP. Two of the the cars could be identified by the red flag on the antenna.

1406 Surveillance of Calico reports that he believes that the meeting is in progress and people left because they could not get into the hall.

1449 FBI reports that Russell Means left Rushville, Neb., at approx. 2:00 pm in a tan Cougar with brown vinyl top.

1506 BIA reports that at approx. 2:40 pm Russell Means was assaulted in front of the Sioux Nation store by Poker Joe Noble and Glen Three Star [chief of the "goon squad]. Gary Thomas, legal aid, also advised BIA that he had just been assaulted by the same persons in the company of two others. Victims advised by BIA to obtain Tribal Court complaints. Injury sustained are minor.

1558 Information from Betty Novak — USM, Sioux Falls — that the Corps of Engineers provides info. that there is a movement of Indians towards Big Bend, Crow Creek Reservation, S.D. NFI [no further information.]

1620 Information subject Banks is in a white car with Hobart Kieth around Billy Mills hall.

1658 Note received at the lobby entrance requesting Mr. Richards to meet Pedro Bissonette at the Calico church.

1750 FBI rpts, Calico area has approx. thirty (30) cars with people is headed to Porcupine and Banks is with the caravan.

1941 Caravan passing at this time, 18 vehicles counted.

1943 Col. Simmons, Pentagon, called and wanted to talk with the Director about status of Marshals and Indians.

1955 BIA PD advised burglary in progress at Wounded Knee store and they are taking all weapons and ammunition.

1957 Call from Community Relations re: convoy going to Porcupine due to lack of space for meeting at Calico.

2005 Merryville of BIA PD re: Woman at Wounded Knee store called screaming that two car loads (about 10 people) are still carrying guns and other goods from the store. PD will have car at scene sometime soon.

2010 Joseph Trimbach, FBI, was advised of above message.

What did you expect to happen?

Ellen: We just thought we'd take this place and we'd sit here with all our people and they could leave and then they'd be back with food and different things so we'd have enough to eat, and we'd have our meetings and get in contact, till we got what we wanted from Pine Ridge. We thought we'd be able to drive back and forth freely. We didn't think we was going to be caged in like a bunch of animals.

Why do you think they turned so much firepower on you?

I know they'd like to shoot us, but we don't care. We didn't come in here for them to be pointing guns at us and everything, but we knew Dickie Wilson from the start. He really can't face honesty — he's got to hide behind somebody. That's why he's got all those goons, those guards, bodyguards, policemen, U.S. Marshals, and all that. He's so scared to do his own dirty work, he stays under cover. That's the kind of thing he is.

Gladys: Since we are here, in Wounded Knee, we've been shot at, over and over, always after dark. But last night we were hit the hardest. I guess the Great Spirit is with us, and no bullets find their way into our bodies. We ran through a hail of bullets one night from that little church. Bullets were whizzing all over us — past us, over our heads, past our feet. But that must be the Great Spirit's doing, to guide us out of the way of the white man's bullet — the pig's bullet — is what I call it. We're going to hold our stand until we are completely an independent sovereign nation, Oglala Sioux Nation.

The village of Wounded Knee.

2.
THE FIRST
TWO WEEKS
AT WOUNDED KNEE

"We're going to win. Cause the people are standing up, and they're saying, 'no!' and they're saying, 'I don't want this, I don't like this.' With that kind of attitude — this is just the beginning."
— Severt Young Bear

THE U.S. GOVERNMENT SENDS AN ARMY TO SOUTH DAKOTA

At the time that the caravan from Calico was reaching Wounded Knee, Aaron Desersa, Oglala and AIM Communications Director, was alerting the news media, hoping that their presence would act as a buffer against a possible Government attack.

Joseph Trimbach, Special Agent in Charge [SAC] of the Minneapolis area branch of the Federal Bureau of Investigation, had come to the Pine Ridge area in mid-February to head the FBI operations there. He filed the following report, describing the events of February 27 through March 1:

At approximately 9:00 p.m., while at a motel room in Rushville, Nebraska, I received a telephone call from a news service who advised that AARON DESERSA had in turn advised him that there would be a confrontation in Wounded Knee that night.

Upon receipt of the above information, I telephoned the U.S. Marshals' Office at the Bureau of Indian Affairs (BIA) Building in Pine Ridge, South Dakota, and furnished the above information to them. They advised me that they had received the same information and that, in fact, Indians were then at Wounded Knee and had burglarized a store and taken a considerable amount of weapons and had obtained several hostages. Allegedly one of the hostages, a Mrs. GILDERSLEEVE was on the phone to the police department advising them of the situation.

I immediately left the motel room, assembled all available Agents, and we proceeded to the Pine Ridge area and from there to Wounded Knee Road. I was advised by radio that the BIA law enforcement officers in the area had been fired upon when they attempted to enter the town site. They had retreated to a place on Wounded Knee Road further south and were standing by.

At approximately 10:00 p.m., I rendezvoused with the BIA Police Officers and ascertained that they had been fired upon and that some of their units were attempting to establish a roadblock north of the town. I suggested to the BIA Police that they reinforce their units on the north end of town, as well as on the east and west side, and the FBI would handle the roadblock on the south end of Wounded Knee Road where it meets Highway 18 . . .

On my instructions, FBI Agents stopped all cars exiting from Wounded Knee and if the occupants had articles in their possession indicating they may have been taken from the burglary, I instructed that the occupants be arrested. I further advised that unless the occupants could explain why they were coming out of Wounded Knee at this time, such as a tourist that might have been caught in the middle of this situation, that the occupants of any such car would be subject to arrest . . .

The second or third car to arrive at the roadblock was a car driven by JOHN TERRONEZ, Field Representative, U.S. Department of Justice, Community Relations Service. I went up to him and said, "Mr. TERRONEZ, to work with these people is one thing, but if I find that you have participated in a burglary with them, I will have to arrest you."

Mr. TERRONEZ replied that he was at Wounded Knee when the burglary and subsequent takeover occured. He said he wanted to leave but they told him they wanted him to wait while they made their demands. I asked him what demands he was referring to, at which time he gave me two pieces of paper which state as follows:

"Demands

"I. Senator WILLIAM FULLBRIGHT to convene Senate Foreign Relations Committee immediately for hearings on treaties made with American Indian Nations and ratified by the Congress of the U.S.

"II. Senator EDWARD KENNEDY to convene Senate Sub-Committee on Administrative Practices and Procedures for immediate, full-scale investigations and exposure of the Bureau of Indian Affairs and the Department of the Interior from the Agency, reservation offices, to the area offices, to

A meeting the first night at the Catholic church. "Either negotiate with us for meaningful results, or you're going to have to kill us, and here at Wounded Knee is where it's going to have to happen." — Russell Means

the central office in Washington, D.C.

"III. Senator JAMES ABOUREZK to convene the Senate Sub-Committee on Indian Affairs for a complete investigation on all Sioux Reservations in South Dakota.

"People we will negotiate with:

"1. Mr. ERLICHMAN of the White House.
"2. Senators KENNEDY, ABOUREZK, and FULLBRIGHT — or their top aides.
"3. The Commissioner of the BIA and the Secretary of Interior;

"The only two options open to the United States of America are:

"1. They wipe out the old people, women, children, and men, by shooting and attacking us.
"2. They negotiate our demands.

Signed:
Oglala Sioux Civil Rights Organization:

President   VERN LONG
Vice-Pres.   PEDRO BISSONETTE
Secretary   EDDIE WHITE WOLF
American Indian Movement
Leader   RUSSELL MEANS

"Before we took action this day we asked for and received complete direction and support of medicine men and chiefs of the Oglala Nation:

FRANK FOOLS CROW
PETER CATCHES
ELLIS CHIPS
EDGAR RED CLOUD
JAKE KILLS ENEMY
MORRIS WOUNDED
SEVERT YOUNG BEAR
EVERETTE CATCHES"

TERRONEZ also mentioned that he was to write the following information down and present it in the form exactly as shown below. He then referred to some notes and said, "Communicate this to whoever is in charge. We are operating under the Provisions of the 1868 Sioux Treaty. This is an act of war initiated by the United States. We are only demanding our country."

. . .

Based on the assurance of Mr. TERRONEZ that he was not personally involved in the burglary or the takeover, I permitted him to proceed out of the roadblock area. I told him that I would see to it that the information he supplied would be furnished to the appropriate authorities.

Supervisor HOWARD A. SHARPE was placed in charge of this roadblock and I then proceeded to the Command Post in order to handle the placement of additional personnel as they arrived from Rapid City, South Dakota.

. . .

At 8:42 a.m. on February 28, 1973, I telephoned the residence of Mrs. GILDERSLEEVE, allegedly one of the hostages at Wounded Knee. A male voice answered the phone and I asked to speak to the person in charge. After about two or three minutes' delay an individual came to the telephone and identified himself as CARTER CAMP, American Indian Movement (AIM) Security Chief. I told this individual that the people inside should stop shooting at our Agents. CARTER CAMP said that he was unaware that any shots had been fired in the morning. I told him that I had been advised that shots had been fired from the west side.

I then asked CAMP if I could meet with him so that perhaps we could avoid bloodshed. He agreed and said I could come into the area. I told him that I would have a white cloth on the antenna of the car.

Later in the morning I went to the roadblock on Wounded Knee Road and after passing through the FBI roadblock I put a white cloth on the antenna and proceeded very slowly north into Wounded Knee. At a point approximately three miles north of the roadblock I saw two burned cars blocking the road.

Behind these cars I would estimate that there were eight or ten men, armed with rifles. These rifles were pointed in my direction. I stopped the car about 100 yards south of the barricade. I then proceeded by foot to a point midway between the FBI car and the AIM barricade. An individual came from behind the barricade and asked what I wanted. I told him I was there to see CARTER CAMP.

In a few minutes CARTER CAMP appeared. I introduced myself and told him I was the Special Agent in Charge of the Federal Bureau of Investigation. I told him that I was interested in avoiding bloodshed and wanted him to take steps to assure that the people inside Wounded Knee did not fire on the law enforcement officers.

CAMP said he wanted assurance from me that we would not advance from our present positions. I told him that I could not and would not assure him that we would never make such an advance; however, in order to cut down on the rifle fire, I would assure him that he or AIM would be notified before an advancement was made. I stressed with him the absolute necessity of eliminating the shooting if we were going to avoid having someone killed. I also told him that if there were further shootings I would come back and discuss

them with him.

CAMP said that he was not in charge and that he was not authorized to make any statement on behalf of persons at Wounded Knee. I told him that I wanted to speak with someone who had authority and he said I could come back later if I wished.

At 2:08 p.m. the same day, I approached the barricade as previously described. Again I was confronted by at least six persons who had rifles pointed at me. In addition, two riflemen took positions in the gullies on either side of the road and pointed their rifles in my direction.

I waited in the center of the road for a few minutes and then was approached by an individual who identified himself as PEDRO BISSONETTE of the Oglala Sioux Civil Rights Association. I asked him about the hostages and what could be done to effect their release.

He replied that he could not speak for the Oglala Sioux and it would be necessary for additional personnel to be summoned. He gave me a card on which was printed the following:

Wounded Knee's Pine Ridge Roadblock.

"FRANK FOOLS CROW
JAKE KILLS ENEMY
EDGAR RED CLOUD
SEVERT YOUNG BEAR
PETE CATCHES
NAMES OF ALL PEOPLE ARRESTED
LAST NIGHT AND THIS MORNING"/

I asked him who these people were and he described them as holy men. I told him I would endeavor to locate these people if they would have some bearing on resolving the situation.

I was also informed by BISSONETTE that one of the elderly hostages was in need of medication. He said the prescription had been telephoned to the drug store at Rushville and asked if I would bring the prescription back in the afternoon. I said that I would handle it. I also said when I returned I wanted a list of the hostages by name and age.

Later in the day I returned to Wounded Knee following the same proceedure as described above. I again parked the car and walked to a distance approximately 100 yards north of the car and about 50 yards south of the barricade. I was approached by a person who identified himself as RUSSELL MEANS. I gave him the medicine for the hostage and I also furnished him with a list of persons who we had arrested the prior evening.

He gave me a piece of paper which listed the hostages as shown below:

"Hostages
Wounded Knee, South Dakota

WILBUR A. RIEGERT	82
GIRLIE CLARK	75
CLIVE GILDERSLEEVE	73
BILL COLE	86
MARY PIKE	72
AGNES GILDERSLEEVE	68
ADRIENNE FRITZE	12
GUY FRITZE	49
JEAN FRITZE	47
Father MANHARDT	46
ANNIE HUNTS HORSE	78"

38

In Wounded Knee.

The FBI's Roadblock 1.

RUSSELL MEANS then related how the white man has been unfair to the Indian and how the hostages were really prisoners of war. He then referred to the area between the barricades as a "DMZ." He then said that many Indians were massacred at Wounded Knee years ago and that if we came into Wounded Knee after him, he and many other Indians would die, but also the hostages would die with them. He said he was not afraid to die.

I told MEANS that there was no way that we would just leave the area, that we had to have him surrender, and that his only hope was to surrender. He expressed great displeasure at this and stated that we were trespassing on Indian land. He said, "We are the landlords and the rent is overdue."

It soon became apparent that MEANS was getting more excited and that I was getting more nervous and I, therefore, decided to leave without engaging in any further conversation with him.

"The hostages are in no danger from the Indian people. The only danger is if the Federal troops attack — their bullets are indiscriminate."

— Russell Means

On the morning of March 1, 1973, I was requested by Mr. RALPH ERICKSON, Special Assistant Attorney General, to see if I could arrange a meeting place for Senators MC GOVERN and ABOUREZK to meet with the Indians . . . I again met with RUSSELL MEANS. I told him that the Senators would not meet with him until the hostages were released.

At this point numerous persons with the news media came to the area and with them were three persons, who MEANS said were on the hostage list. These individuals stated that they were no longer hostages and were free to come and go as they pleased. MEANS said that the other eight hostages were also free to come and go as they wished but that none of the hostages wished to leave. I told him that I would bring this message to the Senators.

It was then decided by the Senators that they would come to the roadblock area. I thereupon drove Senators MC GOVERN and ABOUREZK and the aides to Senators KENNEDY and MANSFIELD to the roadblock on the Wounded Knee Road. I had no further contact with the personnel on the other side of the roadblock on this date.

Abourezk told reporters, "I want to emphasize that we're not going here to negotiate demands, but to work for the release of the hostages. There can be no negotiations with a gun at anyone's head."

McGovern spoke to the press at Ellsworth Air Force Base. He said, "I deplore the tactics that have been used by AIM, tactics of violence, the tactics to disrupt orderly procedure. We can't tolerate that. We're not going down there with any prior notions or concessions, but to talk with AIM leaders and see if we can't arrange for the release of the people they are holding there."

When the Senators finally got to Wounded Knee, they discovered that there were no hostages. Senator McGovern told newsmen, "They don't want to leave because they consider that to be their home." Mr. Riegert, 86 years old and one of the "hostages," told the press on March 3, "The fact is, we as a group of hostages decided to stay to save AIM and our own property. Had we not, those troops would have come down here and killed all of these people. The real hostages are the AIM people."

Once it became apparent that there were no "hostages" the Senators departed, after promising to work for change. They assured the Oglalas that BIA officials Lyman and Babby were already due to be transferred away from the area. McGovern told the press, "We gave them assurances that every effort would be made to get them a fair hearing on the matters they are concerned about."

HOSTAGES

i am a hostage
you are a hostage
the people are a
hostage : bound
held for another's purpose
not free to choose
your own way
NOT FREE !

my body / bound
my mind / confused
my soul / aching
my spirit / searching
my blood rages
in these Lakota hills
as the Wind screams out
purify
purify
be strong
be one
search no longer
be strong
stand
STAND
free me
free you
free the people

— Karoniaktatie

"Now they are afraid and they are scared to hear the truth, because with their military power they think they control everything by force, killing people and hurting people and suffering people and threatening people, 24 hours round the clock."

— Wallace Black Elk

BUILD-UP / FEBRUARY 27-MARCH 2

Meanwhile, the U.S. build-up was continuing. Soon after the caravan had arrived from Calico on the night on February 27, approximately 90 U.S. Marshals and FBI Agents surrounded Wounded Knee, blocking off the roads and arresting anyone coming out of the village. The Marshals' logs state, "[BIA] advises they can handle 60 at the jail . . . send over that number of plastic cuffs." By the next day, 250 Federal personnel were on duty, helmeted and armed with M-16 machine guns. The Marshals' logs report, "All U.S. Marshal personnel advised to fire when fired upon . . . Army convoy arrived with [armored] personnel carriers [APCs – tank-like vehicles used to carry soldiers into battle]."

People inside began digging trenches around the buildings and setting up roadblocks on the edges of the village. Armed with .22s, shotguns, and a few good hunting rifles, they established foot patrols to keep out U.S. agents and vigilante ranchers who were roaming the area. The Marshals' logs note, "BIA advised that the Indians are giving out food and plan to burn the store down . . . three bunkers near the church . . . aircraft are drawing fire." On the first full day of the siege, February 28, Wounded Knee patrols fired warning shots over a car coming within a quarter mile of the village. The Government returned the fire. The next morning, an FBI agent was heard to say, "We just wanted them to know we were there."

By this time, Oglalas outside Wounded Knee were mobilizing to show support for those inside. On March 1, the logs reported, " . . . a demo. – a large crowd behind Billy Mills Hall, led by AIM leader [Oglala Sioux Tribal Councilman] Richard Little." That night, the home of Aaron Desersa, a resident of Pine Ridge village and National Communications Director for the American Indian Movement, was fire-bombed and his wife was seriously injured. Federal agents were using their APCs as bunkers, stationed between the roadblocks on the hills overlooking the village. Firing broke out on the night of March 1, when an APC tried to force the warriors out of the roadblock on the Big Foot Trail.

Ralph Erickson, the Justice Department official in charge at this time, explained the build-up to the press. "There has been a general disregard for persons and property. Agents and Marshals are being exposed to gunfire, and it causes us concern . . . We have discovered the Indians have an automatic weapon which could wipe out a group of men. We believe it's an M-60 machine gun. It doesn't look very promising." Wounded Knee had no such gun.

The Marshals' logs for March 2 note, ". . . call-up of additional 40 personnel . . . the Governor [Richard Kniep, of South Dakota] 'is extremely hesitant' to call up the National Guard and suggests that the Federal installation nearby be contacted . . . 30 or 40 shots exchanged near RB [roadblock] 1 . . . Group of 15 local ranchers (Very irate) state that if we don't do something, they are going to round up all the ranchers in the area and declare war on Wounded Knee . . . cars leaving Wounded Knee by cutting across fields without lights . . . great deal of movement in and around Wounded Knee, armed persons on vehicles and on horseback."

Wounded Knee bunkers in front of the church

"APCs — against .22s and shotguns — who's pointing guns at who?"

THE GOVERNMENT INFORMS THE PUBLIC

International attention was focusing on the confrontation. But from the first, Government policy was to keep the press as far away as possible. The Marshals' logs for February 28 read, "Do not let newspaper personnel in the Wounded Knee area . . . No TV coverage of the Wounded Knee area, authority [of] Attorney General [Kleindienst] . . . No photos of [U.S. Marshal Service] personnel . . ." Reporters who sought to cover the story had to hike into the village over the hills, while the only "official" source of information was the daily press conference in the Pine Ridge BIA building. On March 2, at one of the briefings, the Department of Justice's Public Information Officer, Horace Webb, responded to questions from the press:

Webb: I'd like to bring you up to date on the events of the last evening and certain of the events of this morning. There were four arrests made last night at Roadblock 3. Arrested were Joyce Sitting Bear of Rosebud, South Dakota, Chris Bad Eagle of Rosebud, South Dakota, Linda Staples of White River, South Dakota, and Eugene Hopkins of White River, South Dakota. They were charged with burglary, larceny, and assaulting Federal officers. They are presently en route to Rapid City, South Dakota, for arraignment.

Had they come out of the village?

They had come out of the village last evening and were apprehended.

You said [the] four people were being charged with assaulting Federal officers. Was that in connection with some incident as they were leaving, or with rifle fire?

Rifle fire.

Fire that occurred last night, or fire that has been occurring?

Fire that has been occurring.

Is there any direct evidentiary link on these four people or are you going to lodge such charges against anybody who is picked up?

I am not at liberty to discuss investigative material that the FBI has.

Did they have any evidence in their automobile which would directly link them to the burglary or larceny?

I am not at liberty to discuss investigative material that the FBI has.

Were they armed so that you could directly link them with the firing that's been going on?

We have no evidence to indicate that they were armed.

Could we assume that everyone emerging from there would be faced with the same charges?

No, that's a generalization that I would not suggest you make.

Can you go through the circumstances of the arrest? Were these four people coming out by car?

[They] were coming out, as I understand it, by car. They came to one of the roadblocks, at Roadblock 3.

Where's "Roadblock 3?"

Oh, I'll have to find that out. I don't know.

And they were stopped and arrested at the roadblock?

Stopped and arrested at the roadblock.

. . .

"No TV coverage of the Wounded Knee area, authority Attorney General . . . No photos of personnel . . ."
— U.S. Marshals' log

Also last evening there were approximately 20 rounds of rifle fire taken by one of the armored personnel carriers that moved in yesterday evening that I told you about. That fire was returned by Federal agents. And in connection with that, one canister of tear gas was fired in the direction of the shooting and it ceased.

What time was it?

That was last evening about 8:00 local time.

When did you say the fire was returned, how many rounds, and what sort of range and what sort of —

The number of rounds I don't know. Range I would

estimate within 1000 yards. That's the reason tear gas was used because it was felt the tear gas would go in that direction. And certainly we would rather have the persons firing leave because of that gas than injure some of them.

Is that the first time you returned fire?

I can't confirm that. I don't know.

Since things don't seem to be getting, as far as the gun fire is concerned, any better, has there been any talk or plans to bring in more reinforcements?

No.

Have your people been in touch with the President recently in regard to the situation here in any way?

When federal authorities are used in as many numbers as have been used here, the Attorney General and the White House are kept informed.

. . .

One of the things you should know, we have a five mile perimeter, five miles out from Wounded Knee.

Where do you get your figure of five miles?

Where do I get my figure? From the FBI and the U.S. Marshal Service that have set up the perimeter.

There are those of us that have been to that checkpoint that overlooks Wounded Knee, last night. And there is no way your people are five miles away from Wounded Knee.

You can report the distance as you see it. I will report as I have it reported.

I suggest you see it.

Okay.

It's not five miles.

. . .

Mr. Webb, what about the hostages? Mr. Erickson said last night he was seriously concerned about their safety. Four churchmen on one radio station this morning said that they were quite convinced, having spoken to the hostages, that there isn't any cause to be worried about the hostages.

We still have great concern for the residents of Wounded Knee. Our concern is based primarily on the discussion of yesterday afternoon about one o'clock with Mrs. Gildersleeve in which she indicated although her family is

not being held hostage, she could not speak for the others. And as a result of that conversation, we are still very much concerned about the safety of the persons there.

Force is still not being ruled out?

Force is still not being ruled out. We're trying to maintain all avenues with the hope that the matter can be resolved without further use of force.

Next day at the conference the questioning resumed:

Newsmen that came out of there around noon today said that at least one of the APCs came to a distance less than 500 yards from the bunkers in Wounded Knee both last night and at 9:15 this morning. According to those newsmen, it was the approach of those APCs that precipitated that 9:15 incident you're talking about, and that, by the way, has been documented on film. / Don't you think that destroys your credibility telling us 'two to three miles away' when we have documentation on film that those APCs came to within at least 500 yards of the bunkers? /

The Federal authorities who are on the scene are taking those steps that they think are necessary in order to protect themselves as well as to perform their function and their mission, and they are not in any way taking offensive steps in terms of attacking or moving in. . .

Is it fair to assume that the Indians at Wounded Knee would do anything but try to take some counter-action if they see an APC approaching their bunkers? Isn't it reasonable to expect them to fire at the APC? Why should the marshals be surprised? That seems to be inciting an incident.

We don't think it's reasonable to assume that anyone would fire at Federal authorities. I think that's fairly clear.

Meanwhile, the marshals were receiving assistance directly from the Pentagon and from Army and Air Force units around the country. For example, according to the Marshals' logs, they requested photo reconnaissance missions through then Defense Department General Counsel Fred Buzhardt [who later was to become President Nixon's counsel on Watergate matters]. On March 3, Air Force F-4 Phantom jets came in low over the village. Also according to the logs, the director of the marshals Wayne Colburn and FBI Director Joseph Trimbach had a secret meeting at 4 a.m. with a "military VIP" at Ellsworth Air Force Base. Later that day, a Major Vic Jackson from the "California Civil Disorder Management School," and a Colonel Potter, Sixth Army

Oglala Oscar Bear Runner — a guard at the negotiations.

advisor with the Army's 82nd Airborne, arranged for additional APCs and equipment. In a conversation with the Pentagon, Army officers asked the FBI if they were "shooting to kill." The FBI replied, "Rifles are for that purpose . . ."

Inside Wounded Knee, people who had expected to spend, at most, a couple of days in the village, were adjusting to the unexpected siege. Newsmen who hiked in reported that despite the frequent Government fire, "a friendly pow-wow atmosphere" existed. They "wandered around freely", and were welcome to eat with the Oglalas. Kitchens were being organized in the churches, using the food from the trading post shelves and sometimes a cow. One elderly woman said, "If they accuse us of killing this cow, I'm going to tell them those planes just scared it to death." On the evening of March 3, the AIM leadership announced that they were willing to leave — if all the Federal forces would also leave so that the Oglalas could work out their own problems.

The Government's first reaction had been to try to end the occupation with military force. If there had not been so much publicity, they might have done so. But they were coming under increasing pressure from public opinion, church leaders, and Congressmen to handle the situation without violence. The Government finally agreed to talk with the Oglalas.

On March 4 talks began between the Justice Department and the Oglala leadership. A tipi was brought from the village into the "demilitarized zone," between the Wounded Knee perimeter and the Federal encirclement around it, on a hill near the Government's Roadblock 1. The Justice Department did not reply to AIM's offer for mutual withdrawal. Instead, they proposed that all the Indians in Wounded Knee could go out through the Government's roadblocks without being arrested, but would remain subject to indictment by a Grand Jury. There was no answer to the Oglala's demands for suspension of the Tribal Constitution and an investigation into the broken treaties. Russell Means said, "Sounds like the offer they gave Big Foot."

Dennis Banks and Russell Means burn the Government's offer at a meeting, March 5.

"Blackmail? I call it blackmail when our children are forced to attend boarding schools away from home nine months of the year. When the police jail the drunks but not the bootleggers. When we are forced to deal with white businessmen who dominate our towns. When a tribal chief can hire goon squads with Federal funds. When the Government holds our land in trust. They offer us two choices — jail or death and to hell with our demands. That's blackmail!"

— Russell Means

Oglala leadership meets with the Government, March 4.

Richard Wilson told the press, "I will not be responsible for holding my people back. If necessary, I will join them with my guns." When asked the size of his force, he replied, "Eight or nine hundred — guns."

News of Wilson's press statement spread through Pine Ridge. One Oglala, Mildred Galligo, commented, "We parked right in front of the Tribal office to see who his nine hundred were. He was going to have a big conference with his nine hundred to make plans, so we sat there and sat there. Fifteen half-drunk kids went in — those are his goons. And he's half-shot himself — so he probably kept counting them over and over until he got nine hundred. That's the size of it."

RICHARD WILSON: PROTECTED BY THE GOVERNMENT . . . SOMETIMES

Richard Wilson was also unhappy about the Government's offer. It appeared that the Federal personnel that came out to protect him might now abandon him. Back at Pine Ridge, he gave a rare interview:

Wilson: I was not consulted [by Ralph Erickson of the Justice Department] in this offer of amnesty to any of them knuckleheads out there and I'm just completely upset about it.

What was the tone of your conversation with him then?

I said, *"Why? Why?* Man, they got away with it in Washington, Scottsbluff, Crawford, Custer, Rapid — and it looks like they're going to walk out of Wounded Knee, too."

What do you intend to do about that?

Let me get over my madness and I'll tell you what I intend to do about it.

*What sort of ideas do you have? What **can** you do about it?*

Obviously not much, right now. But if we're going to be free game for a bunch of militants to come in and tear up our reservation, the responsible citizens of this reservation are going to damn sure do something about it.

Do you expect these people to accept the offer?

They probably will. They want out of there and they want amnesty. They've been hollering amnesty all along.

Do you consider this amnesty?

Absolutely. Erickson says they're convening a Grand Jury this week. Now that could be ten years before any of them is ever brought to trial. In the meantime they could take over another store.

How easy would it be for them to get away and not appear before a Federal Grand Jury?

They got a free way into and out of Wounded Knee — there's roads that's never covered down there.

So they could walk out without identifying themselves?

Absolutely. I had a friend of mine come out of there this evening. Stopped by my house and gave me some information about the whole situation.

What about the 900 people that were going to mobilize and go down there?

They're standing by.

Have you talked to any of these 900 today?

Absolutely. Mr. Erickson has too. About over 100 of them he talked to.

Have you had to restrain them from going down there?

The restraints are off as of this moment.

So what ever is game, is game?

Free game.

What are you going to do personally?

I think I'll go home and have a drink.

What are you going to do if they start walking out under these terms?

We have Tribal laws that they've probably violated, but they are merely misdemeanors at this point, and we will try to do what we can to get them jailed.

It seems to me that your obvious concern at the moment is that these people can step out and avoid giving their names to the Federal Marshals. Would it not be a responsible move on your part to mobilize the 900 men you say you have to protect these avenues of escape so they will have to give their names?

It might be a real good idea, and we may do it. That would be classified information, though. I am very upset about the whole situation.

Are you going to nab them right after they get past the barricades and identify themselves and charge them with misdemeanors?

That, too, is classified.

Do you still stick by your statement, "AIM will die at Wounded Knee?"

Absolutely, and I think the Justice Department has failed again, completely failed. If any agency should be cut out, it should be the Justice Department.

Isn't it true, Mr. Wilson, that you and the Council asked the Justice Department's assistance?

We asked the U.S. Marshals, not the Justice Department. If I knew they was coming, I may not have asked for the Marshals. I think the Marshals are doing a terrific job. I am upset with the entire Washington staff of the Justice Department.

Why do you think they've failed? Why haven't they resolved the situation more conclusively?

They got people like [attorney William] Kunstler looking down their throat, and Ramon Roubideaux, and people like that that they're scared of. I think an interesting fact is that everybody's hiding behind the skirts of civil rights, and yet it has never been adopted by this Tribe. We have no mechanics whatsoever to initiate the Civil Rights Act of '68 at all. It's never been brought to our people here, and ratified and put into our code, nor our Constitution and By-laws.

Are you saying you don't agree with civil rights?

I agree with civil rights, but it has to be ratified by the people of this reservation. That's an infringement on our sovereignty if it's not.

Are you implying that Washington is only interested in quieting the present situation down?

Yes, that's it exactly. That's all they want to do. And they want to make the Oglala Sioux people look like a bunch of dogs — so they can run away to their mansions up there and do their thing, I guess. It's very disappointing what has happened this evening. I don't know yet what I can do about it. Many bad situations are solved over a drink and that's where I intend to go now.

Dennis Banks and Tom Bad Cob.

The famous AK-47 automatic rifle.

"We're not going to massacre the white man, we're going to massacre his attitude and his government."
— Leonard Crow Dog, Sioux medicine man

"They can't do anything but kill us, and more will come that way too."
— Grace Black Elk

Bringing in food from the trading post to the church kitchen.

In the church kitchen basement.

"Obviously, somebody is going to die at Wounded Knee. If people do die, well that's the way the ball bounces."
— Richard Wilson

sneaking into
wounded knee
thru the creekbed
meeting headfirst
the spirit of the
women fleeing
83 years ago
with the children
the future
killed
slaughtered
so far from
the field of
"battle"

stones
stained with the
blood of
minneconjou
women
the trees, the brush
every blade of prairie grass
filled with haunting spirit
of a nation slaughtered
    a nation watching
    a nation rising

spirit of the minneconjou
find me worthy
that i may
fight in your place
that i may avenge
(with vengence & rage
grown only of love)
speak to me
so that i
may help
in the rebirth
of this nation
& if need be
show me the true
way to Die!

    — Karoniaktatie

In Pine Ridge, schools had been closed all week, welfare checks were delayed, and all normal BIA services had been disrupted by the Federal occupation of the BIA building. Demonstrations were held to protest the Marshal's presence, and the siege of the village. Opposition to Wilson was still growing, too. Gerald One Feather, the previous Tribal President, announced he was leading a move to upset Wilson's administration. Supporters of the Oglala Sioux Civil Rights Organization were gathering signatures on a petition which asked the Interior Department to immediately suspend the Tribal Government and hold a referendum to establish a new constitution. Although the Department has the legal authority to suspend Tribal Governments, and has done so on several reservations in the past, it now took the position that it could not "interfere with the right of Indians to govern themselves unless there is a total breakdown of government on a reservation."

Wilson, on the other hand, was disappointed that the U.S. had not ended the confrontation with force. Lloyd Eaglebull, Secretary of the Tribe under Wilson, issued a statement for the "protection of the Oglala Sioux Tribe," asserting:

. . . That the Department of Justice, AIM leaders now on the Wounded Knee site, and the National Council of Churches, shall be charged with the full responsibility of, any and all acts of violence, that may result in any injury or death to any person as a result of the present "Wounded Knee Crisis" and stalemate.

This statement to absolve responsibility is based on the following reason:

The three named organizations are involved in the "on-going" and current negotiations and official representation from the Tribal Government has been denied. The fact that the Pine Ridge Indian Reservation has a duly constituted form of Tribal Self-Government has been completely and intentionally overlooked.

ULTIMATUM / MARCH 6–8

Only two people took up the Justice Department's offer to leave. Negotiations continued, and Federal negotiator Erickson repeated he would discuss arrests, but not issues. On March 6, he stated, "Negotiations cannot be made at gunpoint . . . I call upon them to send the women and children out of Wounded Knee before darkness falls March 8." The next day the "call" became an ultimatum. Russell Means spoke for the Oglalas in reply: "We came here and bet our lives that there would be historic change for our Nation. The Government can massacre us, or it can meet our basic human demands. Either way, there will be historic change."

Support for those in Wounded Knee was beginning to come in from around the country. People began to collect supplies and raise money, and early on the morning of March 7 a small plane landed inside the village perimeter, delivering food donated by Chippewa people in Michigan. That night, forty people walked in over the hills, bringing food and medical supplies with them. Demonstrations were held in many cities of the country as the "ultimatum" deadline approached.

Rev. Ralph Abernathy arrives in Wounded Knee to show his support, March 7.

It was tense in Wounded Knee on March 8, as people awaited the nightfall deadline. APCs could be seen creeping up closer on the ridges. Two Air Force Phantom jets flew low over the village. Inside Wounded Knee, a religious ceremony was held and warriors came forward to have their faces painted by the medicine men, signifying their acceptance of the possibility of death. The marshals' logs note that, "a newsman leaving Wounded Knee advises that they observe a lot more weapons than before . . . " Carter Camp said, "We in no way think we can whip the United States Government, but we have every intention of selling our lives as dearly as we can." Many of the Oglala residents of the village had taken up a petition accusing the U.S. forces of holding them prisoners in the village. Now they announced that they were joining with the activists. Pedro Bissonette, speaking for the Oglalas, announced, "One hundred sixty-seven have volunteered to remain and fight with us until we get more top officials in here to negotiate."

As the deadline approached and no one left the village, Erickson rescinded his offer of free passage through the lines. Then, at the last minute, the Justice Department announced a cease-fire and more negotiations. "There will be no charging through the barricades," a Department official said.

Demonstrations of support on the outside during this time helped to pressure the United States Government not to use the full force of the military machine it had assembled outside the village. But shortly after the Government announced the cease-fire, a Wounded Knee roving patrol was fired on by automatic weapons from an APC, precipitating a gunbattle in which two Oglalas were injured.

The Reverend John Adams, of the United Methodist Church, a National Council of Churches representative on the scene, later described his efforts to bring about the cease-fire on March 8 and a firefight that broke out the next day:

Now I tell you that was a war there. There were people who felt that that was another scenario, a charade of some sort. But it wasn't. It was a war . . . And if you don't believe that you should go look at the buildings. You should see the ripping up of the countryside.

. . . So we proposed a cease-fire. I called a man in the Department of Justice in Washington, D.C., and said, "I want you to hear how this sounds." He said, "I'll have this on the desk of the Attorney General at nine o'clock. In the meantime, see how it goes out there."

. . . We took this proposal to the leadership of AIM and the Wounded Knee community. We said, "Now maybe this is a workable instrument for a cease-fire." They read it, and within five minutes they said, "We go with it. If you can sell it in Pine Ridge, we'll go with it."

. . . We went back to Pine Ridge, and by that time we found out that in Washington, they'd go with it. They were favorable. They had delivered an ultimatum, but it was an

ultimatum they couldn't stay with. They had to get out of the box they'd created for themselves.

The National Council of Churches had offered to put some observers in the "demilitarized zone" to try to effect that cease-fire. Now that sounds like a game, but it wasn't a game. In fact, the next night, it became a very real physical exercise. We'd had a negotiation session on Friday afternoon [March 9]. We went into Wounded Knee and were talking with the lawyers and the AIM leadership. We finished a little session and went over into the trading post and while we were there getting ready for a little pow-wow, firing broke out. And it was heavy firing. You could hear the automatic weaponry.

They signalled for the lights to go out. I was standing next to Russell Means and he said, "Let's get out of here." And he called all of them with their weapons outside. A young man came running up to him in the semi-darkness and he said, "They fired on us first."

I said, "Russ, I got to get up to the Federal checkpoint. Can I drive my car up there?" ... He said, "You can drive up, but you can't turn on your lights till you get over that hill over there."

I got up to the Federal checkpoint and they had these brilliant blue lights shining on the car. Brought me to a stop. And an agent came out and said, "Stay where you are. We're under fire." I said, "I know that." He said, "They fired first." I said, "Well, that's what they're saying down there." He said, "Dammit, Reverend, you've really been brainwashed!"

It took minutes to get through the checkpoint to see the agent in charge. When I got to him ... I said to him, Mr. Hoxey, they say you fired first. He said, "Reverend, they fired first." I said, "Well, what are you going to do?" He said, "Well, we'll stop firing when they stop firing." I said, "Okay, I've got to get back down then, to Russell."

FBI agent at Roadblock 1

So I got the car turned around again. They let me turn on the lights after fifty yards and I got back down that hill. And as I pulled up in that darkness, there was Russell standing there. I got out of the car and said, "Russ, they said you fired first." He said, "Dammit, John, they started it first." You start to learn how wars take place and how they keep going.

I said, "Well, they'll stop firing if you'll stop firing." He said, "Big deal." I said, "Would you pull your men back from that one sector, I think that would help." He stood there in that ring of men with rifles, thought a minute, and said, "Okay, I'll do it." I said, "Well, I've got to get back to the Federal checkpoint then."

So I turned the car around again and went through this same exercise. I went back up and by that time the agents were very nervous. One of them said, "You come up here one more time under these conditions and you're going to be

shot! We've got our lives on the line." I said, "Well, I'm not here for my health and I don't even have a gun. I've got to see the agent in charge."

So I saw Mr. Hoxey and said, They've pulled back their men in that sector." And he said, Okay." I said, "Will you signal a cease-fire." And he said, "I will."
. . .
Most of the people who came out to Wounded Knee — and we had a whole parade of people who were going to come out and solve that problem — and do you know what problem they wanted to solve? They wanted to

disarm the Indians. That was the solution they had. I told the AIM leaders, "It's not for me to tell you to take those guns down. I only ask you to use them as non-violently as possible." You had to recognize that that was the only political leverage they had.

It was a serious matter. And there were lives at stake. And if people thought that those who said they were ready to die were just playing, they were wrong. They were ready at that point — not to commit suicide — but to let their deaths be as strategic as possible.

Watching the APCs and helicopters.

THE INDEPENDENT OGLALA NATION

By March 10, the resistance at Wounded Knee had been front page news for two weeks. The Government had failed to force the native people out of the village, and with support for them growing, the military stalemate looked as if it might drag on indefinitely. The Federal officials then agreed to a Wounded Knee proposal to lift the roadblocks and allow free access in and out of the village. The officials had said the "militants" were only "seeking publicity" and would leave if given the chance to do so without the risk of arrest.

But the Oglalas were not about to leave until something had been done about the issues that had brought them there, including Tribal President Richard Wilson, whose "goon squad" was still terrorizing those who opposed his administration. For many Oglalas, it was safer in the village. So those in Wounded Knee were willing to see the siege lifted, knowing that supporters from around the reservation would then be able to join them.

The Federal roadblocks were lifted on Saturday afternoon, March 10. Some people did leave the village, but hundreds of others poured in, including many of the Oglala chiefs and headmen. That night, too, some local white ranchers made their way into the now-open area and set fire to the trading post. The fire was put out quickly and the warriors spent the rest of the night battling vigilantes who were shooting into the village. As a result, the people in Wounded Knee were forced to send out patrols and man their roadblocks once more.

It was a tense night, and the next day the drums beat as the defenders danced and sang, celebrating a victory. But the Government still considered Wounded Knee its own territory, and open to a "police sweep." Several times Sunday morning, according to his official report, FBI agent Trimbach tried to drive into the village. On his last attempt he was told at the checkpoint to ". . . immediately leave the area and that when any law enforcement officers were found at Wounded Knee they were to be arrested."

The Oglala chiefs met all day in the tipi and then announced that they would now be negotiating with the United States, nation to nation.

Oscar Bear Runner, Oglala, and Stan Holder, Wichita, embrace in celebration as Federal lawmen take down their roadblocks.

LET IT BE KNOWN THIS DAY, MARCH 11, 1973, THAT THE OGLALA SIOUX PEOPLE WILL revive the Treaty of 1868 and that it will be the basis for all negotiations.

Let the declaration be made that we are a sovereign nation by the Treaty of 1868.

We intend to send a delegation to the United Nations as follows: Chief Frank Fools Crow; Chief Frank Kills Enemy; Eugene White Hawk, District Chairman [of the Wounded Knee District Council]; Meredith Quinn, international advisor; Matthew King, interpreter . . .

. . . [We want] to abolish the Tribal Government under the Indian Reorganization Act. Wounded Knee will be a corporate state under the Independent Oglala Nation.

In proclaiming the Independent Oglala Nation, the first nation to be called for support and recognition is the [Iroquois] Six Nation Confederacy. [We] request that the Confederacy send emissaries to this newly proclaimed nation immediately to receive first-hand all the facts pertaining to this act . . .

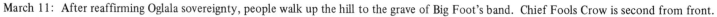

March 11: After reaffirming Oglala sovereignty, people walk up the hill to the grave of Big Foot's band. Chief Fools Crow is second from front.

"The traditional people were already a nation before the white man ever came — with our own laws, our own religious ways, our own tongues, everything. All we are doing is reminding this Government of that."

— a Blackfoot warrior

Two members of the Independent Oglala Nation community spoke about the wider meaning of the fight at Wounded Knee:

Russell Means: For two weeks we've known that the United States Government can come in and squash us, militarily. We never thought that we could beat them, overthrow them. But here's the fact: if they come in or not, whether we're massacred or not, they are still going to have to answer to our treaty rights, not only to the Indian people of America, but to all the countries of the world.

Lorelei DeCora: This is where it's at. Everybody that's ever had a fight for freedom is watching this. And Indian people, the smallest number of people in the country, the poorest people in the country, are making a stand here and are ready to die. All the people that have to struggle for freedom — Vietnam Veterans Against the War, people in the peace movements, are all watching this, because a group of people made a stand against the United States Government, once again.

People even across the world are watching the credibility of American treaties. They never realized — I don't think people in other countries realized — there were treaties with Indian tribes here, and nothing was being done about them.

Dennis Banks, Chippewa, and Russell Means, Oglala, give thanks with peace pipes in a ceremony celebrating victory over the United States Department of Justice.

Three Oglala women, Gladys Bissonette, Grace Black Elk, and Ellen Moves Camp spoke about Oglala sovereignty:

Gladys Bissonette: We want an independent sovereign Oglala Sioux nation. We don't want no part of the Government, Tribal or BIA. We have had enough of that. They don't allow us our rights. We want our old 1868 Treaty back.

We can go back to our old Indian culture, and if we have to start from scratch right here, in this small nation that we have settled on, I think we could make it. They call us lazy, they say we get land sale [money] and drink it up and then we're broke — but that is the way the BIA taught us to be. They have trained us to be dependent.

Grace Black Elk: See, in the beginning we had our own way. But this Tribal Council Government is a substitute for our way. It's run by white people's laws. And that BIA is just a puppet. They hold him by the nose and tell him what to do. So he tries to force his authority on the Indian people whether they like it or not. And that's how come we're balking now. We don't want that no more. We want to think for ourselves. We got a mind — the Great Spirit gave us a mind. We got our own way too. So we're going back to where we used to be.

Ellen: Well, this place has always been a nation, it was always recognized as a nation, and you go back into the 1868 Treaty, it's all in there. That's why we took this stand. . . . At the time, the roadblocks were up so there was people from the reservation that came in and they had a meeting in the tipi, and the people here on the reservation are the ones that had that announced.

Not the AIM people?

No, it wasn't the American Indian Movement people that done that. It was the people here on the reservation that done it.

And by the Independent Oglala Nation you meant the whole reservation?

Well, it's going to be the whole reservation, because all the people will stand with us. We know this. That's why we're here.

The chiefs asked the Oglala Sioux Civil Rights Organization and the American Indian Movement to form a provisional government which could speak for the new nation to the outside world. The Oglalas continued to supervise the everyday functioning of life in the village, and to make overall policy decisions. Lou Beane and Gladys Bissonette described their daily meetings.

Lou: When we have to make a decision, we call all the people together. And we sit down and talk about it, and then we decide on it. And if someone wants to talk about something, they get up and express their thoughts — what we should do and what we shouldn't do — and we agree on it that way.

Gladys: About 40 – 60 people come to these meetings but it will probably be more now. We don't go in the line of raising your hand and voting anymore. If someone doesn't agree, we just keep on going until it's unanimous. Otherwise, there's no decision made — until a further meeting, or turn back and talk about it again. We always come to some kind of agreement. In this Oglala Nation, one doesn't think that they're better than the other. We are all equal and we know it.

The roadblocks are up again. "We no longer have a perimeter to defend — we have a border."

The four "postal inspectors" and two ranchers temporarily detained after being disarmed by Wounded Knee Security.

While the chiefs were meeting, four men who identified themselves as postal inspectors drove to the village "to examine the post office in the trading post." They were challenged at the checkpoint and found to be carrying handcuffs and pistols. They were detained briefly and then released minus their weapons. Dennis Banks, a leader in the American Indian Movement, said, "I don't think they came down here to protect no mailboxes." Meanwhile, FBI surveillance on the roads was extremely heavy and many people had been arrested.

About the same time, several people who had gone to the nearby community of Manderson in a U-Haul van were returning, when, about four miles from Wounded Knee, as one of them described, " . . . a sedan pulled alongside and all of a sudden he hit the siren. I was going to pull over but he put an M-16 out the window and fired." The people in the U-Haul van fired back, wounding FBI agent Curtis Fitzgerald in the wrist. The bullet-riddled van made it safely back into the village.

This series of events enraged the Federal officials who realized that the community in Wounded Knee was strengthening itself. "We were sure they would pack up and disappear into the night," one high official said. The marshals and FBI agents immediately reestablished roadblocks, this time closer to the village, and began to build permanent bunkers fortified with logs and hay bales. Reinforcements soon brought their numbers to more than 300 men, and they began intensive patrolling to seal the perimeter. The next day, March 12, a Federal Grand Jury met in Sioux Falls to bring indictments in connection with the confrontation. Under the renewed siege, the Independent Oglala Nation settled in for an indefinite stay. ■

Safely back in Wounded Knee, looking through the window of the U-haul van.

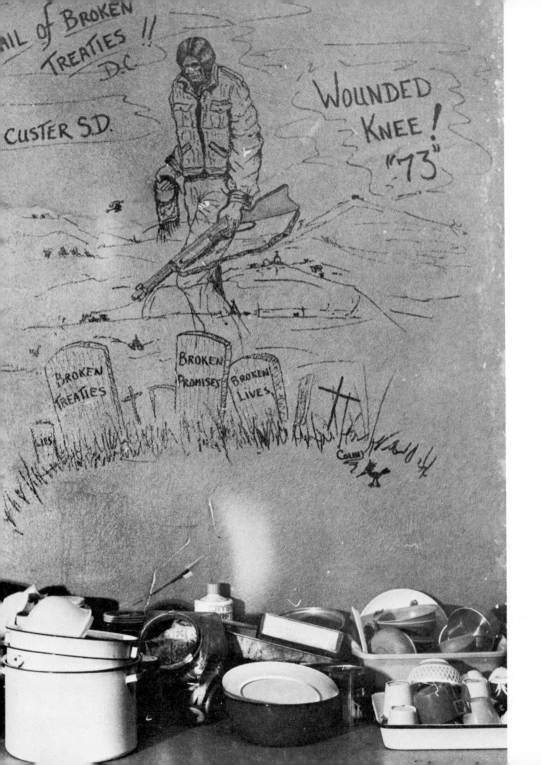

3.
THE AMERICAN INDIAN MOVEMENT

"I lived here 77 years. This whole reservation was in total darkness. And somewhere, these young men started the American Indian Movement. And they came to our reservation and they turned that light on inside. And it's getting bigger — now we can see things."

— an Oglala elder

The press was filled with reports of a "tattered band of renegades" who had come to take over Wounded Knee. Who were these "outsiders," and how did they come to find themselves surrounded by APCs and marshals, often far from their home reservations, risking charges that could bring them years in jail? One evening in March, one of the leaders of the American Indian Movement talked about its beginnings and what brought it to Wounded Knee:

The American Indian Movement was started by a group of men that had been living in an urban situation. Most of them had done time in correctional institutions and most of them were very bitter. They were put in there because of the pressure against Indian people in the cities. They knew the bitter frustrations of trying to exist in a society that would in no way accept them as human beings. They put together this movement to try to correct the things that are happening in the cities. Something had to be done.

They first started to work in the way of many urban organizations to try to gain control of a portion of Federal Government spending. They demanded that the Indian people be given a share so that they could begin working towards a solution to their problems. In that respect, they were very successful. On their first action the American Indian Movement demonstrated against the OEO offices for two or three weeks, and they were finally able to have people sit on the board of directors of OEO and the other funding organizations, and to begin channeling money into programs that would be controlled by Indian people.

Then they realized that one of the main oppressors there was the police and the way they brutally treated Indian people. Friday and Saturday nights, the police would go down into the Indian area of town and pick up bus loads of Indian people and take them to jail, and the next morning, court-appointed lawyers would tell them to plead guilty.

With a grant from one of the churches, they started an American Indian Movement patrol. This patrol was there to see that Indian people were given their rights to justice like any other citizen. They began patroling the Indian neighborhoods and when the police would arrest someone, they were there to make sure that they weren't beaten and brutalized as was so often done. This was about six years ago. It was a very successful thing, and has been an on-going program ever since.

The American Indian Movement worked in Minneapolis for its first year and people who found out what a tremendous help it was for the American Indian people started spreading the word of it. Of course, during its origin, the leaders of the American Indian Movement knew that there was something missing. They could go deal in the white man's courts, they could go advocate for Indian people in the poverty program and that sort of thing — but they still weren't helping the Indian people in the way that they wanted to be helped. The statistics didn't change for the Indian way of life.

At that time, some of the American Indian Movement leaders heard about a spiritual leader on the Rosebud Sioux Reservation named Crow Dog and they made a trip down there to Rosebud to visit with Crow Dog and see if they could gain some sort of spiritual direction that they had realized was so vitally missing.

And Crow Dog told them that if they were to be a true Indian organization, they had to have the spiritual involvement of our medicine men and our holy people. And that is actually when the American Indian Movement was first born: because we think that the American Indian Movement is not only an advocate for Indian people, it is the spiritual rebirth of our nation. It carries the spirituality of our ancient people and of our elder people. So now the American Indian Movement relies very, very heavily on the traditional leaders and the holy men of the various tribes — to give them the direction they need so thay can best help the Indian people.

At times, you will hear politicians or critics say that the American Indian Movement is an urban Indian group,

which is totally false. At one time it was true, but it almost immediately changed. Because along with getting deeply involved in the spiritual direction of our people, they soon realized that the very people that are in cities suffering were the same people that are on the reservation suffering.

Our people would go to a BIA school, and learn a skill

Dennis Banks and Carter Camp in center.

that could only be used in a city. Then they'd return to their reservations and not be able to get a job. They'd stay there for a while and decide, well, they'd try the city since the Bureau of Indian Affairs was giving people relocation money to change from reservation to city status, and trying to assimilate them into the melting pot of the United States.

These people would go to the cities and they could not survive. Indian people can't live in the cities. It's too cutthroat. It's always hurt your brother, or stab your brother in the back, and Indian people can't live that way.

So they would return to the reservation and be faced with the extreme poverty, the inability to get a job. There was no escape except maybe drinking or gambling or things that Indian people, you know, have such a problem with now. Abject poverty was their lot for as long as they stayed on the reservation, and a loss of manhood and pride. Many times, Indian men or Indian families would rotate between the city and reservation for a long time — each time thinking that when he changed his residence, he was changing his life for the better.

We realized that our involvement had to be with a total structure of Indian life across the whole nation. We had to begin advocating for Indians on the reservation and off the reservation — and in Canada and Mexico. Any place that there was Indian people, then we had to be right there to be their champion and fight for them, for their rights.

One time, reservations were, you know, concentration camps for our people. They were a place where Indians were locked in and left to die by this Government after they took away their way of life. And yet, our people, because they live on the land — live so closely with the land — they come to love the place where they were put. That became their home, that became the place where their relatives were buried, and the place where they wanted to be forever. The American Indian Movement realized the way people felt about reservations. They themselves felt exactly the same way about their very own reservations, and they had to be on those reservations to fight for their people.

The American Indian Movement sees itself as a new warrior society for Indian people. There is a varying concept of warrior society. To white persons, the warrior is the armed forces. It's the guy that goes out there and fights and kills for his people. But Indian people have never had hired killers. Warrior society to them means the men and women of the nation who have dedicated themselves to give everything that they have to the people. A warrior should be the first one to go hungry or the last one to eat. He should be the first one to give away his mocassins and the last one to get new ones. That type of feeling among Indian people is what a warrior society is all about. He is ready to defend his family in time of war — to hold off any enemy, and is per-

fectly willing to sacrifice himself to the good of his tribe and his people. That's what a warrior society is to Indian people, and that's what we envision ourselves as, what we idealistically try to be. I'm not saying that we are all completely selfless or any kind of saints. But we try, with the spiritual direction of our holy men, to get ourselves to the point where we don't have the avarice and greed that is so much a part of Anglo — of white — society in the United States.

We believe that the power of this universe is held within our peace pipe. It is a pipe of peace, a pipe that at all costs tries to guide us in avoiding any deaths by our own hands, any violence on the part of the American Indian Movement. And if anyone will check back into the history of the American Indian Movement, though we take a very strong stand for our people, we've never killed anyone. We have never had violence unless violence was perpetrated on us first.

The real violence in America is committed by the Government against our people. The real violence is the fact that on a reservation our women are taken and raped in the back seat of these police cars. The real violence is the fact that our children are never able to learn to live in a society that is completely alien to them, and so they suffer tremendous disorientation in their own lives which many times leads to suicide, or drunkenness — which is another form of suicide — or drugs. The real violence is when the Bureau of Indian Affairs, who is supposedly holding our lands in trust for us — because they say we are incompetent to handle our own affairs — reduces our land base by 160 thousand acres or so every year. And it's violence against our people when they build dams and flood our ancestral lands and disturb the graves of our past generations.

We first started taking direct action on the Sioux reservation around 1969 when some of our people tried to force the BIA to deal with the issues of Indian problems. We were trying to change the educational system. They taught our Indian children that wearing their hair in the traditional manner was bad for them, that Indian people were savages, and that our religion was paganism. We tried to get them to start teaching our children that religion is the very basis of Indian life, and the way we wear our hair or the way we dress in no way interferes with the way we can learn.

In the border towns around here, tremendous oppression against our people exists. In Rushville, Nebraska, an old Indian man was on the street and the police came along, and this particularly sadistic policeman knocked this old Indian man down and every time the Indian man would rise, the policeman would hit him with his club or kick him until he fell to his knees. Rushville is only three blocks long, and he made that Indian man crawl from one end of town to the other, while young high school kids gathered around and spit on the old man and called him names. There were two Indian women there watching, but they couldn't do anything about it. They came to AIM and told us about that. That was in 1970, when America was supposed to be so aware.

Then in Gordon, Nebraska, some white people killed Raymond Yellow Thunder. Raymond Yellow Thunder was an old Indian man, well-respected on the reservation, and looked up to as one of the kindest people, which to Indian people means that he was a real leader of his people. He was in Gordon, and I don't know, maybe he had been drinking — maybe he had and maybe he hadn't — it doesn't make any difference. He was found on the street by a couple of white ranchers, the Hare brothers, young men — young brutish people — along with a couple of their companions. He was beaten severely in an alley and then put into the trunk of their car and driven around for 45 minutes or an hour. They testified themselves that he was taken to an American Legion dance where he was thrown into the American Legion hall while all the people stood around and

"Indians have always had a lot to say. The question was if the Europeans had any desire or ability to listen. The Indian nations will be here long after the United States ceases to exist — and this comes from old people who don't even talk English, who understand what this America is about."

— Tom Cook

laughed about it. The Hare brothers kicked him to the ground and invited the other white people there to kick that Indian because it was so much fun. They took off his pants and degraded him when he was half-naked and threw him back out of the American Legion Hall. They put him back into their trunk again and drove him around, and beat him severely again and finally he died.

At that time, the American Indian Movement was in Omaha, Nebraska, attending a convention of Indian people. The sisters and brothers of Raymond Yellow Thunder tried to go to the local police and were laughed at. They called the FBI and the FBI said that it didn't mean anything to them and they wouldn't give them any help. They went to the BIA, who naturally claimed that they didn't want to help They tried to call their Congressman and had no response whatsoever. As a very last resort, they called the American Indian Movement and told us of the circumstances.

The American Indian Movement was just tired and frustrated that our efforts had not met any kind of success in stopping these degradations against our people, so we mobilized to go to the town of Gordon and demand that justice be done. Over two thousand American Indian people drove in caravans from the Pine Ridge Reservation, the Rosebud Reservation, and then from the convention in Omaha. They completely took over that town for three days that they were there. They demanded that those people at least be arrested, because up until that time, the officials of that town hadn't even filed charges against those Hare brothers. The mayor of the town and the chief of police then capitulated and charges were lodged against these people.

Then this January, in Buffalo Gap, South Dakota, a white service station owner named Schmidt killed Wesley Bad Heart Bull, and the authorities refused to take any action on that. The American Indian Movement was called because the Bad Heart Bull family had faith in what we are trying to do. We had known of murders around the reservation and hadn't taken any action because we needed to have the support of a group of Indian people before we could come in. When the county that had jurisdiction over his death found out that Dennis Banks was in town to investigate that death, they decided that they had better charge the white man with manslaughter — second-degree manslaughter — because they knew that the American Indian Movement was becoming interested in that case and that we were going to do something about it. The Indian people felt that the charge should have

been murder in the first degree because of the way that it all happened.

The American Indian Movement decided to mobilize its forces to try to once again show a town that they couldn't do that to Indian people any longer. On February 6 of this year, they were going to have a preliminary hearing in Custer, South Dakota. When they heard that the American Indian Movement was mobilizing, they set that date off until later in February. We decided that because our forces were mobilized in Rapid City, the actual date didn't make any difference. We were going to go to that town and demand that he be charged with first-degree murder, and that sufficient bail be put against him to make sure that he came to trial, because we knew that we had plenty of evidence to convict him.

The racist government of that town decided that they didn't need to deal with any Indian people; they didn't need to deal with us at all. And while myself and some of the AIM leaders were inside the courthouse building trying to negotiate with the city officials, who at that time wouldn't even talk to us, they attacked our people that were trying to come into the courthouse. They attacked our people and we started fighting inside the courthouse and we beat the cops in the courthouse and beat them out the back door where they mounted a counter-charge and beat us out the front door. So we had quite a set-to in the courthouse, and then our people, thinking that the leadership was trapped inside, started fighting all over the town. They were very mad and they burned the courthouse and the Chamber of Commerce and a couple of other buildings there and generally wreaked havoc on the town of Custer, South Dakota.

That type of action wasn't planned by us and it wasn't something that we decided to go and do before we ever went up there, but it was something that spontaneously came about because of the extreme frustrations of the people.

Then we went back to Rapid City, and realizing that they controlled the feelings of the other towns in the area, we made the town of Rapid City agree to a set of demands and proposals by the Indian people, and caused the mayors of ten other towns in the area, the small towns, to also meet with us and start finding some way for the Indian people to deal with living in those cities.

During this time, the Oglala Sioux people had formed a civil rights committee here on the Pine Ridge Reservation, trying to find a way that they could deal in a legal manner with the Bureau of Indian Affairs and its puppet, Dickie

Wilson. After trying and trying to change the governmental system on this reservation, the Oglala Sioux people called the American Indian Movement and asked us to come down and offer what aid we could. [We had promised not to involve ourselves in the politics or policies of any Indian nation and this looked at first like that's what it was. But when we came down here we realized that the struggle was not at all with Oglala Sioux people — it was with the Federal Government and the Bureau of Indian Affairs. We said then that we would stay and help if they would call together the traditional tribal chiefs and the traditional people around the reservation — the real leaders of the Sioux people — and if they wanted to take direct action, then we would.]

They came together and decided to take action, and they left the mode of action up to the Oglala Sioux Civil Rights Organization, who in turn asked the American Indian Movement to help in the planning of some type of demonstration. Our original thought was to go to the Bureau of Indian Affairs in Pine Ridge and physically throw out the Government. We soon realized that this was impossible, because they had the place completely fortified and had Federal Marshals and BIA pigs all around it, and sandbags on top, machine guns, and fortifications all over the town. So in order to avoid that kind of pitched battle, we decided to come to Wounded Knee, because of its historic significance to our people, naturally, and the fact that it lies right in the heart of the Pine Ridge Reservation. We felt that by coming here, occupying this town, we would be telling the Sioux Nation that they had someone there to fight for them, to help them fight and protect them.

The Oglala people sent about two hundred people here with us. The American Indian Movement provided about fifty people, mostly warriors. We came to Wounded Knee and seized the town and started telling the Government that if they wanted this town, as part of the United States, that they would have to start dealing with the Indian people on the issues of replacement of the Bureau of Indian Affairs officials, Stanley Lyman of Pine Ridge and Wyman Babby of the Aberdeen Area Office, and we also told them that we would have to have a re-call election to replace Dickie Wilson. They refused to do that, and we solidified our position here, and we have stayed here and held Wounded Knee and held off the Federal forces that surrounded us with armored personnel carriers, and, you know, machine guns and the whole works. They have us completely surrounded.

Two weeks after we had been here, the Oglala Sioux had a general meeting of the leaders of this Oglala Nation of Pine Ridge. The leaders flocked in from all over — the traditional chiefs, Charlie Red Cloud and Frank Fools Crow, came in to give their guidance; holy men like Pete Catches and Leonard Crow Dog and Wallace Black Elk, along with the district leaders like Severt Young Bear, Birgil Kills Straight, all the primary leaders of the Oglalas came here to meet in council. The American Indian Movement and the Oglala Sioux people decided that AIM people should be excluded from this meeting because we were here at the request of the Oglala Sioux people, and we felt that they should make any decisions about the future of their lives and their reservation themselves without any interference from outside participants. We excluded ourselves from this meeting and were in fact very surprised by its outcome.

The traditional leaders decided that this was probably the only time in history that they would have a chance to regain their sovereignty as a nation. They came out of an all-day meeting inside a council tipi, and told us that they were declaring their sovereignty as an independent nation. They had voted to send delegates to the United Nations, and to address the White House in Washington, D.C., on the fact that they were going to be independent from now on. They asked the American Indian Movement to effect that change. We were eager to help them. We set up a government here and strengthened our positions to try to repel any invaders.

The American Indian Movement and the Oglala Sioux people here have what every race in America dreams of having. We have a land base, we have a government here, we have the support of the mass of Indian people on the Pine Ridge Reservation. And what is at stake here at Wounded Knee is not just the lives of a few hundred Indian people. It is a way of life that we believe could lead to the complete salvation of the United States and of Western civilization. We're trying to make everyone realize that from here, a true revolution in the way people live can start. ■■■■■■■■

4.
A COMMUNITY
OF RESISTANCE

"We're trying to regain what we had in the past, being human beings and being involved in society."

— Stan Holder

In the first two weeks of the take-over, a community developed spontaneously as people worked together to set up sleeping quarters, bunkers, and communal kitchens. Then, after the affirmation of Oglala sovereignty on the weekend of March 11, the newly-formed provisional government of the Independent Oglala Nation established committees on housing, medical care, food supply, customs and immigration, internal security, information, and defense.

Some of the better-equipped homes, belonging to the white missionaries and trading post owners who had left the village, were taken over to serve as sleeping and eating quarters and as a clinic. Communal kitchens were set up in some of the church buildings. Little communities formed in different areas of the village with people eating and sleeping near their bunkers in case of an alert. The trading post itself became a meeting hall where people gathered each evening to discuss military and political matters, to hear reports of the committees, and to visit with friends after a day's work.

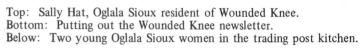

Top: Sally Hat, Oglala Sioux resident of Wounded Knee.
Bottom: Putting out the Wounded Knee newsletter.
Below: Two young Oglala Sioux women in the trading post kitchen.

From the bunker in front of the Catholic church facing South towards downtown Wounded Knee. The long building in the center of the downtown area is the trading post. To its left is the Security building. In the field at the right edge of the photo is the tipi, and sweat lodge on the 1890 massacre site.

A description of Wounded Knee — written at the time by a member of the alternate press:

Wounded Knee is set into a little valley in the rolling South Dakota prairie. It marks the meeting of four roads, coming from the reservation communities of Manderson, Porcupine, and Denby to the west, north, and east, and the administrative center of Pine Ridge to the south. At the center where the roads meet is the huge, sprawling trading post, owned by the Gildersleeves and the Czywzcynskis, two white families who also own much of the nearby land and housing. Before the occupation, prices there were even more expensive than in nearby Pine Ridge village. Since February 27, the food has been given out to the kitchens to feed everyone in the village.

A five minute walk to the east from downtown is the the most luxurious house in Wounded Knee, where the Church of God missionaries lived. In the same compound are their two churches, (called the "white church kitchen" and the "tipi church,") and the three buildings now house and feed about 100 people, many of whom work in the bunkers nearby, Little California and Denby.

To the north of the trading post up on a hill stands the Catholic church, now made famous by news photos, built near the mass grave where Chief Big Foot's people were buried after the 1890 massacre. People now eat and sleep in the basement of the church, although the church takes a lot of fire because of its high position.

Further to the north is the Episcopal church, which now houses the squad for Hawk Eye bunker, dug in front of it. The front of the bunker — made of 2 by 4s packed with earth — is peppered with slugs — as if the marshals had tried to eat it away with their machine guns.

Down a slope to the northwest, on the edge of the perimeter, is the cluster housing project, where most of the local Indian families live. Many of them have stayed. Their children can be seen playing around the bunker, which is manned entirely by Oglalas. During the firefights they are caught in between the Wounded Knee bunker and the Government roadblock, and their cardboard-thin walls have taken quite a beating.

The valley of Wounded Knee is round, and around the perimeter lie seven bunkers — Last Stand, Hawk Eye, Little Big Horn, Denby, Little California, Crow's Nest, and Star. — built to defend the village from an assault by Federal forces.

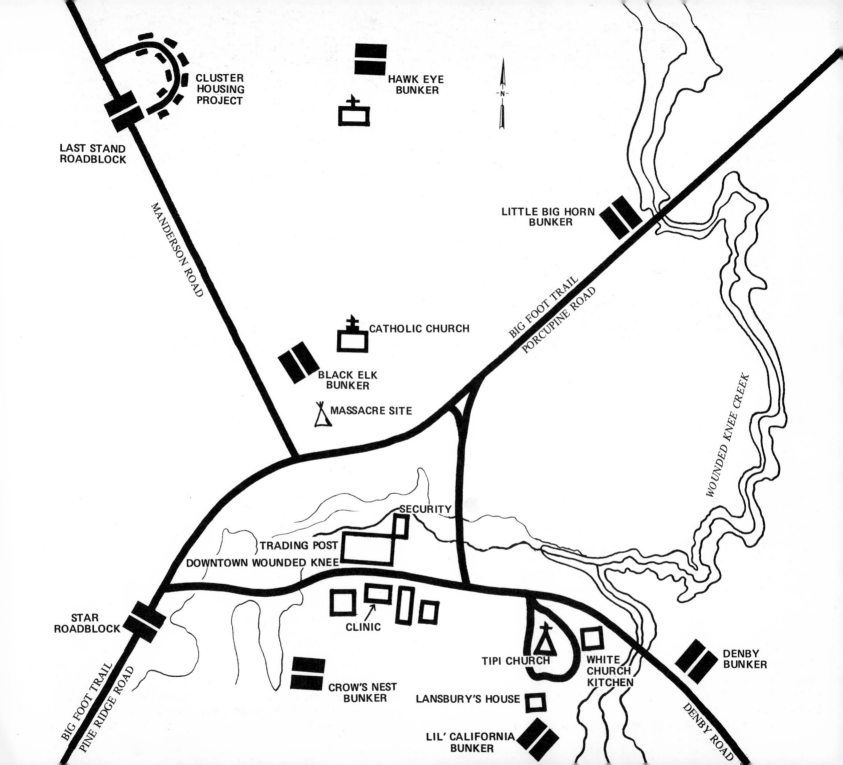

THE CLINIC
"It's like a hospital on the lines in Viet Nam — we're under fire almost every night . . ."

A clinic had been set up in the small two-bedroom house across from the trading post. Now doctors and nurses were organized to come in weekly teams from free clinics and people's health organizations around the United States, while Indian people ran the clinic and worked and trained as medics. The clinic also ran one of the main kitchens.

One night a bunch of people were sitting around the clinic's kitchen table. Three warriors from Little California bunker came in for their midnight break just as the coffee ran out and had to make some sage tea instead. Lorelei DeCora, a Minneconjou Sioux and State Director for Iowa of the American Indian Movement, walked from the kitchen into a quiet back room, sat herself down on a box of medicines, and talked about the functioning of the clinic.

Madonna and I, we are the head women of the clinic. We use Western medicine and Indian medicine to cure colds and things like that. It's like a hospital, like on the lines in Viet Nam because we're under fire almost every night and we have to turn the lights off — one room with the lights on

for emergency surgery or whatever we have to do. We have a few patients here that stay and we have medics that go out when the firing starts. We have food here — we also cook for Security. It's a hospital and a home at the same time.

Mostly we have colds, strep throat, some pneumonia, fevers like the flu. We had three guys that got shot — two were Oglala Sioux. One was shot in the leg with an M-16. The other was shot in the hand with an M-16 but the bullet went right through. And just a couple of nights ago, a Chicano medic who was here to support us, when they started to fire he ran out with his medic's bag and he got hit in the stomach with an M-16 too. They're all okay. The medicine man took the bullets out.

We have a capable staff here. Any group of medics that come in, we brief them on what's happening, what to expect, what not to expect, the rules, and whatever. We've really been fortunate in all the crews that have come in here — really been hanging in there. We had a crew here from California. They left and another team came in from Seattle, Washington. There are a lot of veterans that were in Viet

Nam as medics. They stay here until the next crew can come in — it's negotiated by the National Council of Churches. They also hustle a lot on the outside for the supplies that we need.

We need medical supplies in here badly, like for colds. We have no cough medicine or antibiotics or drugs for guys that are really in pain. The last few days they've cut off even bandages, and things like that, that people have sent from all over the country. They're just piling up out there and we need them in here badly. Marshals and FBI are cutting them off. We're going to need that support from people on the outside sending in supplies. What I really like, is three big box loads came in from the outside — medical supplies — and on the outside of the box it said "Power to the People." There really are a lot of people on the outside.

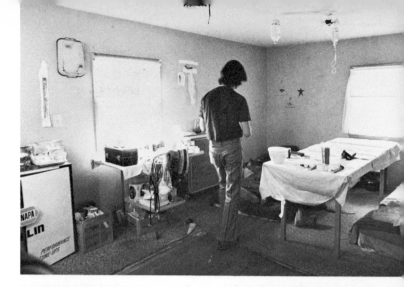

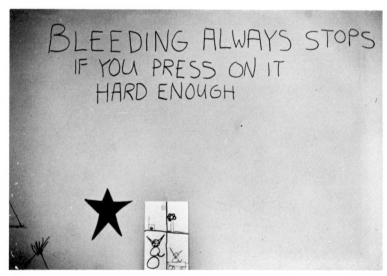

Left: Lorelei DeCora; medical drill.
Above: Sign in the clinic.
Right, above: Operating room.
Left, above: Volunteer medics in the clinic kitchen.

"This clinic we have here, I think is something great. And we are very proud of these volunteer medics. We don't want any of the Public Health Service from Pine Ridge coming in here. They have killed us Indians right and left."

— Gladys Bissonette

HOUSING

"People realize that when they're pounding a nail, they're pounding it for the Indian people . . ."

For two weeks people had been sleeping wherever they could find a space, curled in blankets on church pews and empty floors. One afternoon, Duane Camp, a Ponca, head of the new housing committee, was in the back of the trading post, where people slept, helping to nail up a partition. At the other end of the building people were singing around the drum. Yelling a little to be heard, Duane described the housing situation.

The housing's adequate right now — it's nothing fancy. We have a sanitation problem, lack of water and the plumbing's all fouled up. But the people are reasonably warm and reasonably comfortable. They are aware that we're a city under siege and consequently the complaints are negligible.

But in the earlier days, when 90% of the people that were here were warriors and they needed a place to lie down to get out of the bunkers, it was more of a challenge. We got the job done, thanks to the guys that were willing to lay down their guns and do something that had to be done. They put up units to house 200 people, in four days. And that takes a certain amount of dedication.

We have two different crews. One of the crews is basically rebuilding bunkers for better quarters during the bad weather and the other is making sleeping quarters. We call them apartments sometimes as a joke. They're just four aisles and we're lucky if there's bunks in there. There is not anyone sleeping cold but there is none to spare.

There is a lot of lumber that was here, unused lumber, good lumber. Then of course we use all the lumber when we tear down walls and so on. We even take the nails out and straighten them because we're here for such an indefinite period that it's real hard to plan ahead. So we try to make use of everything.

Each crew varies from day to day from four to six fellows. The guys just work as late as they have to and we don't have a very — you know, we don't punch in in the morning. So we all just get together during the day when there's no meeting going on.

We have real good teamwork. The people here realize that when they pound a nail, they're pounding it for a cause, for the Indian people. And so consequently, everybody works together real good — sharing the hammers and saws — different work crews. They have a sense of history. This is the makings of a new nation, and each nail represents a part of that.

Opposite page —
    top: Duane Camp.
    bottom: Work shed
behind trading post.

This page —
    top: Putting up clothes line.
    left: Installing Security radio antenna.
    right: Working on Black Elk Bunker — "downtown" is at left.

SECURITY

"So it's an army, but it's an army born purely out of love for the Indian race, and not hate for the white race . . ."

The nightly attacks by the Government continued, and the Independent Oglala Nation strengthened its defenses. Warriors arrived bringing some better weapons – still few against the machine-guns of the U.S. forces – and the skills many had learned in military service. Leaders emerged as groups came together for defense of vital areas on the village perimeter. New bunkers were dug, and existing ones reinforced. Stoves were installed in them for heating and cooking, and some had sleeping platforms. Bunker squads pulled 12 and 18 hour shifts, and each crew slept and ate close by its station.

The Wounded Knee Massacre Site Museum, a sturdy log building attached to the trading post, was made into the headquarters for the Security forces. Here, roving foot patrols checked in periodically as they walked the perimeter watching for infiltration and attack. Citizen's Band radios were used to communicate between the Security building, bunkers, and patrols. On the wall above the radio desk was hung a huge, bright orange hand-drawn map of the area, detailing the ION and Government positions. In the back of the building, near the large stone fireplace, were newly-constructed bunkbeds, and an old ditto machine used to run off announcements.

One evening Stan Holder, a Witchita, head of Wounded Knee Security and a Viet Nam veteran, discussed the philosophy behind the defenses:

We were born out of defense for this nation. We're not an offensive striking force at all, but we will move when we have to, to defend this nation. We try to keep as much of the European style of military expertise out of it, and stick with our warrior societies, working on a basis of trust, not corporal or disciplinary punishment. It's more of a brotherhood, than an army with a chain of command.

Indian warrior societies were born out of the community life that the Indian existed in. He didn't live in a regimented society. There was no army. When the nation he belonged to needed defense, the warrior societies vowed to do this fighting. That's basically the same way that our army is set up. I don't keep rolls, I don't keep names, I don't have to because we're adult Indian males and we have enough respect and love for each other that we don't need that.

There's a spiritual aspect to it, too. We have our own medicine personally, and then we have the medicine that is given to us as a warrior society. These are usually conceived from visions, fasting, or the animal and plant life, things of nature that we see when we come out of our spiritual ceremonies. We're still searching for something to designate our warrior society here. We've taken the magpie as our sign, our coup feather for deeds done. But that's still tentative. And we're going to get together as soon as this nation gets a lull in this war that the United States is waging upon us. We're going to fast and we're going on a vision to find out exactly what our medicine is, and the way that we'll integrate it into this new warrior society.

There's no discipline in this warrior society except self-discipline. I don't raise my voice at the men that I supposedly command because I don't command them. We haven't had any trouble at all with this, because people realize the need for this, they realize that once there is a breakdown in this trust we have, that there will be no Independent

Oglala Nation. So it's an army, but it's an army born purely out of love for the Indian race and not hate for the white race.

It's a 180-degree change from the U.S. military. The men here — they don't gripe, they don't say, "It's cold out," or anything like that. They realize that there's a need to defend their women and children here, and a need to defend the sacred land that we're living on, and they do it. They keep their respect for nature. They don't go around wanting to defoliate, as the United States did in Viet Nam. They don't go around wanting to indiscriminately kill people, because they realize that the loss of a life, whether a white, black, red, or yellow, is still the loss of a life and it's a loss to nature, it's upsetting the balance.

The American fighting forces and the American Justice Department are so dehumanized that they can't even bring the personal aspect into their wars. They just want to wage wars on a mass scale and keep identity totally out of it.

Grass fires on the Wounded Knee perimeter.

That's why they rake the entire town with fire when they open up on us, or they rake an entire field with fire. And they're not only killing or wounding human beings but they're wounding the animal life. They just have no personal feeling at all. They can't see the human aspect in this fight. If they did see it, they'd realize that they should lay down their guns — that this is a fight for the survival of the world.

. . . We've been receiving automatic-weapons fire — M-60, it's a 7.62 NATO round; M-16, the weapon used in Viet Nam by the United States Armed Forces; .30 calibers, which are either mounted or built into these armored personnel carriers. Then the 30.06, a normal hunting rifle that the white ranchers and vigilantes use — who the Government says aren't there. Also, shotguns used by the BIA police, and .38s, .44 magnums, things of this nature — weapons you'd find in any sporting goods store, and your military weapons utilized by the Federal Marshals. They've also been using gas, which they say they haven't been using.

They've burned off large areas of land by utilizing flares fired directly into the dry grass. The winter has taken all the moisture out of the plant life around here and it's very easy to set it off. They're destroying something that was totally beautiful and totally pure for reasons that have no backing other than pure aggression.

We're trying to regain what we had in the past, being human beings and being involved in society. We're going to accept some forms of technology to defend ourselves until such time as we don't have to defend ourselves at all.

Stan Holder.

The following Government transmissions were monitored by Wounded Knee Security on their UHF radio receiver after an hour-long firefight in mid-March. Red Arrow was the Government's field command post, operating out of a luxury Winnebago "Red Arrow" model motor home on the top of a hill on the eastern perimeter. Warriors' comments inside the Security building as they listened to the status report are printed in italic.

Red Arrow: The last ten minutes or so have been quiet.

> ***Warriors in Wounded Knee Security Headquarters:** We want some grits and butter up here . . .*

Red Arrow to Command Post: Headquarters 18 report continues: "No injured, no one hurt on our side . . ."

> ***Warriors:** Tell 'em we're okay over here too. That would freak them out!*

. . . Estimated number of rounds received: 250. Estimated number of rounds returned: 250.

> *Tit for tat. Two hundred fifty? Hell! There ain't 250 rounds in camp . . .*

. . . Most of the fire came from the large bunker; some from the small one. Amount of damage: windshield shot out of jeep . . .

> *Yeaaaaaaa!*

. . . The blue van has one round in it . . .
> *Heeeeeey!*

. . . No injuries on our side. No injuries on our side. Other side, unable to advise. For the last ten minutes it's been quiet.

> *Indians, zero — Feds, zero!*

WAR

war
when will it ever
stop

what else would you call it:
assimilation
acculturation
relocation
education . . .
as long as we have known the whiteman
we have never known
peace

only in the Longhouse
the Kiva
only in the lodges
when the sacred smoke
is carried by the wind
for all the Creation to see
only then
are we at peace

the people
are cold
poor?
not so poor as
without the dance,
the chants,
the thanksgivings
the children, the
laughter, the burning
desire of freedom

you do not wage war
on a poor people, whiteman
we have power
we have strength
we have the will to live
we have the will to die

since we have known
the whiteman
only this have we learned:
death   needless & lingering
           drunk & far from home

now
death   honorable
           as a warrior

— Karoniaktatie

A Navajo Viet Nam veteran spoke inside Wounded Knee Security headquarters, to a background of Government radio reports:

Now that I'm down here in George McGovern's great
state of South Dakota, all I've done is get fired up about going
back to New Mexico and organizing, trying to raise people's
consciousness to the point where they realize that they don't
have to take it. Just like the people here finally realized that
they don't have to take all the shit from the man.

There's a tremendous amount of coolness, considering
that we're outgunned, that even if we do knock off a pig,
there's always one more, or ten more in his place. We're
facing a huge machine that has replaceable parts, thousands
of them. And considering our odds, you might say that this
is really something else. *(Government radio in background
interjects: "Roadblock 4 reports hearing gunshot between
their 10-20 and yours. Can you confirm?")* This is really a
tight little band of people, considering what we're up against.

But people stay because they believe; they have a cause.
That's why we lost in Viet Nam, cause there was no cause.
We were fighting a rich man's war, for the rich man, being

used as cannon fodder, with no regard for what happened to us at all.

In Wounded Knee, we're doing pretty damn good, morale-wise. Because we can still laugh. *("That's 10-4, Red Arrow. Negative on our side. Try and pinpoint a location.")* These marshals out there are becoming quite edgy. You can tell by the inflections in their voices on the radio that all is not cool with them. The strain on them is worse than it is on us.

A Chicano Viet Nam veteran:

I just came out here because I'm against the thing, and if I'm against it, the only way I can fight is to come out here and put my ass on the line. I ain't got a lot of money. The only thing I got to give is whatever I can do — help 'em out physically.

Most of them pigs are out there cause they get paid for it. It's really a sad thing — they got to depend on their APCs and shoot from a distance. I'd rather see it hand-to-hand.

It's just like the Air Force. Guys that fly the B-52s. They drop their load and blow everybody away, women and kids, and they never come in contact with them. "Well, I flew a plane and pushed this button and the bombs dropped out . . ."

If I want to do somebody in, I want to make sure I do him in, and not some little kid that was standing next to him. I don't think I could handle that kind of a trip.

One Chicano warrior kept a diary of his time at Wounded Knee. These are some of his entries.

March 8. Being followed by pigs all the way from Montana border through Wyoming. One mile from our contact, pigs flashing M-16s stopped everyone. Sad to see all Indian pigs doing this. Searched every inch of cars.

Waited till dark and made it to Porcupine after some hassles. Brothers and sisters there under heavy surveillance — expecting a raid tonight. About 30 of us waiting to go into Wounded Knee.

March 9. Went to an afternoon meeting at Porcupine. Ate a fabulous meal almost precisely like the meals I ate as a child — *caldo de res,* Indian fry bread *(bunuelos),* and a pudding of berries that took me back 20 years.

After the meeting we collectively made the decision to cut across the hills this p.m. to enter Wounded Knee, in spite of last night's shootings. No clear idea of what to expect, visions of danger prevalent in everyone's mind. Most conversations center around possibility of dying — yet all are anxious to depart on long hike. Expectations of hike: 8 miles. Actuality: about 20 miles, over incredibly difficult terrain. Left at 10 p.m. eagerly, 13 people.

March 10, 4 a.m. Four hours on the road and constant flares in the distance. Hills look harmless from a distance, but they're m-fkers. Hitting dirt after every flare. Guide is

very young and inexperienced. We lose main group several times. Some snow and ice on hills and no smoking — what a bitch. Finally walk into occupied area at 6 a.m. totally fatigued. Lots of excitement and overwhelming satisfaction to finally see the area I had tried so long to visualize.

March 11. Doing guard duty on northern perimeter, after digging beautiful trench. FBI pig injured at checkpoint. Conflicting stories and tensions running high. Talked to main person involved and hard to tell from his story just what happened.

March 12. Duty on bunker after declaration of independence by Wounded Knee nation. Evening meeting regarding make-up of provisional government. Many, many cameras (national TV). Sack time after long Indian spiritual ceremony.

March 13. Meeting with many announcements that lifted morale tremendously. Organization is improving every day but has a long way to go. Work brigades are getting better and security is best organized group. Got assigned to bunker number 2 from 12 to 6 p.m. Very quiet with heavy fog. Fifteen APCs are stationed around zone — we're facing two, about 500 yards away.

Looking for housing since present quarters are unbearably crowded and a heavy smell of fuel oil in church prevents breathing. Haven't seen a newspaper or news program for third straight day.

March 14, 3 a.m. Could not believe the weather — rain turned into an out-and-out blizzard. Got completely soaked and by 6 a.m. had lost almost all feeling in my legs. Slept most of the day before going back on guard duty at 6 p.m. Blizzard still on.

Mass meeting this p.m. Full report by many committees on details and problems of their work. These include: housing, security, military, police, medical, supply officer, customs and immigration, negotiations. Almost 300 people at meeting and morale appears high in spite of snow and wind. It appears that the pig Government is not going to allow medicine or food in, in spite of TV reports to the contrary. It figures. Thirty-one indictments handed down by Sioux Falls Grand Jury (names kept secret.) No negotiations today, due to snowbound roads. Apparently all leaving Wounded Knee can expect to be arrested.

Very good meeting, especially the open question part. Cleared up a lot of rumors. Lots of jokes and good humor among leadership. Meeting ended in beautiful spirit of solidarity. There was special thanks given to Chicanos in and out of Wounded Knee. Finale was AIM song with drums.

March 15. Got up late to the sickening news that a Chicano brother was wiped out in Rapid City. His brother is in Wounded Knee. Security meeting.

Bad weather over, with whole place being a mud bath. Strange calmness prevailing. Symphony of coughs dominates entire encampment. Many bad colds.

March 16. Helped build a beautiful bunker on northern perimeter, most sensitive area of all. Everyone pitched in and the results are a tribute to the people's spirit.

Evening meeting full and exciting. Citizenship granted to residents of new Oglala Nation. Three types which include 1. Oglala; 2. Dual citizenship for other Indians (Dig this: including Chicanos); 3. Naturalization for non-Indians. Beautiful Indian ceremony followed.

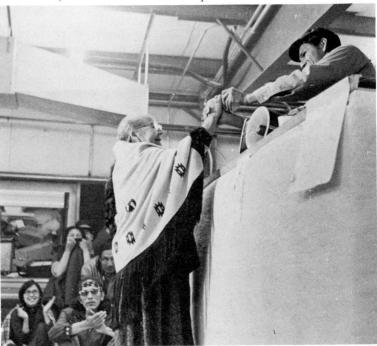

182 Oglalas, 160 Indians from other tribes, and 7 whites became citizens of the Independent Oglala Nation. Below, Grandma Wauwasick, Potowatomi, receives her ION citizenship.

From the Knee / To all their Relations

There was a young security guard who asked me
not to use his name 'cause he felt shy
   who had been walking from his bunker back towards town.
The darkness and the cold were all around him
but the way he is
he dint give a damn   and walked on towards the center.
   In the sweat lodge he remembered Crow Dog talk to them
of spirits, of relations and all life and where things fit
                  and in the rest of that second
   it scared him sharply to hear those noises, frightened voices
of women and small children towards that creek.
It seemed he heard them clearly, and he stopped and stared that way.
He lit a smoke and stood for a short while
                  but there was only silence and the night.
He continued on and swears he heard again
a crying and a movement there that went away again.
   He told no one about it, until one time he heard an older warrior
murmur very humbly that he knows there's wailing voices
out that way. Three others right there told of how they also
felt those spirits many times and heard their voice. And one said
that he knew it to be true   that they were our relations
who every now and then will speak to us.
And no one said a lot because they all knew where they were.
   It came from medicine people at the Knee
that in the oldest ways, all the life spirits with their strengths
and messages were asked to come here   and speak to those who listen.
   It come to be apparent that many people knew about the presence of
much strength that came from somewhere else.
   And the grandmothers and grandfathers of our people, and even
those who yet are coming towards us, watch there in the bunkers
with our men, and visit with them about what things must be done.
   And even now you will not hear it over any networks,
for it is said to be a knowledge in the bunkers at this place
   that networks cannot listen to "such things" for they are Indian.
And the people here who keep the others strong
continue to maintain, that none can know what the Knee's about
unless they think in Indian.
So we continue
to speak in Indian, of where things have been and are
and to send the words out
to all of our relations on this land.

                                        — Kanatakeniate

SISTERS AND BROTHERS OF MANY TRIBES

"I'm here to learn how the Sioux deal with the Government, and perhaps I can take back some knowledge and be of some help to my own people when we have another fight . . ."

Like the occupations of Alcatraz Island and the BIA building in Washington, Wounded Knee brought together native people from many different tribes. Everyone did what they could — some came for just a few days, others stayed throughout the siege. They brought with them the experiences of their own people, to share with others as they gathered in the trading post for meetings, sat around a wood stove on long nights in the bunkers, or washed dishes in the kitchens.

Monica, of the Klallum tribe in Washington State, spoke about the fishing rights struggle there:

Our treaty in 1855 guaranteed us fishing and hunting rights in the usual and accustomed manner on the accustomed grounds. But two dams have been built and they've changed the course of the river. Now it's off the reservations, and they claimed it's the State's right to regulate our fishing.

Is this all in violation of the treaties?

Yes, very much so. Some of the boys at home have been picked up by the game wardens for fishing out of season. Sometimes they use helicopters to watch the rivers for nets or fishermen. But they haven't forced any issues with us yet, because they're fighting a battle on the Nisqualy and Puyalup Rivers. They threaten the men at home with jail — they'll go to jail if they don't stop fishing. Some of the families, that's the only source of food they have.

My aunt has a really big family — sometimes she has twenty people living in her house. If you have an Indian family, it doesn't only consist of father and mother and kids, it's all your relatives. Her husband used to be a logger, but he's too old to work now, and so the only source of food

they have most of the time is salmon. And her boys have been hassled by the Game Department — for fishing out of season.

Is there still a lot of salmon in the rivers?

Not as much as there used to be. We're being blamed for that, but there's mills along the straits that spill their waste into the water, which kills off the sea life. And the Russian and Japanese fishing boats come just off our rivers, inside the international limit, and fish there, and nothing has been done by the State or by the Federal Government about these foreign fishermen.

Are there big American companies that also fish up in that area?

Yes, there's commercial American fishing fleets, and there's sportsmen, which is the strongest lobbying force in Washington State. The sportsmen say that we're depleting their sources and they fight against Indian treaty rights.

What have Indian people been doing about this?

The only organized fight has been on the Nisqualy and Puyalup where the people openly challenge the State. On my reservation it's been individual fights. But on the Nisqualy, every fishing season they openly set gill nets on the river. And every fishing season the State comes in and confiscates their nets and takes the people to jail, for illegal net fishing. You see, a gill net is set across the river, and you catch salmon when they're coming up the river to spawn. Most people think that when you do that you take every fish that comes into the river, but that's not true. People misunderstand Indian fishing — we only take what we need. We smoke it and it lasts until the next run.

Trudy, a Schaticoke, spoke about her people in Connecticut:

My tribe is the Schaticoke, an off-shoot of the Pequot-Mohican tribes. You have to understand that the history for the Eastern tribes is somewhat different because what happened to us happened so long ago, almost three hundred years ago when we were pretty much destroyed — King Phillip's massacre took place in 1695. Whole tribes in the East were destroyed.

My own tribe, for instance, was a fugitive tribe. It was made of three groups — Pequots, Putitucks, and Mohicans — who came together and were called the Schaticoke. They were on the run for a long time. They didn't even have time to retain the culture and our language was pretty much lost by the 1800s when tribes in the Southwest were struggling and fighting and still had it together.

Do you live on a reservation?

No, I wasn't even brought up on a reservation. My grandfather left after he had his fifth child. They were extremely poor and he had no way of providing for his family unless he left. The tribe that I come from and most of the Eastern tribes are not Federally recognized, so there are no services or benefits on the reservations.

Does your tribe have a land base?

Yes, the State says we have about 400 acres, but they have never surveyed the land. We started out with over 21,000 acres which runs over into what is now New York State and up through part of Massachusetts. They started by taking a little bit of land here and there, 15 acres, 20 acres. There was an Indian Agent on the land, up until around 1900. He was like an overseer. The "wards," the "children of the state," you see, need a father type to look over them. He was in charge of the land and the Indians on the land. For instance, for food and medical supplies that was needed — when there was no way of paying for this at the end of the year, it was all totalled up and he took land which he felt was in proportion to the money we owed. So it kept dwindling and dwindling.

Did he keep the land for himself?

No, it was sold to the white settlers. And sometimes it was sold without the okay or the signature of Indians. I looked over the land sales, and many times I did not recog-

Trudy, Schaticoke; Judy, Winnebago (in rear); and Monica, Klallum.

nize the signatures as being Indian names, so I know that the land was sold illegally.

Is this selling of the land still going on?

No, the 400 acres is now pretty much intact. But what they have done — my grandfather, when he died in 1940 the State came and bulldozed down the house without anyone's knowledge. This happened to many of the houses there. As people left to find outside work, the State would come in and bulldoze down the house. This was to discourage returning. So that many of us almost lost our land base — we certainly lost our culture. And our being together, which we are now attempting to very strongly revive.

What kind of things are you fighting for now?

For our land base. For instance, Connecticut Light and

Power has been leasing our land since 1925. Some of us weren't even aware of this. And when some of the people went to find out where was this money going — because it certainly wasn't going to the tribe — they were told that they had no legal right, that this was none of their concern because they were individuals. So we are organizing as a group, with a charter and so forth, to fight this. It's a rather small tribe, there are only about 65 families. But we do have, compared to others, a pretty large land base, 400 acres. Even more if we win our fight against Connecticut Light and Power. And they've been leasing our land for so long that they owe us a great deal of money.

Most of us would like to return to the land and live on it and become self-sufficient. That's our plan and our hope. Our people are scattered around through Connecticut. Some are farmers and some have regular jobs. Others have left to try and get an "education" to try and do something. It's been very hard but there's been a strong revival in the past few years, of getting it together, and we're determined now to do something about it.

Clyde Bellecourt, Chippewa.

Chippewa Clyde Bellecourt, one of the founders of the American Indian Movement, described the situation on his home reservation.

In the central part of Minnesota there's a reservation where the Indian people have been deprived of their rights for years — their rights to hunt, fish, gather wild rice, and trap free of State law. I've seen this violated over and over, time and time again. And I've seen the Indians try everything — they've been through the courts, they've had Federal Court rulings which guaranteed them this right, yet the State continues to violate it.

I can go up to my tribe and tell them that I want to buy or lease some land, and it goes to the Area Office, and on to Washington, D.C. It has to go that far to get an OK on it, and they just don't sell it to Indians. White ranchers or farmers, anybody — they can come on the reserve. Resorters, people that are influential and have money, sportsmen's clubs — they come on. At Leech Lake, Cass Lake, it's all wooded and forest, sandy beach. Indians can't get in there to swim no more. They own all that property. It's all leased to those sportsmen's clubs, and they get maybe $29 a year for it, 99 year leases, unrevokable.

But I see the same thing happening on this Chippewa reservation as is happening here in Wounded Knee. A nation once again being established where Indian people recognize their own sovereignty and rights — and not the "rights" that have been established for them by the United States Government.

Connie Martinez, an officer of La Raza Unida, a national organization of Chicanos, talked about her people's role in the native struggle.

We use the word *Chicano* to identify ourselves because we are not legally recognized as Indians, we're not recognized as Mexicans, we're not recognized as Americans, either. So we use the word Chicano as a tool for identity, although we are Indian people who lost most of our traditions and most of our culture. I think most of us had a similar religion, a similar culture to that of most of the tribes here. It has been supressed, mostly wiped out. It has been so many years ago that the Indian got conquered by the white man. Before the Spanish came with their Bible and their crucifix, and their religion, we had our own. We were able to live

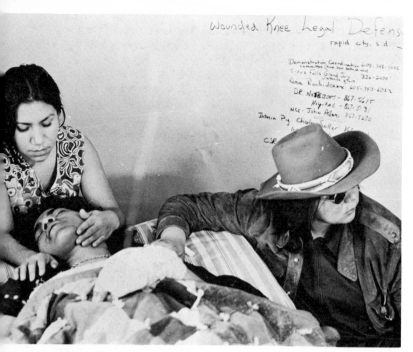

Connie Martinez, Chicana; Armand and Martina White Bear, Winnebagoes.

off the ground, we were able to survive, and it was beautiful and we were healthy human beings. Then came the Spanish saying that we should feel guilty about a man that was crucified. Now we are really screwed up.

The Aztec had a prophecy that said one day the land would go back to the people. And maybe this is part of the prophecy. If we happen to get killed here, at least we are going to die fighting, with honor. We have been abused, and used, humiliated so much all of our lives, something like that wouldn't bring our spirits down. It just gives us more of a reason to fight.

We are only fighting for our survival as a race. And I don't see why anyone should have to go to jail for it. They try to tell us how to live and they don't even follow it. In the Constitution it says men are created equal — but the person it was written by, he had black slaves. And so how in the hell do they expect us to want to live by a phony piece of paper? I could tell you that I love you and I could write it down on a piece of paper, "I love you, I'll die for you, if you're hungry I'll feed you, if you're thirsty I'll give you water." That's only words on a piece of paper. It doesn't mean anything. The action is what means something — and the action that we have seen — we know that there is no love in the white man for us.

Stan, an Ochimawe, spoke about the similarities between his people's fight for their land on the California coast, and the conflict in South Dakota.

I'm an Ochimawe, better known throughout the country as Pit River, from northern California.

Ochimawe people's ancestors have lived in this particular territory, on the Pit River, for centuries, and the ground is now claimed by the Federal Government as Mt. Lassen National Park and National Forest. But the Pit Rivers never had treaties with the Government and never gave up their land. So we occupied this land.

. . . We're having confrontations right now with the logging industry who are sending loggers up there to cut that timber. It's our land. Where the loggers denude the timber it destroys the fishing, it destroys the environment of the land itself. It'll be erosion, destroy the wildlife. And also the Indians feel the land was given to them by the great Earthmaker, to live on and protect and to hold and that's the name of the game.

. . . The California Indians organized 30 or 40 years ago, after they found out there were 18 treaties that were hidden more than 50-60 years, that had never been ratified. The California Indians formed their own organization, hiring lawyers and sending them back to Washington. It took them 20 years just to get permission to sue the Government, and almost 50 years before they got a settlement. And it amounted to only 47 cents per acre. That's what they were paid early this spring, which amounted to about $676 a person.

When the Government paid the California Indians off, the Pit River Indians refused it and organized themselves and claimed this land. We're on it and we're going to stay on it.

Why did you come to Wounded Knee?

When Pit River had their first confrontation with the loggers, about four years ago, quite a number of Sioux came out there and helped physically fight with the officers and

rangers. At that time the Pit River Indians had no idea whether it was going to come to regular blows and they had no weapons other than sticks they could pick up — where the officers had mace and riot guns and machine guns. They clubbed hell out of us at the time and even broke the back of a 70-year-old Pit River man and beat women, knocked them down, and kids and clubbed over their heads, which is fairly well known throughout the area.

Now the Indians are willing to arm and fight back and do exactly what was done here in Wounded Knee. And I'm here, not because I was sent here, but I'm here to learn how the Sioux deal with the Government and perhaps I can take back some knowledge and be of some help to my own people when we do have another fight, which I expect. And this time the Pit River Indians will have more help. It will be more organized, and we'll be able to stand up and take up whatever they send against us. It won't be hardly police officers, it'll be the private logging industry that will send what we call "goon squads" to try to protect their logging trucks and loggers while they're trying to cut the timber.

I'm sure Wounded Knee is a precedent. I'm sure the Sioux people are going to win the treaty rights. Every tribe in the United States has had bad dealings with the Government through treaties which were never ratified and through the very bad way they've been killed and diseased, wiped out, and never really been able to get up, but we're beginning to fight back for the things that were taken away in the past.

. . . They had their Bibles in one hand and their soldiers with their swords in the other, and the California Indians had such a peaceful existence — everything was there. They weren't fighters. They were tame, and they welcomed the pioneers. But the pioneers wanted to convert the heathen Indians to Christianity and in doing so they built these missions and they enslaved the Indians. And they were just like prisoners, building these missions.

Then when gold was discovered in 1849 the miners came over and swarmed in there and they tried to put the Indians working in the mines, make slaves out of them and the Indians weren't the type that wanted to work. They'd run away and the miners would hunt them down and kill them. Between 1840 and 1860 they killed over 50,000 California Indians, not for anything other than just running them down like they would shoot animals for sport. We had massacres in California similar to Wounded Knee, where they'd wipe out a whole community of Indians.

There's a tribe of Paiutes in Nevada round Pyramid Lake and they had a chief called Winnemucca. When the first early travelers came through in their covered wagons they had to cross a terrible desert all the way from Utah, and sometimes they just weren't making it. So the Paiutes would go out there under Winnemucca and bring them food and water and show them where the water hole was and help them through. A lot of settlers settled in the valley of my home town, and Winnemucca brought his little band and camped in the meadow below the town, intending to trade with the white people. He figured that they were a lot of the people he'd helped cross the desert, saved their lives. So he thought he'd be welcome. While he was

Stan, Ochimawe.

camped there in this meadow, the people in town got to drinking booze and they got their guns and went over the hillside where the Indians were camped, and they started shooting the Indians like shooting rabbits, just killing them for nothing, just for sport. Winnemucca got his band back to Nevada, and went on the war path. He massacred wagon train after wagon train whenever he could. Before, he had helped them. He got his revenge for what people in my hometown did. And some of the leading citizens in our town, town fathers, and some of their fathers, they're the people that done this.

THE GHOST DANCE

"How to be unite together — how to bring the power together as one? I pick out the way I could learn, I teach my relations. We have ceremonies, the tipi, the fire, and the sweat lodge. It's really hard to be an Indian. It's there that I find out."

Medicine men Crow Dog and Black Elk helped bring people together in the traditional Sioux spiritual ways, and for many, Wounded Knee meant a coming home to Indian religion and tradition. Religious ceremonies were held every few days, often when important decisions had to be made or when unity was flagging. These were Sioux ceremonies, but all tribes and all races were welcomed by the medicine men. These ceremonies were not simply rituals, but rather a reaffirming of the community's solidarity and the relationship to the land. Most involved some physical sacrifice — at the very least, sitting up all night, or as in the sweat lodge, staying through a very hot sauna through long prayers. All ceremonies were conducted in a circle and in all there was a time when every person in turn spoke out their most honest feelings and prayers, both to the Great Spirit and to each other. The ceremonies served to unite the nation, much as the Ghost Dance had in 1890.

Now the grandchildren of Big Foot and his generation performed the Ghost Dance again. People pieced together ceremonial clothing from what they could find in the camp, and for four days rose at dawn and went to the gully where the massacre took place to dance in the snow — a slow, strengthening dance, a circle of people holding hands. Late on the eve of the Ghost Dance, Crow Dog spoke to those who would participate.

Tomorrow—
Ghost Dance.
Nowadays you guys walk around, you're tired.
You're not gonna say, "I'm gonna rest."
There's no rest,
there's no intermission, no coffee break,
we're not gonna drink water.
So that's gonna take place
whether it snows, rains —
we're gonna unite together
no matter what tribe you are
we're gonna be brothers and sisters.
Mohawk, Chippewa,
whatever you are

we're gonna be together.
We're not gonna say,
"I'm a different tribe," or, "I'm a different man,"
or, "He's a white man," or "He's a black man."
We're not gonna have the Government,
the white man attitude.

If one of us gets into the power —
the spiritual power —
we will hold hands.
If he falls down, let him,
on the other side of the ring,
or inside the ring.
So anybody that gets into the spiritual power,
looks like he's gonna get into convulsions —
don't be scared.
We won't call a medic
the spirit's gonna be the doctor,
so anything happen like that,
back up and keep going.
Hold hands.

There's a song that I'm gonna sing.
The song
is gonna be the spirit —
the drum
is the Mother Earth
and the clouds will be the visions.
And the clouds — the visions — will go into your mind.
You will see the visions.
We elevate ourself from this world to another world.
From there you can see
our Grandfather.
We're gonna remember our brothers
that been killed by the white man

and we're gonna remember our chiefs.
You will see your brothers,
your relations that died,
you will see them.
Ghost Dance Spirit will appear.

The peace pipe
is gonna be there
the fire
is gonna be there
tobacco
is gonna be there.

We're not gonna go on a trip like on drugs.
It starts physically and goes into
spiritually
and then you will get into the power.
It's gonna start in Wounded Knee in 1973
and it's gonna continue.
We're gonna unite together as brothers —
we're gonna Ghost Dance.

Everybody read about the Ghost Dance,
but nobody ever seen it.
That was something that
the United States of America prohibits —
they're not gonna have no
Ghost Dance
no Sun Dance
no Indian religion.

But this hoop has to be not broken —
for the whole unborn generations.
So decide tonight
if you want to dance with me tomorrow.
You be ready.

Medicine men Wallace Black Elk and Leonard Crow Dog.

After the Ghost Dance, Russell Means spoke to the community:

   The white man says that the 1890 massacre was the end of the wars with the Indian, that it was the end of the Indian, the end of the Ghost Dance. Yet here we are at war, we're still Indians, and we're Ghost Dancing again. And the spirits of Big Foot and his people are all around us. They suffered through here once before, in the snow and the cold, and they were hungry, they were surrounded at that time with the finest weapons the United States had available to them, brand new machine guns and cannons.

   What came to me was that Big Foot and his band were like a grandfather. It was time for them to go to sleep, but they had a child that was just born. And this child had to grow and learn all kinds of new things before it once again could return here to Wounded Knee. World War I came along, and the United States asked the American Indian if they would fight their war for them. So we went out and saw around the world what was happening, and we came back. Then another war happened. This time they not only took Indians into the army, but into the defense plants all across America, and into the big cities. And we learned the ways of the white man, right here in this country, found out

about the white man to bring that knowledge back for the use of our people. But we still had patience, and all this time we had been watching the white men.

When armed white men were fighting in the labor movement, riots and armed clashes with the pigs, we watched that. And in the 50's when the Communist scare was going throughout the country. And white man was fighting white man, arresting him and putting him in jail. And in the 60's, we watched the black man, that black cloud that Black Elk prophesied would cover this country. Then the 1970's came. And as a people we are beginning to see . . .

While the Ghost Dance was taking place, some warriors reported hearing over the Government's radio that the marshals became worried and called in a "BIA dance expert" to tell them what was going on. He informed them, inaccurately, that it was a war dance that "had not been performed since just before Custer's massacre . . . "

Later that week, Wallace Black Elk spoke at a meeting, thanking those who had participated in the dance.

So we are all here tonight
and this little place called Wounded Knee
is now turned into a world-known place.
The whole universe has focused on this place.

The sacred pipe
represents the whole universe;
that staff
represents the tree of life.
And that tree
represents all nations, Indian nations, all red nations.
That sacred hoop was broken.
We want that sacred hoop to come back —
and now it's come into reality.

So I am very thankful
that those of you have taken part
in this sacred spiritual dance.
I want to thank my brothers
like Russell Means —
he took off his shoes
in that cold, wet snow
to dedicate himself and experience
like some of the people that suffer that experience.
Chief Big Foot and the family,

they were massacred here
on the 29th of December, 1890,
and they were lying there two or three days, all frozen.
So that's why my brother Russell
he dedicate himself
and walk that snow.
So I am very thankful —
I thank him very much.
Along with my brothers here, and my sisters too.
I'm very glad and I'm very happy
that we see the power.
The power's still here —
the power that
I saw there
with my naked eye —
there was a tipi,
and the sacred tree of life was standing there,
there was a tipi
and all my people were going in circles —
there were many people going into that tipi. ▬▬▬▬▬

5. SUPPORT
"Little Wounded Knee is turned into a giant world."
— Wallace Black Elk

The trading post, largest building in the village, was rearranged to meet the needs of the ION community. Way up front, behind the podium and the "Wounded Knee, Independent Oglala Nation" sign, was a kitchen which served meals — usually beans — to anyone who came by at meal-time. In the back were partitioned sleeping quarters and a pile of blankets and old clothes for whoever needed them. In the large central room, counters were pushed up against the walls to make room for the 300-400 people who came to the nightly meetings. It became a visiting place in the evening when people gathered for the meetings, which usually started a couple of hours late, "Indian time," and went on into the early morning.

At one evening meeting Dennis Banks read letters and telegrams of support which had come to Wounded Knee from Australia, Finland, Germany, Italy, Japan, England, and all over the U.S. and Canada. One message came from some of the Attica Brothers, who face long jail terms for their prison rebellion of September, 1971. An excerpt from their letter read:

The Brothers of Attika salute the American Indian Movement in their struggle against oppression and facism. We send you our support, our love and power, in the supreme confidence that you shall win your struggle! . . .

We who once stood in the same position; surrounded by Amerikan Authority waiting to kill, to restore the power and order of Amerikan Administration; with a shortage of food and water, experienced the savagery of Amerikan Steel, send to you our understanding and awareness. Our thoughts are with you, and with the dead of Wounded Knee and Attika Prison .

You fight for our Earth Mother and Her Children. Our spirits fight with you!

In struggle together, Charles Pernascilice (Catawba), John Hill (Mohawk), and Attika Brothers at Erie County Jail, Buffalo, New York

Newcomers to Wounded Knee would bring in the latest information from their area, often of events and expressions of solidarity that were not reported in the national media. The news would be related at the evening meetings. On Wednesday, March 24, demonstrations had been coordinated around the country, calling on President Nixon to recognize the 1868 Treaty and end the attempt to starve out the Indians. More than 10,000 people demonstrated in cities across America. In North Carolina, 2000 Lumbee / Tuscarora Indians along with blacks and whites marched on the town of Lumberton. They said they would "blow Lumberton off the map" if the Government attacked Wounded Knee. A cheer went up as people in the trading post heard about these support actions. Then the talk turned to other, more serious incidents which had cost some supporters of Wounded Knee their lives.

In New Mexico, Larry Casuse, a Navajo activist, had been trying to bring attention to the Mayor of Gallup's treatment of Indian people. Mayor Garcia was the chairman of the state's anti-alcoholism program, but at the same time owned a tavern on the edge of the Navajo reservation. Shortly after the occupation of Wounded Knee began, and partly in a gesture of support, Larry and Robert Nakaidine forced a confrontation with Garcia, taking him hostage and intending to bring his actions to public attention. In the course of the incident, Larry was shot and killed; Robert was held in jail on $85,000 bond on kidnapping charges. On March 3, 1000 people attended Larry's funeral in Gallup.

Demonstration in Gallup, New Mexico.

"Porque todos somos indios y todos nos ven igual. Todos somos cafe, y el pleito no solo esta en Wounded Knee."

In Denver in mid-March, 2000 Chicanos marched in support of the Independent Oglala Nation. Soon after that, the offices and apartments of the Crusade for Justice, organizers of the rally, were raided by police. Luis Martinez, who had recently returned from Wounded Knee, was killed in an alley as he fled the gunfire.

On March 13, Graciano "Chano" Juaraqui and four friends from D-Q, an Indian-Chicano University in Davis, California, were in Rapid City on their way to Wounded Knee. The police allege that they attempted to rob a tire store. They were challenged, and in the confrontation that ensued, a policeman was stabbed. Chano was shot and left to bleed to death as an ambulance took the policeman to a hospital. A Chicano brother spoke at a memorial rally for Chano held later in California:

He went to Wounded Knee with other brothers and sisters from D-Q University and [U.C. at] Davis, just to see how he could help. And Chano run into a cordon that the Federal Government has put around the whole State of South Dakota. Graciano got shot in cold blood, by a Rapid City policeman. But it isn't only the Rapid City policemen who was doing it. It was the U.S. Government that was ordering every pig — every little lackey that they have — to kill anybody that walks in, or wants to drive in the place.

There are 353 treaties that have been violated by the United States. The *Guadalupe Hidalgo* also, that was signed by the Mexicans, has been violated many times. And the U.S. Government supports it and covers it up. I would just like to pinpoint — and I'm going to say it in Spanish —

Porque Chano era mexicano tambien, y era indio, y era navajo y era chicano, y era todo lo que quieran decir — y por eso me quiero dirigir a toda la gente de habla hispana en toda el area de la Bahia. De que todo el que sea mexicano, indio, o lo que se llame deber soportar a lo que hacen en Wounded Knee hermanos ahi, porque todos somos indios, y todos nos ven iqual. Todos somos cafe, y el pleito no solo esta en Wounded Knee — esta en todos lados donde hay indios en que el gobierno los opresa con hambre en reservations.

Because Chano was a Mexican too, and was Indian, and was Navajo and Chicano and anything you want to call him — that's why I want to address all Spanish-speaking people in the Bay Area. All that are Mexicans, Indians, or whatever, ought to support whatever the brothers are doing in Wounded Knee. Because we are all Indians, and they see us all the same. We are all brown, and the problem is not only in Wounded Knee, it is everywhere where there are Indians, as the Government oppresses them with hunger on reservations.

Eso es todo — gracias.
Thank you — that's all.

Demonstration in Denver, Colorado.

In the first official statement of the ION, the Oglala chiefs had called for the "support and recognition" of the Iroquois Six Nation Confederacy. On March 19, an official delegation arrived in Wounded Knee from the Six Nations, and they addressed the community meeting that night. They read from a statement of support which their Grand Council had sent to the U.S. Government in Washington, D.C., soon after the take-over:

The Six Nation Iroquois Confederacy stands in support of our brothers at Wounded Knee . . .

We are a free people. The very dust of our ancestors is steeped in our tradition. This is the greatest gift we gave to you, the concept of freedom. You did not have this. Now that you have taken it and built a constitution and country around it, you deny freedom to us. There must be some one among you who is concerned for us, or if not for us, at least for the honor of your country. In 1976 you are going to have a birthday party proclaiming 200 years of democracy, a hypocritical action. The people of the world would find this laughable.

The solution is simple: be honest, be fair, honor the commitments made by the founding fathers of your country. We are an honorable people — can you say the same? You are concerned for the destruction of property at the BIA building and at Wounded Knee. Where is your concern for the destruction of our people, for human lives? Thousands of Pequots, Narragansetts, Mohicans, thousands of Cherokees on the Trail of Tears, Black Hawk's people, Chief Joseph's people, Captain Jack's people, the Navajos, the Apaches, Sand Creek Massacre (huddled under the American flag seeking the protection of a promise), Big Foot's people at Wounded Knee. When will you cease your violence against our people. Where is your concern for us?

What about the destruction of our properties? The thousands of acres of land, inundated by dams built on our properties, the raping of the Hopi and Navajo territories by the Peabody strip mining operations, timber cutting, power com-

Iroquois delegation leaving Wounded Knee

panies, water pollution, and on and on. Where is your concern for these properties?

The balance of the ledger is up to you. Compare the damage of the BIA and Wounded Knee against the terrible record and tell us that we are wrong for wanting redress. We ask for justice, and not from the muzzle of an M-16 rifle. Now what is to occur?

Remove the marshals and the FBI men. They are hostile, and eager to exercise the sanctions of the United States to subjugate the Indian people. Do not prosecute the Indians for the methods used to gain your attention, for the fault actually lies with the Government of the United States for ignoring Indians for so long . . .

We have not asked you to give up your religions and beliefs for ours.

We have not asked you to give up your language for ours.
We have not asked you to give up your ways of life for ours.
We have not asked you to give up your government for ours.
We have not asked that you give up your territories to us.

Why can you not accord us with the same respect? For your children learn from watching their elders, and if you want your children to do what is right, then it is up to you to set the example. That is all we have to say at this moment. Oneh.

The Six Nations delegation spent four days in council with the Oglalas. Then the Iroquois chiefs announced that they would leave by walking out through the roadblocks, protected by their treaties which guarantee them free passage through international borders in North America. So on March 23, at a time when the Government was allowing only a few reporters and one lawyer through the roadblocks and others had to sneak in and out at night, 14 Iroquois were escorted to the edge of the village by approximately 100 Oglalas and then passed through Roadblock 1 without incident. Shortly afterwards, they were ordered off the reservation by the BIA police.

While he was in Wounded Knee, Chief Oren Lyons spoke about his Iroquois people and the traditions which still govern their territory:

We support the Oglala Sioux Nation or any Indian nation that will fight for its sovereignty. We recognized immediately the implications of such a nation and its fight, so we responded. The issue here at Wounded Knee is the recognition of the treaties between the U.S. Government and the sovereign nations that were here before. Regardless of how fraudulent some of these treaties are, we're stuck with them. However, so is the United States stuck with them. A bad bargain for us maybe, 100 years ago, but not so bad today, when you're looking at half of New York State and you see that we gave up half of Ohio, Pennsylvania, and part of Canada, for half of New York State — 18½ million acres. They don't have legal title to it. That explains why they are so hard on us, why they don't want Indians. As soon as they terminate Indians as an entity, they terminate the obligations of the United States Government to our people. And then these claims on land and sovereignty weaken and become something to put in a museum, safely.

Sovereignty is freedom of a people to act and conduct affairs of its own nation. We the *Hotinonsonni* [People of the Longhouse], the Six Nations, have our sovereignty. We conduct on our territories and we act for our people. And so we have the Oglala Sioux, who should be conducting their affairs here because this is their territory, but who now has its government interfered with and who now have another form from another power acting within their territory.

I come from Onondaga, the capital of Hotinonsonni, and I have an ancestry that goes back beyond a thousand years in one place. Our people were governed by *rotiianer,* chiefs, which when translated means "the good minds," or "they keep the peace." Each chief comes from a certain clan. Each clan has a clan mother, who chooses a candidate when a position has to be filled. And then she must present her choice to the other clan mothers, then to the council, and then to the fifty chiefs of the Six Nations, and they inquire. If he passes this, then he is presented to that one of the Six Nations for which he is going to stand. And every person has the right to make a statement on his eligibility to be a chief. If he passes all of this then the horns are placed on his head — the symbol of the leadership he must carry all his life.

We have no single head man who has authority and power. The power lies with the unanimous consent of the council who govern for their people. And the unanimous consent is the key word here. There's no vote.

We chiefs receive no funds other than what we receive when we have to travel. We live exactly as our people live, by our own abilities one way or another. We don't have to campaign for our re-election, so we're not forced into compromises. We can be removed immediately from office by the action of our clan mother and our nation.

So a different type of individual is brought forth than one who is seeking the offices and the monies and prestige that would be in such an office. A chief must have compassion, an understanding for his people. He must be honest. As a chief, I don't have any authority. My duties are to uphold the constitution of the Confederacy, to keep a place of life for the coming generations. We're just caretakers. . . . Before our white brothers came here there was a great

Oren Lyons in the trading post.

peace in this land, great peace. We used to always get together. The trails that people travel now, we used to travel to other people's territories once or twice a year to trade and exchange. Down in Acoma, in New Mexico, they have a song they call an ancient rain song. I know every word because it's Iroquois. We travelled. We were at great peace.

. . . The problems that the United States is having now come from the centralization of its government. Indian nations have consistently never grown too large. They automatically divide when they come to a certain number. They remain Sioux, or whatever, but they branch out and become Brule Sioux or Oglala Sioux. The reason why they branch out is to maintain

this acquaintance among their people.

It's a hard thing, it's a sad thing, when you live in the United States today. Each house is a little fort, and you surround yourself first with a fence, and then with the insurances to protect yourself. Against who? Your neighbor. What does that mean? It means he's an enemy, or at the very least, he's got to be watched. If you're lucky he's fine, and he doesn't fall down in front of your house and break his leg and then you lose the whole house. Or bump your car and hurt his back and charge you. This is the fence system of the United States. The white man says, "This is mine." Indian says, "This is ours." That's the two ideologies; this is the conflict. We must be concerned for the welfare of all human beings. When we function on that level and concern ourselves with the welfare of coming generations we can all move in the same direction. The creator has made us all brothers and we should be all of one mind.

I would say the awareness is growing. The abridgement of human rights and freedoms are now coming out in the open so that people can see the dangers that are enveloping them and they are responding to these more and more. You take the present excesses of the Government in Watergate. Power and greed is the motivating force behind the present U.S. Government. People are now becoming aware of this and

On the same day that the Iroquois left Wounded Knee, Angela Davis came to the reservation on a visit of support. She was prevented from entering the village by Federal officials. Here, at the roadblock, she greets members of the Iroquois delegation, William Lazore, Oren Lyons, and Louis Papineau.

are actively doing something about it. And people really understanding their own power in this U.S. could change this thing in one night or in one day. The power always lies within the people, and the governing body should be functioning only for the welfare of these people.

These people here at Wounded Knee are fighting for the right to conduct their own affairs. We've been fighting for our freedom all these years. It has just now come to attention. But it's not revolutionary, it's consistent. In our eyes it is an on-going conflict that we must continually address to maintain our individuality and our sovereignty.

Now in numbers we are small compared to the nations that surround us, and our brother of the thirteen colonies, who we held in our arms as a child to grow, now have superceded us in numbers and power. It is a very great and outsized brother we have, and he leans heavy upon us. He has forgotten who it was who is the elder brother that was holding him. So now we have to remind him. It's a difficult period, for he is very strong and he's willful. And I don't know what the outcome will be.

SUPPORT ON THE RESERVATION

While people in Wounded Knee had to contend with food shortages and firefights, their supporters on the reservation were facing different forms of harassment. Soon after the confrontation began, the house of Aaron Desersa, a Pine Ridge village resident and AIM communications director, was firebombed, destroying the house and injuring his wife. Barbara Means, a Tribal employee and opponent of Wilson, was shot at several times. Eugene White Hawk, head of the traditionalist Inter-District Council, lost his job and was badly beaten after he returned from the East Coast where he had gone as an Independent Oglala Nation representative to the U.N. Many others were harassed by the "goon squad" in equally serious ways.

From the first day of the occupation, people on the reservation had mobilized to support Wounded Knee. A woman who opened her house as a drop-off point for people and supplies coming in and out of Wounded Knee spoke about the underground nature of much of the support.

The people, especially my people in Wanblee, are for the people that are in Wounded Knee, except that they're all, you know, so afraid, that they can't come out and show themselves too well. But we get information from them. And actually we can't do anything by ourselves, because we're not rich, we're poor people. If it's not for our people that are behind us we will never go through this. They've been giving us gas money here and there and that's the only way we can help out.

They're all so scared of the goon squad. They're afraid to get arrested if they so much as mention Dick Wilson. And there are roadblocks up all over the place. But they can't get us now. We can go around. We know all the roads. And the Great Spirit is guiding us all the way so nobody can touch us. So that's my belief, helping my people down in Wounded Knee. At the end I know we will win.

The Government's policy was to prevent anyone from entering Wounded Knee, and to drive out those still inside by cutting off all access to food and medical supplies. This policy applied to local residents as well, many of whom supported the occupation of their village. Once these people left, for whatever reason, they could not return.

In this way, the Government created a large number of refugees, who were left stranded in Pine Ridge village, sleeping in various institutions and church back rooms. At the same time, both Federal and Tribal officials publicly blamed the American Indian Movement for having disrupted the lives of the local people, creating the impression that it was AIM and the ION that was keeping the refugees from returning to Wounded Knee.

One woman who left Wounded Knee to deliver her child at the hospital in Pine Ridge village related her family's unsuccessful attempts to get back home:

Why did you leave Wounded Knee?

On the night of March 11, I went into labor, so my husband brought me out. The next day, the roadblocks went back up. So when he was going to go back in, he couldn't. So after that, he and my oldest boy and my little girl – they lived in a car, staying around the hospital. They came over there to get meals, or went over to my sister's to eat, and during the evenings they visited me. Then they went to sleep in the car. After I got out last Friday, we tried to go back into Wounded Knee, but we were refused [by the US roadblocks].

When I got out we were told to come down to the BIA office to talk to a US Marshal, to get a permit to go back. We came down to the office, but we never talked to the US Marshal or whoever it was that we were supposed to see. We were directed to a Marian Taylor of the BIA welfare. She called a number of places and we were told that nobody was allowed to enter Wounded Knee.

We tried every day since then to go back in. They tell us to see this person and that person. They ask us why we want to go back. It's our *homes* in Wounded Knee. That's why we want to go home. And this living like a gypsy — I've never done that before. It's very embarrassing.

How many families are in this same position?

There's 58 families.

Did people leave by choice?

The day that the roads were open, some of them had to come out to do their shopping. And then when they went back, the roadblocks were back up. And they couldn't get back in. And some of them left for fear, because of all those guns the U.S. Marshals set up . . .

Our place is about a mile from Roadblock 2. We wanted to peek over there because we left the door unlocked and we have some pups. But the minute we drove close, the U.S. Marshals had their guns pointed at our car. We explained why we was there, to peek over the hill to see if the place was all right. They asked us to get off the car and they searched the car. What they were searching for, they never did say. They went right through the whole car. We asked

them if there was any way to get back over to our place, to lock it up, and they said, no, there was no way.

Do you know why they're not letting you back in?

Yes, I've heard rumors that they want to get all the local residents out, and after they got all the local residents out and accounted for, they were going to go in and get the AIMs, to arrest them once and for all.

What do you think about what's going on there?

I think the things they're fighting for, it's true — to get the Tribal President out, the treaties that were broken, and all of that. And the AIM people, they have just small guns, .22s. And then you see the marshals — they have those great big old armored deals. I said to my husband, "They must be afraid of this handful of people to bring all these guns pointing at them." They even have those jets flying over. The US Marshals acted like they was fighting in Viet Nam. They would set fire to the land with those flares, grassfires all over the hills. I got the feeling that these people were just out to kill the Indians. You can just tell their hatred for the people. I heard one of the US Marshals say, "If I had my way, I'd go right in there and pow-pow-pow!"

One of the refugee families staying in the Pine Ridge Old Folks Home.

Refugees in the Episcopal church in Pine Ridge.

Federal Roadblock 1

A woman from the town of Sturgis, not far from the reservation, entered Wounded Knee when the U.S. removed its roadblocks and free passage was allowed on the weekend of March 11. Later, in an affidavit, she described the harassment she received on leaving the village:

On March 12th I entered Wounded Knee around 4 p.m. to deliver food donated by myself and another Sturgis resident. I came in through Denby, South Dakota. I delivered the food, remaining about 45 minutes, and then drove out again on the same road. About one mile outside Wounded Knee I came up over a hill. I saw three armed personnel carriers blocking the road. Four armed marshals with rifles came running down the hill to within about 50 yards of my car, dropped into firing position, pointed guns at my car, and yelled, "Stop." I immediately stopped. They then ran to both sides of the car, two on each side. They escorted me up the hill at gun point, telling me to proceed straight towards the tank in the center of the road and if I sped up or made any false moves, they would open up fire on me. I was also told to be quiet. I drove slowly to the top of the hill and parked between a tank and a pickup. I was ordered out of the car with guns still pointed at me and told, "Take off your coat. Turn off your motor. Open the trunk." I asked what to do first and was told, "Shut up or you will get shot. Just shut up." I took off my coat and placed it on top of the car as I had been ordered. I gave my keys to the marshal who opened the trunk and searched it. Three marshals then searched under the hood and inside my car,

brushing seats and dashboards, knocking several things out including an address book belonging to a friend, and kicked these items under the car. While searching, they questioned me, asking who was in the cars parked in the hills, how many people were in the church and the trading post and where security was located. I said I saw nothing and knew nothing. While being questioned I heard a communication over a small two-way radio held by a marshal somewhere to the right of me which said, "open up fire on the muddied-up van first. Then next on the wild Indians in the bunkers. From there on it will be easy going." During the search I asked for my coat, explaining I was sick and cold, and was told, "It's not that cold, just shut up."

Then they said they were turning me over to an FBI man. An FBI man stepped forward from the pick-up, picked the address book up, and placed it and a black case on top of the car. He then gave me permission to put my coat on. He questioned me about what I was doing in Wounded Knee. I told him I brought food, and he asked me what kind of food. I named several items. He then asked why I had brought food. I said, "Because when somebody is hungry, you feed them." He stood there writing down my name, address, etc., then said

he was going to let me go if I promised not to bring any more food. He said if he saw me there again I would be arrested. I said okay. I asked for the address book and was told he could not give it back.

I got in my car and went on, one or two miles farther, when I saw three more APCs. Marshals again ran up and dropped down pointing guns at me and yelled, "Stop!" Then they came up to the car and again told me to get out, take off my coat, and give them the keys. I did so and told them I had already been searched. They asked where and I said two miles back. They said I had to be searched again and did so.

A man jumped out of the tank, ran to me and asked where I thought I was going. I said, "Home." He then asked if I had been to Wounded Knee. I said, "Yes," and he said, "You're going back." I said that the FBI man told me I could go and I didn't understand why they said I should go back. I asked that they contact the other marshals and FBI. They stepped to one side and huddled together. They then decided to let me go, saying I wasn't important. They returned my keys, and I left immediately.

Marshals and FBI personnel
at Federal Roadblock 1.

A major base of support on the reservation was Porcupine, which had first invited AIM to Pine Ridge after the Yellow Thunder murder a year before. Eight miles north of Wounded Knee, it is a community with a high proportion of traditional people and a history of resistance.

At the beginning of the siege, Porcupine had offered its community center to outside supporters who could not get into Wounded Knee because of the Federal blockade. For over two weeks, Indians from around the country had been sleeping, eating, and meeting in the center. On March 16, nearly 100 Indian people were in the center when a force of over 30 marshals and FBI agents in APCs, and 15 BIA police cars, came in and ordered all the occupants to leave the reservation under threat of arrest. According to one observer, the marshals refused to answer repeated questions as to their authority to do this, and the "BIA police were clearly taking orders from the marshals."

In late March, Severt Young Bear recounted the harassment he had undergone as Porcupine District Chairman:

I got throwed in jail because I was AIM leader and AIM chapter chairman. I was a political prisoner. They held me on $50,000 bond, and that afternoon they reduced it down to $20,000. Then that Friday before I got out they reduced it down to $10,000. That Monday they came down to five. That Tuesday 2 o'clock they came down to a thousand. So I got out.

Is Wilson the one that brought the charges against you?

FBIs, I think, pressed the charges. They had eight charges against me, saying that I was at the Wounded Knee takeover, and that I destroyed the post office in Wounded Knee, and that I was an AIM organizer and that they used my house as a supply center and they seen boxes of weapons and ammo and food being transferred into my house on March 7. But on March 7 I was in Rapid City. I knew right from the first day FBIs were watching me — I had a binocular and I caught them laying on top of hills watching my place. So right from that day I stayed away from that house.

And as far as the takeover of Wounded Knee and destroying the post office, the police went after me at my house that night to help them. I went to the police station and Special Officer Colhoff said, "I want to go in unarmed and talk to the leadership and get those hostages out of there." So I drove to Wounded Knee and met with Dennis and Russell and those guys. They said, "Okay, you tell Colhoff to come in, we'll clear him. He'll come in unarmed and take the people out. So I went back out and the police on top of the hill radioed in to Pine Ridge. And I waited on top of the hill till four in the morning and Colhoff never showed up. The superior officers wouldn't let him out of Pine Ridge . . .

Do the people in your district support the takeover of Wounded Knee?

About a month ago, the district passed a resolution in full support of all the action taken at Wounded Knee. Then, a couple weeks later, this court order came out of the Tribal Court, asking the Porcupine people to set up a roadblock between Porcupine and Wounded Knee. They're asking for "volunteers" that will man this roadblock voluntarily, no pay or mileage per diem. Then they had a few legal terms in there, and towards the bottom — "Anybody who refuses this Court Order will be thrown in jail with a fine of $300 or 30 days in jail." And they're asking for volunteers.

So the Porcupine district had a meeting and there's over a hundred people there and they refused it. They told them that they had no business doing that. And all the older people talked in favor of AIM. And a couple of weeks before that, Porcupine district passed a resolution that they're in full support of all actions taken by the American Indian Movement down in Wounded Knee.

Why do people on the reservation support AIM and the take-over?

We're sick and tired of BIA, Tribal Government, and there's a lot of issues that we want cleared up. The only people that can do that is AIM. Our district chairmen can't do it, the Tribal Council can't do it, BIA can't do it. Nobody else can, because of political ties, or red tape, or you got a cousin that's involved in some dealings under the table. There's relationship involved.

Do the people on the reservation see this as the beginning of something?

If you go out and talk to the old people, they are for AIM but they're keeping it inside of them. Like this one old man told me, he said, "I lived here 77 years, this whole reservation was in total darkness, throwing a blanket over it and we're living in darkness. And somewhere, these young men started AIM, and they came to our reservation and they turned that light on inside. And we seen a little light," he said, "in our reservation. And that light's getting bigger, now we can see things."

What kind of hopes do you have?

We're going to win. It's not going to end at Wounded Knee, even if they throw me in jail, or they throw Russell Means and all the leadership in jail. That's not the end of it. Cause the people are standing up. They're standing up, and they're saying, "No!" and they're saying, "I don't want this, I don't like this." With that kind of attitude. This is just the beginning. It's not going to end tomorrow or the next day.

6. COMING HOME

"Now, this is a turning point. The hoop, the sacred hoop, was broken here at Wounded Knee, and it will come back again."

When groups of new people hiked into Wounded Knee, they were usually taken to meet Wallace Black Elk, Lakota medicine man. Wallace and Grace, his wife, lived in a wooden building near the Security building, formerly used for storage. Their door was always open, and friends often dropped by to visit — relaxing in the comfortable room with a bed, couch, table and wood stove. On the walls hung a few clothes, and medicine bags which Grace made from deerskin filled with sage, cedar, buffalo hair, and earth. Nearly everyone in camp wore one.

One day in late March Wallace was preparing for the first peyote ceremony to be held in Wounded Knee. As he worked on the skin for the peyote drum, stretching it to get the stiffness out, four new medics stopped by. He stood up to greet them and Grace gave each person a medicine bag. Then everyone sat down on the plank floor and Wallace welcomed the medics to Wounded Knee, and spoke to them about the Lakota philosophy:

. . . This fire comes from the sun and from the Great Spirit. He talk to the fire, he talk to the trees and all green vegetations. And he talk to the stones and all the minerals, and the water and the creatures — the creeping things, the crawling things, four-legged creatures and flying creatures. And this sacred pipe was carved and the Great Spirit put all his knowledge and power in it and gave it to the red nation. And its sacred altar is this Western Hemisphere. This land is sacred, it is an altar, and we know that we have the spirit here at all times, and we have been talking to him. And so our altar, our floor, our green carpet is the green vegetations, our ceiling is the universe of universes, our night light is the moon, and our director is the Great Spirit, the sun. So it's very simple as that. Yet there's mysteries, wonders — "How the creation? How this green formed?" — like now the greens are coming up — and the living creatures take formation. There is spirit working, every day, every moment, every second. So it is beautiful.

And we are a part of his creation. I eat the buffaloes that eat grass, so I nourish through his blood and flesh. And I wear his clothes and he gives me shelter — the tipi — so that buffalo's alive for me. And all the other, the pumpkins and corns I eat, fruit, and the rest serve as a medicine, the trees give me protections. So we are a part of the tree of life. I burn these sticks to keep warm. I burn that deer meat there and then I eat, so that fire is sacred to me.

We were civilized. That time, we didn't have no roads, or hospitals, or schools, or penitentiaries, policemen and marshals and FBIs and them kind. We didn't have them, we were civilized. We were educated, and we had direct communication with the spirit.

Now the Christian people came over — "We'll Christianize you and educate you." They call this civilization. You don't see nothing civilized. They try to destroy our philosophy, they try to totally wipe it out, exterminate all the Indians, drive all the Indians into the Pacific Ocean, like that. Them kind of attitudes are still here.

We were civilized, and these people, we never invite them in the first place. They come over and they want to survive, and in fact we welcomed them with open arms and they survived with our philosophy. We taught them how to live. How to live by nature. But they use force, they kill our buffalo, and they use armament and military.

And these Christians that come over, invade our territory, this sacred altar, they brought the Bible and they start dividing my people's minds. Here you see Chief Big Foot's grave. They dug a trench and they dumped those bodies in there and just covered them up and the Catholics took over and built their church. But them people was never baptized, and they've got them right in the center of the graveyard.

Christianity keeps dividing and dividing my people. People are against each other because those believing in the Catholic hate the Presbyterian group, and those believing in the Episcopal hate these two groups here. When the treaty was signed, the white man said, "I have a religion, and if you wish to use the Bible, I've got three ministers here, Episcopal, Presbyterian, and Catholic." "Well, we got our own Indian religion, but if our people wish to use the Bible, well, it's up to them." They should have said, "No, we got a sacred pipe, we have our sacred beliefs," that's what they should have said.

My grandpa was baptized in all three churches. The Christian people came racing down to the reservation — they

"...Here you see Chief Big Foot's grave..."

"Now, the massacre of Chief Big Foot and the family — these tourist people come here and read about it, and they were ashamed of the United States, what he done to the first American, the primitive people. So they changed the name to 'Wounded Knee Battlefield.' But still when they come by they asked, 'Who's doing all the fighting?' The Indians have no weapons, nothing. Men, women, and children — they were disarmed. So that 'Wounded Knee Battlefield' wasn't true. Then, just recently, in the fifties, they put 'Wounded Knee Tragedy.' See that sign there? 'Tragedy' — it was a 'mistake.' But now they're back here again and start reenacting it. So that's another lie."

— Wallace Black Elk

came to my Sioux people and the Episcopal minister told my grandpa, "If you believe in the Ten Commandments and the Lord's Prayer and the Seven Sacraments, you go to heaven, and if you don't, you go to hell." So, "Okay, I guess it won't hurt to join you guys." So he was baptized. Then shortly after, the Catholic came, and told him almost identical except that Jesus, Mary, Joseph, and the Apostles were all Catholic. My grandpa got curious and said, "Hey, Father, there's two besides you, what about those two?" "No, don't pay attention to them, them are false god churches. This is the only true church." So, "Well, I joined the pagan church. I made a mistake, this time I'll join the right church." So he joined the Catholic and was baptized again. Then the Presbyterian came and said, "There are seven gods and the super-king is named Jehovah, so if you believe in the right God, you'll go to heaven but if you believe in the false god church, you'll go to hell."

So my grandfather held three tickets. And he went back to the Episcopal Church and they said, "Hey, you don't belong here, I saw you get baptized in the Catholic." "No, I was baptized here first." And he showed them the ticket, a baptism card. "I've got a ticket to see the body and blood of Jesus Christ, I got a right to come in, eat that bread and take a shot of that blood." So, "Well, okay, you win." Then he goes to the Catholic and they say, "Hey, I saw you over in the Episcopal last Sunday." And then he showed them his ticket, he has a right to go in the Catholic and receive Communion. So next Sunday he'll go to Presbyterian — "Hey, you don't belong here, I saw you at Catholic and down at Episcopal too." "No, I belong here too, " so he showed his card to them. So that's where these churches divide my people, separate them from the Indian religion. We got 285 chartered churches in the United States, and if my grandpa lived today he'd be going down the line. But the funny part is, see, he kept his Indian religion too. So that's how come we still have our religion.

I had a pretty rough time during my boyhood. I went to a mission school and they give me a rough time, they told me that what my grandpa — and what we're doing here — we're devil worshipers, witchcraft and voodoo magicians, and I don't know how many names. But today it's funny — I realize now what they were trying to do, trying to make me believe that false indoctrination. They're holding a cross in one hand and holding a gun in one hand, and they cheated and robbed me of everything and they caused me to live in poverty and hunger and sickness. So when I wandered off from my sacred pipe religion and all my medicines, I suffered death, I suffered hun-

ger, I suffered cold — just plain suffered. Poorest man. These are things I witness in my own life. So my life is a real testimony for what I have said.

Where I went to school they gave me some pictures of Jesus Christ. I brought these two pictures home and studied it and I discovered that one had blue eyes and the other had brown eyes. But the real spirit don't have brown eyes or blue eyes. He has purple blazing eyes, fire. That's where his eyes are. We have a naked eye and we have a mind eye, but the white people, they are blind to these sacred things. That's ignorance, disregarding the sacred powers.

Like one FBI come over and said, "What are you doing to that dead bird, what's this fire mean, what's that tipi, what's that sweat lodges about?" But they're not dead to us, the feathers and shells we wear. This is animal from the bottom of the ocean, and he carries that color from the sun, so that sun is here. We hold the highest creature, the eagle, who controls the weather — tornadoes and blizzards. In the Wyoming area a lot of eagles were murdered. I picked up one that was murdered, and I fast with him and he come back in spirit and he talk to me. So that feather is much alive, and them whistles and claws, they are much alive. Now this eagle was adopted by the United States and became a national emblem, and they got it on the money and you see the United States seal, and it sits on top of the United States flag, but still they don't talk to that animal. And we talk to that eagle when we come to a ceremony. That eagle will come right in, fly right in, and when he sits down he speaks every language, that one we talk to.

Now my being here as a medicine man, that's what I want to explain. I'm not here to say, "Praise the Lord and pass the ammunitions." I'm not here for that. I'm here to tell the highest society that they're wrong.

A medicine man is like an instrument. They call me a medicine man or a holy man but actually that's just another way of saying by the white people — the *real* medicine man, it come from the powers and the Great Spirit. The medicine man he comes in the form of root, the green, the tree of life and all the green vegetation. The medicine we have, they're spirit, they are the ones that direct us as to how we're going to live thorugh the white philosophy.

Now if Christianity was true and their technology was so true, why are we getting sicker and sicker every day with more hospitals? And the same time, they are using our drugs. Ninety-five per cent of the medicines are taken from the

Western Hemisphere and from the Indians. These vegetations, different shapes and forms, each one has a sacred rule. When we find the sacred rules and regulations, sacred commands, they come and they doctor us. We have that way of talking to the spirit, and he comes to us — to heal us, comfort us, and give us courage to go on again.

So it is not separate like white people — technology and Christianity, they don't mix. Ours, the religion comes first. Wherever we go we carry our medicine with us. So I'm here with my people, trying to make these people understand.

Our philosophy is very simple, yet there are mysteries and wonders inside where a man will never get to understand all. So our philosophy has no end.

We are going back home now. We are tired of going this way with technology and science. This way we're going to blow our heads off. Their philosophy is just like a dead end street. It's going to come to an end and they'll be very sorry when that time come.

I pray for the people that are sick in mind. They are really sick people, this highest educated society standing around with their guns, APCs and machine guns. They're supposed to be humans and they're really sick people.

It all boils down to two philosophies, now, the white philosophy and the Indian philosophy. The white philosophy we understand. Their philosophy is based on money. Our gold, they stole our gold. They ripped off the whole Western Hemisphere and they stole all the minerals. They took our gold and they stamped Great Spirit's name on it, "In God We Trust." So that's their god, and they forgot the real spirit.

Now as you see today, their philosophy and constitutions and bylaws and rules and regulations are set by the Government to channel and funnel all the money into his own belly. So he's greedy. In his Bible, his Christianity and

teaching, greedy is a mortal sin. "Thou shalt not steal — " and that is exactly what he is doing every day, every moment, every second.

There's a word in our language for greedy, greedy when you feed a dog with your hand. If you move, that instant, he'll let the meat go and he'll try to bite you. Either kill you or warn you or bite you, to leave that piece of meat — that's for him alone. So the Indians interpret that when the white man — Nixon's outfit, or the BIA, or the Justice Department — when they're eating, don't put your hand in there. Because they're growling and they're eating our gold and silver and all the cattle and food. If he fills up, then he'll wiggle his tail, then he might come and lick your hand. "Thank you, good man, you're kind, thank you." But if the next meal don't come, he's standing there ready to attack you because you got to keep continuously feeding him. So there's an interpretation of what greedy means.

And now what he's doing, he's using the Bible to exploit and manipulate in the name of Jesus Christ. You go and see, in any court in the U.S. he has a Bible and they say, "Raise your right hand," and swear like hell. But not like it says in that book. You have to bleed to death to uphold the constitutions and bylaws set by the white people.

But the sacred rules come from the Great Spirit. It's not man-made rules. Unwritten spiritual laws — we grew up with it so we don't need to just stipulate it and put it in a file and open that book and look whether it's there or not — "Well, I'm guilty," or, "I'm not guilty," or, "Well, I'll have to see a lawyer," and then the lawyer will take a book and start looking in the book to see if it's there.

We actually grew up with it. Like I have these little nephews, when they come to the sacred altar, them kids just sit there with big eyes and look around because they know the

---

"Now they punish me for not serving these dictators, this Dick Wilson. They add a little more hungry, keep out medical supplies and food. Well, they already destroyed my buffalo — my source of life — so what little junk is this sacks and canned stuff, corn meal and rice? What you see here is all we got left to our name. They took everything. Now they want my life."

spirit's going to come. But I got another sister, a high educated, lives in a big town. And their kids, when they come back home, when the sacred altar is assembled, them kids will just run right through and kick them pipe and step on the dirt. And, "Hey, don't go there, act down, sit down, behave yourself." You have to force them, you got to practically pull a gun or bring an APC there and hold them at bay or put plastic handcuffs on them and chain them down, by force you see. And they use that profanity language, "What's this, what's that? What for you got this on here?" Pull on it and break it, and see, that's disorderly, because their mind is not trained. But ours sit there with their ears kind of pulled down, they humble themselves because the spirit's going to come and they respect that. So that's why I say the unwritten laws are observed. We actually grew up with it, we don't have to be reminded every day.

Now you will study real careful, these people don't believe in God. They believe in just material things. They are the super-kings, they're superpowers. They create deadly weapons and everything. They use threat tactics to be adored and be worshiped. So you have to slave for him in order so you could eat the crumbs that fall off from his high society table, the OEO programs and all the little programs. We eat the crumbs, the Indians that are getting welfare and ADC, that's the little crumbs that fall off the table. These Christian people start sweeping up and they are feeding the Indians — just barely, just to keep them alive.

As long as you get up seven o'clock, work to four o'clock, five o'clock in the afternoon, paying taxes, giving your tax money for Uncle Sam's Cadillac, why, "He's all right, you're a good Joe." But the minute you slack off you're an enemy — "Boy, you're dumb lazy, you can't work. Get the hell out of here, " or they'll shoot you or put you in jail.

I've been with white people in many areas and they too, they told me, "By golly that treaty is right, you own this land, we know that, but the Government forced us to come here, be homesteaders, gave me a hundred and sixty acres and I work like a slave and plow that field by hand on foot and walking a team of horses, and I work from sunrise to sundown, and whatever I make, when I sell my crop, it goes to the Government. And the Revenue are on my tail all the time, I have to pay tax on this land, every property, every machine I got, they check my chickens, they count my hogs, they count how many sheeps I got, and they'll even tax the dogs. They keep tab on me and if I don't pay tax and I don't support the U.S. Government, they'll throw me in jail. So I'm not free.

Same time I have to contribute my boys to fight and I lost my boys in the war, so I'm slaving and bleeding to death for the United States Government.

You've seen people, hundreds and thousands of people demonstrating from coast to coast — "Stop the war, stop the war, we're not going to support you, we're tired of giving our money to buy aircraft, rockets and guns and bombs, we need that money to build homes, better roads, our kids go to school and we need clothes, we need teachers, we need more schools — instead of buying APCs and machine guns and tanks." So I know and I've seen it, and this is not just one or half dozen people that I've talked to.

And like Kissinger said, "Peace is at hand." I said, "Hell, it was in their hands thousand-nine-hundred seventy-three

Entering the sweat lodge.

years ago when Jesus came and said to Israel 'and peace on earth, good will towards men.'" So they had everything there.

The white people have to surrender their arms to the Great Spirit. They have to be sorry for what they have done, murdered their own Jesus Christ. Totally murdered him. And they will be judged according to that. He preaches me the Ten Commandments, "Thou shalt not kill," and that is exactly what he is doing, escalating wars and manufacturing, with his technology and science. In order to get himself richer and richer and fatter and fatter every day. And he don't really care what happens to his people — his own people — or the black people or the yellow people or the red people. They just fight each other and stumble over each other to get ahead no

matter whether it's your brother or sister.

Now they are afraid and they are scared to hear the truth, because with their military power they think they control everything, by force, killing people and hurting people and suffering people, every day and night, 24 hours around the clock. And they don't care to talk to the Great Spirit because he's going to tell them that what they're doing is wrong. They don't care to hear that, and they are conscious of it.

Real soon, now, this is a turning point. The hoop, the sacred hoop was broken here at Wounded Knee, and it will come back again. The stake here that represents the tree of life, the tree will bloom, it will flower again, and all the people will rejoin and come back to the sacred road, the red road.

We have a tree of life. A tree stem grows and branches here and another leaf branches out and pretty soon that tree gets bigger and pretty soon we're a big family, a big tree family. So I believe we come from the same ground and the same roots of a tree. The white people branch out of that tree, and another branch branches out into black people, another into yellow people, another into red people. We are the same root.

We're not condemning the white man — we're condemning his attitude towards the American Indian people. So I hope and pray that this is the time, now, the turning point. We are going through that dark cloud, and now we're emerging from that dark cloud, and the eyes and ears of the whole universe are now focused on Wounded Knee. And little Wounded Knee turned into a giant world. And tomorrow, the world, — the people of the whole world — will come to their sense, that the Indians, the red man, they are human beings too.

This purification is coming real soon, and all the guns and gold will be melt. The holy spirit, the atom, the power of god, will melt those guns and tanks and poison gasses they create and boil down so they won't have no gun in their hand. They will be standing by themselves and then they'll be calling me, "Chief! Chief!" But by then it will be too late. They can't wait up until the last second and say, "Gee, I'm sorry, I'll take it all back. Sure made a mistake. I killed a million people. Gee, I'm sorry. I ripped off the whole Western Hemisphere from the Indians." That won't come in the last second. When the time comes, there won't be no amnesty.

We're going back to the beginning of time. It is better to go back and honor our Grandfather, honor our sacred Mother Earth. When we was there we didn't have no roads, we didn't have no Tribal Offices, no Dickie Wilsons and goon squads. Since we wandered off from the sacred altar we had a really hard time. So I tell my people now, "It's better to go home, so let's all go home." The spirit is directing us and guiding us through torments and terrorizing by the white philosophy, and we're on a

hard trail. Some of us got shot on the way home, some of us got sick and tired and hang himself, some are just plain tired and sick and died on the way home.

But I have no fear, I have no slightest fear whatsoever. Even if I have to face death like Chief Big Foot, it's very beautiful. Big Foot and the family, they survive — they are as much alive today as we are. They are with us and we talk to them.

We hold the key to eternity, where it is beautiful and it is everlasting for everyone. That's where we're going. We're going home. And finally, we will be back in the Great Spirit's hands again — Grandmother's arms again. She'll cradle us in her arms again. ■

Wallace Black Elk.

7. ESCALATION — MORE GOVERNMENT STRATEGIES

"We saw what's happened at Wounded Knee. They never try to negotiate — that is, Wilson, the BIA, and the FBI and the marshals. Instead of that they try to kill them just like in Wounded Knee massacre 1890."

— Oglala Sioux elder

ANOTHER GOVERNMENT OFFER

From the beginning of the occupation, the people in Wounded Knee made their demands clear to the Government. As FBI Special Agent in Charge Trimbach reported, the very first night he was handed a statement signed by the Oglala and AIM leadership in Wounded Knee and calling for congressional investigations of the broken treaties and the Bureau of Indian Affairs and the removal of Wilson.

However, Federal officials told the press that they were unable to determine the Indian's demands, and that furthermore, they could not negotiate "with a gun pointed at their heads." They hoped to frighten the people out of the village and thus end the confrontation without a public airing of the issues. Richard Wilson also objected strongly to any negotiations, noting that to deal seriously with the Independent Oglala Nation meant an undermining of his own authority.

But military pressure by itself did not work. The people in Wounded Knee made it quite clear that if the Government did not negotiate their demands they were prepared to stay indefinitely, even risking a massacre. Because of the strong resistance at Wounded Knee, now reinforced by the chiefs' affirmation of Oglala sovereignty on March 11, and because of overwhelming public support for the defenders despite misreporting in the press, the Federal officials were forced to publicly show some interest in negotiating the conflict, rather than fighting it out.

On March 13 new negotiations were arranged and Wayne Colburn, Director of the U.S. Marshals, and Harlington Wood, Assistant Attorney General and previously the Justice Department's negotiator for the Mayday 1971 anti-war demonstrations in Washington, were escorted into Wounded Knee for a meeting. Independent Oglala Nation spokespeople

Assistant Attorney General Harlington Wood (center rear, without hat), being escorted into Wounded Knee for talks.

demanded that Washington suspend the Tribal Government and hold a referendum for a new form of government. Wounded Knee supporters on the reservation had collected 1400 signatures in favor of such a referendum since the siege began, almost as many as had voted for Wilson in the previous election. However, the Federal officials wanted only to discuss law enforcement and disarmament. Following is an excerpt from one of the meetings with Harlington Wood:

Harlington Wood: The Federal Government did not come here to kill. They were sent here to enforce the criminal laws. If there was something they did not handle properly, that should be investigated.

Russell Means: According to all these violations, you guys should be surrounding Dickie Wilson.

Ramon Roubideaux, ION attorney: Why does the Government always get into the position of protecting a corrupt dictator like Wilson?

Dennis Banks: Like in Viet Nam.

Wayne Colburn: We have tried very hard to remain neutral. We were asked in here because the law enforcement in this Agency was inadequate to cope with their problems. Mr. Wood has outlined a program that I think is very fair, and with his career on the line, I might add.

Dennis: I realize that his career is on the line. My life is on the line.

Colburn: We must defuse this situation. We must bring in the Civil Rights [Division of the Justice Department], bring in the HEW people. Let's saturate this area and see if we can come up with a viable plan that will satisfy everybody.

Ramon: While such an investigation is going on, you've got to suspend the Tribal Government.

Wood: Isn't there a way to do that under the Constitution [of the Tribal Government]?

Ramon: Right! And we've got the signatures. We want these petitions acted upon, and an election called. Most of the reservations all across this country are under this same type of government — that's the type of government where they say, "we're giving you self-government" — but that's government by *permission,* and that isn't self-government.

Wood: Well, I think we can expose that —

Ramon: Well, you better expose that now, or you're going to have Wounded Knees all over the country, and you have to understand that.

The Government had stated, "There will be no movement on the part of U.S. forces to take control of Wounded Knee while negotiations are in progress." But in fact, the military build-up they had been mounting continued. And even while the talks were taking place on March 14, South Dakota Senator George McGovern said in Washington, "Every reasonable effort at negotiations has failed – every concession made by the Government has been matched with yet another AIM demand. They are seeking violence. The law must be enforced. There is no other way in a society such as ours."

After two days of talks, Harlington Wood left for Washington, raising hopes among the Oglalas that they had managed to convey some of the problems and that higher-level Government officials would be sent to negotiate with them. But while Wood was gone the Government continued to apply their hard line, indicating that they were treating negotiations as just one of many tactics to get the people out of the village. Stanley Lyman, Pine Ridge BIA Superintendant, approved a Tribal Court Order giving the BIA police a free hand to evict any non-Oglala they chose from the reservation. And in Washington, Secretary of the Interior Rogers Morton released a written statement of his views on the situation.

Wayne Colburn (in badge), and Harlington Wood.

Morton's statement read, in part:

. . . Their demands are vague and change from day to day. They do not represent a constituted group with whom the Government can contract or serve ./. .

. . . I have maintained a wide open policy of communication with all Indian groups, Federally recognized or not.

It is not a problem for them to sit down with me, the Department, or Members of the Congress or officials in other agencies of the Government and discuss ways and means to improve the Indian to society or Indian to Government relationships. All of the so-called "rights" problems which the militants dramatize fall into one of these categories . . .

There is one thing of which I am very sure. Nothing is gained by blackmail. You cannot run this Government or find equitable solutions with a gun at your head or the head of a hostage. Any agency of government that is forced into a fast deal by revolutionary tactics, blackmail, or terrorism is not worth its salt. These are criminal operations and should be dealt with accordingly.

There is no way that I or any other Secretary can undo the events of the past. If it was wrong for the European to move on to this continent and settle it by pioneerism and combat, it was wrong. But it happened and here we are ./. .

I pray that [the Indian] will feel himself part of the spirit and strength of America, not a burden to America. It seems to me this a prayer than can be answered — not only by the actions of a committed Government and people — but more by the Indian himself climbing steadily rung by rung from a base of opportunity unmatched for any group in the society of the world.

On March 17, Wood returned to Wounded Knee with what he termed "the Government's best offer," and left it with the ION for discussion. Several hours after he left the village, a firefight broke out. Ron Ridenour, a correspondent for the Los Angeles Free Press, *described it:*

"Take cover!" a bandoleer-carrying Chicano sentry yelled out. Automatic fire could be heard singing nearby. Federal marshals stationed a few hundred yards away had opened fire from their armored personnel carriers on a nearby hill. Fifty caliber machine-gun fire broke up the land like a plow. Tracer bullets cracked and lit small areas. M-16 bullets could be heard at the southeast end of the new nation, striking the tipi church, once known as the Church of God.

AIM soldiers responded with light weaponry. The battle lasted 30 minutes and at least 300 rounds were fired, mostly automatic fire from the feds.

The security chief told the press later that the marshals had opened fire first without provocation. ABC cameramen thought that the marshals may have wanted to learn what kind of weapons the new nation had.

The sentry fired upon first described it this way: "I was at my position when they just opened up. They fired heavy stuff, about ten rounds before I returned fire." The Indian Viet Nam war veteran, who lost his foot in battle there, said, "Well, I don't mind it when they [bullets] sing. But when they crack, that's when they're close."

I stayed in the street and watched the battle. A Chicano medic, Rocky Madrid, was escorted to the front lines by a platoon of four men to see if anyone was wounded. Minutes later he was returned on a stretcher with a bullet wound in his abdomen, the only casualty of that battle.

Although there were scores of soldiers and weapons in the Indian compound [the village center where many of the houses are], there was no firing from that congested area. People were disciplined and serious and together. No one panicked the entire time. It was their fourth battle of any consequence during the three weeks, and everyone knew it would not be their last.

Harlington Wood's smile of six hours ago lingered in my mind. I could see it growing broader as he probably watched the battle from afar.

Wounded medic, Rocky Madrid, in the ION clinic.

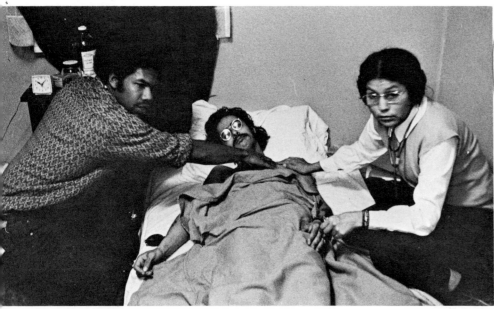

The next day, March 18, at a meeting in the trading post, the Wounded Knee community rejected Harlington Wood's proposal, charging that it was a blueprint for their surrender. It called for ION leaders Russell Means, Dennis Banks, Pedro Bissonette, Clyde Bellecourt, and Carter Camp to meet with Marvin Franklin and William Rogers of the Interior Department in Sioux Falls, for three to five hours. Before and after the session, a one-hour press conference would be held, at the end of which the ION negotiators would be arrested. Simultaneous with the beginning of the talks, the occupants of Wounded Knee were to stack arms, walk out, and submit to arrest.

The ION issued a counter-proposal requesting a special Presidential emissary to "deal with our sovereignty and our separate governments' relationship under our treaty." Carter Camp explained the status of negotiations:

When we first came to Wounded Knee they wanted to deal with us strictly as a police matter. They said at that time that if we would lay down our weapons, they would give anyone that wasn't charged a ride 150 miles away from here. And the people that they were considering charging wouldn't be charged until a Grand Jury met. At several points during the occupation here at Wounded Knee the Government has come with that same offer worded differently. The last offer reduced it somewhat. They wanted to arrest us immediately.

I think what the Government is missing is that the ION is no longer dealing on the issues that first brought us here. At first we were primarily dealing with the Bureau of Indian Affairs, and their mismanagement of Indian lands and funds — that is, essentially dealing within the system. Since then, the traditional chiefs of the Oglala nation and the district leaders from throughout the reservation decided to declare themselves an independent nation of Oglala Sioux people.

Yesterday, Mr. Wood offered us a way to disarm, if we would submit to the whole system of the United States — justice or injustice, whichever it may be. We don't feel that we any longer have anything to say to the people in the Justice Department or the people in the Department of the Interior. By taking the action to declare ourselves an independent nation, we feel as though we have fallen back on our rights as Indian people. The Sioux Treaty states very clearly that the President must involve himself personally and we can name an emissary from him that should come from the Indian nation.

The 1868 Treaty guaranteed that a vast area west of the Missouri River would be in control of the Sioux people "as long as the grass was growing and the water flowing." So far both of these things are still happening and we feel as though they still own this vast acreage of land. These treaties were never to be abrogated without a three-fourths vote of the Indian males on the reservation. But in 1934 the

Government passed the Indian Reorganization Act without the consent of the Indian people, which took away our treaty rights. The legality of our situation is obvious to us. We just have to make it obvious to the United States.

It don't matter to us which way the Government wants to deal. We can deal with them in the violence of the trenches, or we can deal with them at the negotiating table. That's the two choices that the U.S. Government has. The people of the U.S. have choices also. You can remain in your living rooms and watch this on television, and be entertained by the fact that another war is going on — except this one is a little closer to your home — or else you can begin applying the type of pressure that this Government is supposed to be responsive to.

In a meeting at the trading post on March 22, American Indian Movement spokesman Dennis Banks, a Chippewa, voiced the new resolve with which the community responded to the unsuccessful negotiations.

They're stopping all the news media. They let in our lawyers when *they* want to. They let in a little bag of groceries when *they* want to. If we fail to correct that kind of policy, somebody is going to get shot because we can't divide enough insulin among three or four people, because the Justice Department or the Interior Department restricts the amount of medical supplies coming in. They busted Archie Fire out in California because he was bringing medical supplies. They're busting people up here at Sturgis, Rapid City, in Colorado, who are coming here with supplies, and we're depending on these people to reach here. They're steadily trapping us into a situation that's going to be very dangerous.

The nightly meeting at the trading post gets under way.

Tonight *we* close the doors. Tonight *we* dictate who goes through those doors. Tonight our own Phase I has already begun. Fourteen people are already on their way to Manderson and Rosebud to begin trucking in food every night. From now on, we're going to get our bread in here,

"The same gullies that our ancestors went through, our people are creeping around there today. My grandmother used to tell me, 'This was the way we ran, that was the direction we took.' And now another generation is going through the same thing, and those officials are saying, 'Lay down your guns and come out.' You think we're going to be foolish enough to do it? They're crazy! We're not."

— Mildred Galligo

Dennis Banks.

we're going to get our medicine. We're not going to beg from those people any longer.

This man here, who weighs 140 pounds, last night he packed 80 pounds of food to us, 15 miles. I'm sure it was more like 50 miles to him. We had one man who started out Saturday and walked for 3 days, 50 miles, to get here. We have another right here in the red blanket, got out of a Federal prison last week to come here. We've had 3 injuries, 3 wounded men, who are back on duty now. Every one of them are warriors, and we're going to start acting like warriors from now on. If anybody wants to leave, we'll get you safely out of here. You don't have to worry about getting arrested. It's hard to run a community in a military fashion, but those people are out to kill us.

From now on, we will dictate our own future. Because sooner or later they'd have us fighting because we don't have enough to eat. There have been too many Indian people that have died in back alleys, beaten to death because of promises, because of begging over a loaf of bread, or a dollar bill. We can't let that happen here.

This decision was reached with the Oglalas here, in council with members of the Six Nations [Iroquois Confederacy]. We talked it over and we realized that whatever we do here is not only going to effect the Oglala Sioux and our nation here, it's going to have far reaching effects into the Navajo Nation, the Leech Lake Chippewas, the Winnebagos, the Six Nations.

We've got 50 tons of groceries waiting out there. We want 11 volunteers and 11 backpacks for them. Now they're empty — you're going to bring them back full.

MILITARY ESCALATION

In the week following the breakdown of negotiations with Harlington Wood, the U.S. forces tightened their perimeter. Two of their road-blocks were moved in until they were virtually on the edge of the village. There were firefights nearly every night — at first around midnight, but then beginning soon after sunset and lasting for several hours at a time. Carter Camp:

They had agreed previously that if we didn't increase our perimeter, they wouldn't decrease theirs. In fact, in the last two days, they've moved to within two to three hundred yards of our perimeter. They took one of our bunkers, which was up there on Strawberry Hill, and are now using it for themselves. They had three APCs and two helicopters up there this morning. And on the other side, they put in another emplacement and one more APC. What they've done now is in effect a crossfire, whereby they no longer are zeroing in on the soldiers that are out there in the trench. They've zeroes in now on the civilizn population here in Wounded Knee. Every house so far in the last three nights has taken fire. One of our ladies down there in the church, her chair was hit. It was lucky *she* didn't get hit. The churches, the round church in particular, tonight they've zeroed in on that with a crossfire. That's where our women and children sleep. It's the warmest place, but now it's not the safest place.

The Pentagon supplied the marshals and FBI agents with clothing and equipment necessary for night-time fighting. Their roadblocks had the expensive and super-sensitive "starlight" scopes developed for use in Indochina. In order to tell where their machine guns were hitting, they

used belts of "tracer" ammunition, in which every fifth round is illuminated. The APCs were equipped with high intensity search lights with which they criss-crossed the village, looking for targets. Truck loads of flares and flack vests were sent for their use, as well as three sniping rifles with special night scopes for field testing.

The following is a transcript of Wounded Knee's radio transmissions and warriors' conversations during a long on-and-off firefight between 8 p.m. and 1 a.m. in late March. After the sudden start of the firefight, some warriors were being shuttled to their bunkers in cars with headlights off. The defense forces were being directed by one of the warriors from the Security building next to the trading post. (Radio transmissions are in standard type and conversations between people in the Security building or in bunkers are in italic.)

Star bunker on the radio to Security: Were any of the bunkers hit?

Security to Star: Shit yes! They're slamming Denby [bunker] all around. They shot up the Security building and a car right out front.

Warrior dashing into Security building: *Some rounds just now went right over our heads.*

Denby bunker to Security: Hey listen! You better cut out some of them lights down there, man, because tracers are bouncing off 'em.

Security to Denby: We should leave the lights on so people can see.

Denby to Security: No man, that ain't gonna do no good. I can sit up here and scope in on people running across that street. Most of that light is coming out of that trading post door. Every time you open up that door, it lights up that whole street, the hospital, and the trailer.

Security to Denby: Roger, over.

The firing from the Government bunkers stopped. Some of the warriors had gone to the road in front of the trading post. Groups of people were coming out, heading for the nightly meeting. The sky was laced with flares, so bright and common now that people called them midnight suns.

Then a heavy automatic weapon fired from a Government bunker and the warriors crossed to the clinic:

Warrior: *There comes that spotlight on again. You guys got a radio over there?*

Denby on the radio to Security: Send someone out to Manderson bunker. They're out of radio contact with us. There's an APC about 400 yards straight south of 'em.

Security to Denby: 10-4. I just sent a guy out there. They have no radio. They can't see that APC from where they're sitting. All they see is the movement of cars on Denby Road.

Denby to Security: Right on. We'll stand by.

Warrior to another warrior coming in from a bunker: *Freezing, huh? (laughter)*

Second warrior: *No, I ain't freezing. Anyone around here know where I can get some .22 shells?*

First warrior: *Did you check in Security, brother?*

Second warrior: *Yeah, they got one bullet.*

First warrior: *Check in the trailer. I thought I saw a box laying around in there.*

The firing ended again and the village returned to normal. In the Security building some of the warriors were warming up at the huge fireplace as Red Arrow radioed a report of the damage they received to their Headquarters.

Head of Security: *We got one round in there. Of all that fire we got one measly round! (laughter)*

Third warrior: *That's all right. We put some close enough to scare 'em.*

Security: *Yeah, I think so. I told 'em just to return fire, not to initiate any. But if that big spotlight keeps giving 'em trouble, shoot that sonuvabitch out.*

Third warrior: *That's what I was shooting at.*

Security: *Were you in range of it?*

Third warrior: *I was in range of it. I was lying way out back in the field. I came close enough to it that they started spray-*ing way the hell out there. It worked to draw the fire off the village.

Security: *You should have heard Banks shouting when a warrior opened up from right behind his house. "Stop that firing — you can't see a thing!" He cracked me up. Somebody was firing right from his yard.*

Red Arrow had just reported that their bunkers expended 3,312 rounds of Charlie 35 [.30 caliber machine-gun tracer ammunition]. A few minutes later Red Arrow reported they were taking rounds again. Wounded Knee figured the Government was monitoring their radio so they called the bunker that had been under attack and spoke as though they had sophisticated weapons also:

Security, on the radio to Denby: You guys read me. This time open up with that .30 caliber. I told you to open up last time. Goddam it this time we mean it, open up with that .30 cal.

Carter Camp and several warriors in front of the trading post.

Last Stand bunker and check-point.

Warrior: No, tell them the .50 cal. Tell them we're bringing the .50 up.

Security to Denby: Denby, listen — if you are afraid to open up with that .30 cal, we're bringing up a .50 cal. Better have a MAN up there to fire that .50.

Warrior rushing in the door of Security: Cut the lights! Shut the door! Quick as you can!

Another warrior: You guys get them lights off in there and let's go. We just gotta get up there, to the bunker, man.

Security (outside in the street): Look at that spotlight up there! Knock that spotlight out if you can.

Warrior: Listen to those M-16s. There's no sense in wasting ammunition, we can't hit it now in this fucking wind. We don't have the weapons to do it. (A round hits very close to him.) SHIIIIT!!! I'm going across the road to the ditch, dudes. I almost got dusted going to Little California earlier, and that's no lie. (laughter)

Another warrior: WAHOOO! Those fuckers just won't quit. God damn! They're shooting the fuck out of us over here!

Warrior: Let's go back inside.

Warrior: This side of the car is a lot better.

Denby on the radio to Security: . . . we're under heavy fire . . .

Security to Denby: I read you. Go ahead and return it.

Warrior: Here they go again!

Another warrior: They're firing tracers at somebody — they're firing tracers on that hill over there. They got somebody in their sights.

This firefight, the most intense yet, depleted the meager ammunition supply of the Independent Oglala Nation. No one had been hit in all the rounds that passed through the village that night. The next day people made necklaces from some of the expended projectiles they found in the houses and trailers.

THE BLOCKADE TIGHTENS

In the first days of the siege the press had been banned from Wounded Knee, though some enterprising reporters managed to slip between the roadblocks. Later, after much protest, the Government's policy was eased somewhat and press people were allowed in and out on Interior Department passes, after being screened by the FBI.

Then, on March 21, the Government began to tighten media access once again. First, reporters were ordered to leave the village by 4:30 p.m. each day, which prevented them from observing the nightly meetings and firefights. The list of those granted passes was pared down daily, and restricted to major networks and news services. Several days later, the Government stopped granting passes altogether, and only the networks' mobile studios, which had never left the village, and representatives of alternate media, remained. Shortly after that, even these people were ordered to leave. The networks did so, and from then on the only reporters in the village were those who hiked in and stayed, risking arrest like any other member of the ION community. Some of those harassed by the Government's shifting press policies described their experiences.

Mike Falk: I had credentials from *Liberation* magazine, and Betsy Dudley had them from WBCN radio. We saw this press officer from the Interior Department — I think his name was Harpster — and he said, "Well, I'm sorry, we can't give you press passes. You're not full-time correspondents and we've had so many people here, and somebody who wasn't a full-time correspondent ripped off some toilet paper and we have to lock the johns now besides which . . ." and a whole story like that. But he invited us, more or less, to go into Wounded Knee by ourselves, to go around the roadblocks, which we did the next day — and were arrested coming out. We were charged with obstructing a federal officer in the line of duty during a civil disorder.

Network vehicles in Wounded Knee.

Betsy Dudley: The FBI who were manning the roadblocks did the arresting. They turned us over to the BIA police, who then issued a Court Order ordering us off the reservation. They were working in conjunction with each other. It was a convenient means of getting people far enough away that they couldn't be effective.

The person from the Interior Department that we talked to gave out the impression that the Indians inside Wounded Knee in fact didn't want the "fringe press" to be in there, that we were bothering them. It was very clear that *he* didn't want people from the "fringe press" going in. After we got inside, we were made to feel very welcome.

Mike Schuster, of Liberation News Service (LNS): I have press credentials from the New York City Police Department — Working Press cards. Well, I went down to the BIA building and signed in, expecting to be able to go into the Press area and see if I could get a daily pass. And I was informed that if my name wasn't on the list, I couldn't even enter the building. And I thought, "Well, my name would be on the list because usually the list are those people who've had passes from the previous day." And they said, "No, this is a special list that was drawn up this morning."

I looked at it quickly and all I could see were names of people from major newspapers and wire services and the networks. I was informed that no one else would be issued press credentials from now on. I sort of got angry and asked them whether they thought what they had done was legal, or constitutional, or discriminatory, and they just said that it had been their orders and it was their job to carry out. And I said, "You mean there's no appeal? I can't talk to anyone?" And they said, "Absolutely not."

Tom Cook, president of the American Indian Press Association, and associate editor of *Akwesasne Notes*: Two reporters from *The Renegade*, a Washington State newspaper which belongs to the American Indian Press Association, were arrested this afternoon [March 20] at 2 p.m. They are here as reporters and newspeople are here, and this is clearly and outrageously discriminatory to the Indian press. These two people had been given Justice Department passes, which

is required at the FBI barricades. This means of course that it could happen to NBC, ABC, *The New York Times,* but it also means that it will not happen to those people. If it did there would be a big stink, a big issue created of it.

Later, Cook himself was arrested by BIA police and evicted from the reservation. When he returned to the reservation at the time set for his Tribal Court hearing, he was again arrested "for being on the reservation."

The mass media in Wounded Knee.

In another effort to hide the major issue at Wounded Knee, Oglala resistance to U.S. domination, the Federal Government tried to use Indians to fight Indians. In a move resembling its "Vietnamization" policy in the Indochina war, the Government brought in BIA policemen from reservations around the country to occupy the more visible positions in Pine Ridge and free the marshals for direct military operations around the Wounded Knee perimeter. They also recruited Indians to act as undercover informers. Leroy Little Ghost, of the Fort Totten Reservation in North Dakota, was one of those. But once inside Wounded Knee he made the following statement to the people of the Independent Oglala Nation:

On or about March 3, 1973, Bud Warren, a U.S. Marshal, did contact me on the telephone . . . What Bud Warren wanted was, he wants me to come down to Wounded Knee and get all the information for him as to what all they have here, as to what is going on, etc.

. . . He stated definitely that if I fulfilled his orders or requests, that he would pay me $2,000, or either the amount of $20,000, and the sheriff of Jamestown, North Dakota, did buy my bus ticket from there to Rapid City, South Dakota. He gave me the amount of $20, and out of that I paid for the bus ticket $17.50 and upon arrival at Rapid City depot, another marshal from the State of Wisconsin picked me up and brought me down to Pine Ridge. At Pine Ridge another marshal picked me up and gave me the sum of $10, and told me to get drunk or whatever I wanted.

I walked out of there as far as the Pine Ridge Airport and I caught a ride out of there in a yellow camper as far as the line or blockade. I took the canyons and there I came directly to this area. I did run into another U.S. Marshal and he directed me to here.

Please be advised that I do want to come to this place, even with all the unexpected incidents I had to go through. I am a Sioux Indian and I want to stay true to my people. I cannot harm or sell out my people. I wish to be here with them to the best of my ability to fight for right and justice. At the present I do wish my own family was down here in Wounded Knee, South Dakota. I do wish to have the Civil Rights Association of this reservation and the AIM to check on my family, who are staying home at Takio, North Dakota, to make sure they are all right and will be protected . . .

In a nationwide effort to cut off support for the Independent Oglala Nation, the Federal Government arrested people in different parts of the country who were on their way to Wounded Knee bringing supplies. One entry in the marshals' log reads, for example, "Mr. Seymore, Department of Justice Information Center, Washington, D.C., called CP [the Marshals' Pine Ridge command post] in reference to Mr. Thomas, U.S. Attorney, Cheyenne, Wyoming. Confirmed that seven cars and two vans were en route to W.K. with foods and supplies for W.K. . . . Also, that Mr. Thomas would attempt to arrest and would set bond high . . ."

In an affidavit, Scott Burgwin, who with four friends attempted to deliver contributions from Oregon communities, described an experience which is typical of the harassment many others encountered.

. . . We picked up food and clothing in Eugene at about 10 p.m. [and] continued that night toward Bend, Oregon. The truck broke down. We started out again at 1:30 p.m.

Oglalas meeting with the WKLDOC lawyers March 25 to discuss the new court order.
From left —
Tom Bad Cob,
Francis Mesteth,
Phyllis Mesteth,
Ellen Moves Camp,
Gladys Bissonette,
Lou Beane.

on Saturday, March 24. As we were leaving Bend, at about 4 p.m., about 10 – 15 FBI Agents, state troopers, and local police officers, including a matron, caused us to stop. We were ordered out of the truck by the FBI Agents who proceeded to have all five of us searched and then handcuffed. The two women were together and the men were all taken in separate police vehicles. Two agents questioned me in the police car. They asked me what the food was for, where it was going, why the five of us were taking the food. I told them I was taking the food to the Pine Ridge and Rosebud Indian Reservations. They told me it was against the law to do what we were doing. I was booked and fingerprinted. Bail was set at $16,000 for each of us. About two hours later, while still being processed, a U.S. Marshal came and we went into a conference room with him, the three men and the two women in two separate groups. He told us that we were charged with intent to aid and abet a riot by using interstate commerce (highways) . . .

To handle the continuing arrests, and to break through what they termed an illegal siege, a group of lawyers and legal workers formed the Wounded Knee Legal Defense/Offense Committee [WKLDOC]. They announced that they would seek court action "to prohibit the Federal authorities from preventing Wounded Knee residents from returning to *their homes and to permit general access to the area." At the Committee's Rapid City office, attorney Beverly Axelrod commented:*

People from all over the country, from a wide variety of states, have been busted on ridiculous charges of having food in their car with the intention of contributing to the so-called civil disorder here. People have been arrested in Oregon and California, in Nebraska, in many different areas.

It's really a reign of terror — anyone who is suspected to have any connection at all — however tenuous — with the Indians at Wounded Knee, or in any way trying to help them, are subjected to this kind of terrorism. And there is no doubt that this constitutes conspiracy on the part of various agencies of the Federal Government. And we intend to bring a lawsuit to prove it.

On March 25, the Defense Committee obtained a Temporary Restraining Order [TRO] from Federal Judge Andrew Bogue, against Pine Ridge BIA Superintendent Stanley Lyman, Secretary of Interior Rogers Morton, Harlington Wood, and Attorney General Richard Kleindienst. It required that the defendants immediately instruct "all U.S. Marshals, Federal Agents, Sheriff's personnel, police officers, and all law enforcement personnel and persons carrying out law enforcement functions of any kind or nature in and around the Pine Ridge Reservation" to allow six lawyers, each with a carload of food, to come into Wounded Knee each day from March 26 through March 31.

WKLDOC lawyers —
Fran Olsen,
Ramon Roubideaux,
Mark Lane,
Ken Tilsen, and
Beverly Axelrod.

United States Marine Corps Ret. to take command.

Fellow patriots, the Oglala Sioux needs you. Come in and sign up. There is no doubt that Wounded Knee is a major communist thrust. They have established a beach-head. Now it is up to us to Get Them Out. We will organize and train while the Fed. Gov. is negotiating with them. And when the Fed. Gov. has yielded, conceded, appeased and just short of surrender, we will march into Wounded Knee and Kill Tokas, wasicus, hasapas and spiolas. They want to be martyrs? We will make it another Little Big Horn!! and any one of their beatnik friends can be a stand-in for Yellow Hair.

The supporters of AIM come in all shades and the National Council of Churches are very vocal because the

Richard Wilson's men responded quickly to the court order. They circulated a letter on the reservation.

FELLOW OGLALAS AND FELLOW PATRIOTS:

The time has come for all good citizens of the Pine Ridge Reservation to lay aside their petty differences and squabbles and unite. Unite against the American Indian Movement and their planned takeover of our Reservation.

What has happened at Wounded Knee is all part of a long range plan of the Communist Party. First they divide the people, get them to fight among themselves . . . Disrupt the normal function of a society. Demand the removal of key officials. Demand the resignation of Heads of State, and so you see, the jigsaw puzzle begins to fall in place.

To combat this unpleasant nuisance we are confronted with, Oglalas, we are organizing an all-out volunteer Army of Oglala Sioux Patriots. (We need all able bodied men over the age of 18 years.) You may sign up at Pine Ridge by contacting one of the following: William Rooks: Courthouse; Francis Shangreau: Public Health Service Hospital; Glenn Three Stars: Tribal office; Earl Deon: at his home; Bat Richards: Foster Grandparents office; Paul Furman: Al Hemingway Service Station; and Gene Rooks: Housing Authority office. (We are requesting Gen. Chester Fuller,

Members of Wilson's roadblock seizing food from the car of WKLDOC lawyer John Keller on March 26.

Liberal Press and the T.V. News media is right at their elbow. No news reporter or t.v. camera man has ever won a war, but they can destroy a Nation by the propaganda of lies and hate that they broadcast for every Crackpot, Screwball, and Communist-front organization who wants to take a swat at our American way of life, take a blast at the U.S. Constitution, spit at the American Flag, burn it, wear it as a poncho, or hang it upside down.

Since the American Indian Movement at Wounded Knee is supported by non-Indians, we are enlisting the help of all non-Indian residents of the Pine Ridge Reservation. So come on in and sign up, so we can get this show on the road.

WILSON'S ROADBLOCK

With the new court order, the Government was required to let in food. But Wilson's vigilante supporters set up their own roadblock, preventing WKLDOC lawyers from even reaching the Federal positions. The marshals noted this in their logs and even acted as observers, but made no attempt to remove the roadblock or to stop the theft of food from the attorneys' cars.

— "March 26 . . . 10:35 am, Command Post advised that Oglala Sioux Tribe will establish a roadblock on the Big Foot Trail leading into Wounded Knee about one mile above Highway 18. State no one will be passed. Their opinion is that Court Order of Judge Andrew Bogue not valid on Sioux Tribe."

"These so-called 'apples' — red on the outside, white on the inside — just haven't realized what's going on. The white society has washed their minds so bad they don't want to wake up. They're going to realize what's going on after it's all over, that they were wrong."

— Bobby, a Wounded Knee warrior

The roadblock, Richard Wilson in center.

"It's been a problem holding the responsible citizens of this reservation down to low key. They're uptight, they're ready, they want to go, they want to move in, they want to take Wounded Knee back."

— Richard Wilson

U.S. Marshals' bunker on
the eastern perimeter of
Wounded Knee.

The morning that the Tribal roadblock went up, Monday, March 26, the only phone line into Wounded Knee was once again cut. NBC, the last news network in the village, pulled out on Government orders. Less than two hours later, Federal forces began firing into the village.

Marshal Lloyd Grimm, a retired Air Force officer, was hit early in the firefight – possibly before it had even begun. The warriors in Wounded Knee were convinced that he had been shot by a vigilante or by another Government position, and that contention is backed up by the fact that no information was ever released describing the bullet which hit him, and no one from the village was ever charged with shooting him.

The firing went on until late Monday night and picked up again at an unprecedented 6 a.m. the next morning. The situation was serious: vigilantes were firing into the village and on the marshals; the Special Operations Group of the marshals used the excuse of the firefight to move forward of their bunkers for the first time in the siege, even though it put them in a more vulnerable position in respect to the vigilantes. From their close position the SOG shot accurately into the housing areas and closed in on some of Wounded Knee's outlying bunkers in what appeared to be an attempt to take the village. The Federal forces were held back by the Wounded Knee Security forces, their small stock of ammunition having been resupplied by people hiking in during the night.

Around noon the Government finally called a cease-fire, and Government negotiators began a series of frantic meetings with Wilson's people, who had used the firefight to establish two new vigilante bunkers behind the marshals.

Ken Tilsen, an attorney with the Wounded Knee Legal Defense/Offense Committee, was in Wounded Knee when the firing began Monday and was not able to leave for two days because of heavy firing into the village. "We estimated the village took 20,000," he later said. "The Government says 5,000. The press says nothing." Tilsen analyzed the complex relationships between the different parties involved in the fighting:

The best analogy [to Pine Ridge] is South Viet Nam. There are a lot of similarities. Most obviously, there is a corrupt government of "natives," who are set up, armed, supplied, financed, propagandized for, and maintained in power by the U.S. Government. Richard Wilson, whom the Government and the press repeatedly style "the elected leader of the Pine Ridge Reservation people," plays a role like that of Thieu and Ky in South Viet Nam — ruling and repressing the people of Pine Ridge in the interest of a foreign power — and in the interest of personal gain.

This role of Wilson and his recruits is obvious to anyone who is in the area for any length of time. More evidence is provided by the following facts: at a public meeting in Rapid City on March 28, the highest Government official in the area, Kent Frizzell, the U.S. Interior Department Solicitor-Nominee, openly admitted that an agreement had been made with Wilson not to arrest his vigilantes for their law violations and violence.

This agreement allowed them to set up an illegal roadblock, allowed them to violate court orders requiring passage of food and medicine, and allowed them to continue, unarrested, firing from surrounding positions into the streets and houses of the village. Frizzell said the agreement not to arrest was that Wilson should "try to get the vigilantes under control," because their crossfire from between and outside the Federal lines was endangering the lives of FBI men and Federal marshals. (It is generally acknowledged that a vigilante most probably shot marshal Lloyd Grimm accidentally, Monday night. Many reports have implied the defenders of Wounded Knee shot him, despite the direction of fire making this impossible.)

. . . It seems clear that U.S. officials actually want the vigilantes there to do the dirty work. The officials do not really want court orders enforced that would permit communication between Wounded Knee and the outside world, legal representation, press presence, food and medicine to enter . . . Arms, ammunition, supplies, and U.S. Government trucks and other vehicles have been supplied in large amounts to those vigilantes — we could see the equipment they were using with our own eyes.

Main street Wounded Knee. When the shooting starts, two warriors duck behind a car for shelter. Two others run down the ditch towards the white church kitchen. The Wounded Knee "Bus" is caught out in the open. At the left edge of the picture is Denby bunker, a little ways up the hill. On the ridgeline, Government positions are barely visible.

Just after the firefight ended, a plane brought supplies into Wounded Knee.

NEGOTIATIONS WITHOUT THE ION

Monday night after the firefight, Dennis Banks and Russell Means hiked out of Wounded Knee. They went to the Crow Dog family's camp, 80 miles away on the Rosebud Reservation. There, several hundred Indian people were stockpiling food and training a security force, intending to back up Wounded Knee in case of a Government attack.

Government officials heard that Dennis and Russell had left and used the information to fabricate a story. Talking to the press which had been denied access to the village, Assistant Attorney General Kent Frizzell told them that a faction of Oglalas inside the village wanted to surrender, and had used the absence of Banks and Means to "get the drop" on the more militant ones, but that following their return, Banks and Means "reasserted complete control." The Associated Press carried this dispatch:

(PINE RIDGE, SOUTH DAKOTA)---NOW THERE'S TALK OF MUTINY AMONG THE MILITANT INDIANS HOLDING WOUNDED KNEE IN SOUTH DAKOTA. A GOVERNMENT SPOKESMAN SAYS AN INFORMANT INSIDE THE BESIEGED HAMLET REPORTS THERE WAS A FALLING OUT BETWEEN THE LEADERS OF THE AMERICAN INDIAN MOVEMENT AND LEADERS OF THE OGLALA SIOUX...A CONFLICT THAT REACHED THE POINT OF ARMED CONFRONTATION. THE SPOKESMAN SAYS THE MILITANT GROUP HEADED BY RUSSELL MEANS AND DENNIS BANKS IS STILL IN CONTROL, BUT THAT ABOUT 100 OF THE INDIANS MAY DECIDE TO LEAVE WOUNDED KNEE.

-28-

After talking with the support group at Rosebud, Dennis and Russell hiked back into Wounded Knee on Tuesday night. They went right to a meeting in the trading post, where Russell reported on the stories circulating in the press, including one that he had fled the country. He went on to talk about how the Government was attempting to convince outside supporters that the Independent Oglala Nation was no longer worth fighting for because of violent conflicts within the leadership. The Government had also asked Oglala supporters on the outside to negotiate in Rapid City, hoping they would negotiate a surrender, thinking that was what the Oglalas inside wanted.

After the meeting, Dennis, Russell, and Pedro Bissonette, chosen by the Oglalas to speak for them, videotaped a statement of unity which was carried out of Wounded Knee at 2 a.m., taken to the nearby village of Manderson, and then driven by local supporters to Rapid City. It was shown to the Oglala negotiators just before the negotiations were to begin, and they immediately agreed that the only thing to be discussed with the Government was an opening of communications with Wounded Knee.

The next morning, Assistant Attorney General Kent Frizzell, now heading the U.S. negotiating team, gave a press conference in Rapid City as the negotiations were about to begin.

Kent Frizzell: We understand Banks and Means are again in control after that confrontation.

If AIM says that this is not a negotiating session, what do you hope to accomplish today?

Frizzell: I'm optimistic and hopeful, because I'm convinced that the civil rights group comprise the majority of the people that were there. Our information is that there remains approximately 160 people in Wounded Knee. And of that figure, approximately 100 are residents of this community and we're hoping that they will come out peacefully. And we welcome them . . .

Mr. Roubideaux [an attorney with the WKLDOC] said that the confrontation simply did not take place.

Frizzell: Well, as I indicated, I wasn't there and I don't think Mr. Roubideaux was there either, and our sources have been reliable in the past.

When the negotiations began, Ted Means, an Oglala activist, played the smuggled videotape for the Government negotiators and the press.

Ted Means: In response to the rumors that Banks and Means are missing and the leadership has been switched — this is in response to those rumors.

Dennis Banks, speaking on the videotape: "There's been reports circulating around the country that both Russell Means and myself have left Wounded Knee. We want to tell our Indian brothers and sisters all across the country that we are safely here in Wounded Knee, and that we intend to stay here."

Pedro Bissonette: "We also understand that there are reports that some negotiations concerning the Independent Oglala Nation may be taking place in Rapid City. Let us assure the public that we have no intention of allowing negotiating concerning our future to take place without our consent, or outside Wounded Knee.

Today we presented a proposal to the Justice Department: 1) continue the ceasefire; 2) enforce the Court Order and let in the food; 3) install the phone and permit the press to come in; meet tomorrow at 3 p.m. in the tipi in the DMZ; delegates from the Independent Oglala Nation to be permitted into Wounded Knee: Frank Fools Crow, Matthew King, Frank Kills Enemy, Eugene White Hawk, and Severt Young Bear."

The videotape gave evidence that the split in Wounded Knee was a Government fabrication. With the Oglalas on the outside firmly supporting the ION's position, the Rapid City negotiations were called off. That afternoon, South Dakota Senator James Abourezk and Ted Means commented on the situation at separate press conferences:

Abourezk: We're now in the process of trying to set up a meeting in Pine Ridge, between the Justice Department and a group of Indian people, some of whom are inside Wounded Knee and some of whom are outside of Wounded Knee.

When would this meeting be set for? Tomorrow?

Abourezk: We don't know yet.

Is the impediment getting the permission of the Tribal Government?

Abourezk: I'd rather not talk about any of the details now. We just want to try to get the thing moving again. Apparently the negotiations have broken down, and the meeting that was supposed to come off today did not come off because the people that we had been told were representatives of the people in Wounded Knee were in fact apparently not representatives. We're just trying to get a process set up so that we can meet with them now.

Are you optimistic about a settlement?

Abourezk: Not as optimistic as I was yesterday.

Showing the videotape at the Rapid City negotiations.

Ted Means (center) and Vernon Bellecourt (left) at the press conference.

. . .

Who's running things in there now?

Ted Means: The Oglala people.

Was there a confrontation in there?

Ted: There has never been a confrontation within. You all saw the videotape — there has been no rift. This rumor has been spread by a system that does not want to come to grips with Indian people. Those rumors were spread by a system that has the old divide and conquer tactic. There is no power struggle.

Is it true that Banks and Means had guns pointed at their heads by the Oglala Sioux?

Ted: No.

Why did the Justice Department say there was?

Ted: The old divide and conquer tactic. They were trying to pit Indian against Indian.

With the failure of their latest attempt to isolate Wounded Knee, the Government was finally willing to negotiate an end to the confrontation. Ironically enough, it was the Federal command which was quarrelling, not the Wounded Knee leadership. The marshals and the FBI, with their separate organizations, were running into contradictory instructions from Washington, while Wilson's men were becoming angry enough to shoot at the marshals' roadblocks from behind. Frizzell agreed to negotiate directly with the Independent Oglala Nation and to discuss the 1868 Treaty.

Shortly after the Government agreed to negotiate, Pedro Bissonette expressed the hopes that many of the Oglalas held:

I believe this time we are starting to talk about our treaty rights. We'll start getting some successful answers, and we should be getting one of the top officials to be here. The Oglala people's demands were removal of Richard Wilson and BIA Area Director Wyman Babby and Superintendant Stanley Lyman. But now we don't care if the BIA offers to remove them people. It's just too late. This is going to be solved in the Independant Oglala Nation. And we're going to stand on that, our treaty rights, from now on.

Every time we approached the BIA in a nice way, normal way, they shut the doors on us. They're scared to talk to us about the treaty rights. They're in trouble when the Government starts talking about treaty rights. They'll indict us and they won't even talk about the charges. They'll try to end this in some easy offer.

This time it is happening on the reservation at one of the historical sites, and I myself see with my own eyes the young group, and the older group, and the kids are all here. And the local residents are willing to fight for our rights here. There was that 1890 massacre here and we aren't about to lay our arms down before we start talking about that treaty.

I believe that people are waking up — Indian people, and Chicanos, and blacks, and white people. We have a lot of supporters. The inside story don't seem to get out with the news media, but the picture is starting to show around. It's getting to look better all the time.

The situation is that we want to lift the roadblocks and let the food and medical supplies in, and then set a later date, another time and place and date, to negotiate on our 1868 Treaty. We would like to meet with Nixon ourselves, and have our traditional leaders from Pine Ridge Reservation here with us. And I believe that when we talk about our treaty rights, it's not only for the Oglala Sioux. It will be the beginning, and all different tribes will come in. And that's what Nixon's afraid of right now.

8. NEGOTIATIONS

"And when we talk about our treaty rights, it will be the beginning — and all the different tribes will come in . . ."

Laramie Treaty Commission, 1868.

Duplicate

Article I.
From this day forward all war between the parties to this agreement shall forever cease . . . .

Article II.
The United States agrees that the following district of country, to wit, viz: commencing on the east bank of the Missouri River where the forty-sixth parallel of north latitude crosses the same, thence along low-water mark down said east bank to a point opposite where the northern line of the State of Nebraska strikes the river, thence west across said river, and along the northern line of Nebraska to the one hundred and fourth degree of longitude west from Greenwich, thence north on said meridian to a point where the forty-sixth parallel of north latitude intercepts the same, thence due east along said parallel to the place of the beginning . . . shall be, and the same is set apart for the absolute and undisturbed use and occupation of the Indians herein named . . . and the United States now solemnly agrees that no persons except those herein designated and authorized so to do . . . shall ever be permitted to pass over, settle upon, or reside in the territory described in this article . . .

Article XII.
No treaty for the cession of any portion or part of the reservation herein described which may be held in common shall be of any validity or force as against the said Indians, unless executed and signed by at least three fourths of all adult male Indians, occupying or interested in the same . . .

Article XVI.
The United States hereby agrees and stipulates that the country north of the North Platte river and east of the summits of the Big Horn mountains shall be held and considered to be unceded Indian territory, and also stipulates and agrees that no white person or persons shall be permitted to settle upon or occupy any portion of the same, or without the consent of the Indians, first had and obtained, to pass through the same. And it is further agreed by the United States that within ninety days after the conclusion of peace with all bands of the Sioux nation, the military posts now established in the territory of Montana shall be closed.

— Excerpts from the Fort Laramie Treaty of 1868

The negotiations finally got started on March 31. The ION negotiators arrived in some old cars and their "APC" – AIM Personnel Carrier – a well-worn green van. The Government team landed in a helicopter which waited in Pine Ridge village until Frizzell was radioed that the ION representatives were waiting for him at the tipi site.

It was a cold, windy South Dakota spring afternoon when 27 people, many wrapping themselves in blankets, met in a tipi in the demilitarized zone about a mile from the center of Wounded Knee on the Big Foot Trail. Seated in a circle were 13 Oglalas from the reservation, including Gladys Bissonette, Lou Beane, Ellen Moves Camp, Eddie White Dress, Grace Spotted Eagle, Francis and Phyllis Mesteth, Russell Means, and Pedro Bissonette, and Sioux medicine man Wallace Black Elk. Also representing the Independent Oglala Nation were two leaders of the American Indian Movement, Carter Camp and Clyde Bellecourt, treaty expert Hank Adams, an Assiniboine-Sioux who was a central negotiator for the "Twenty Points" outlined in the BIA takeover in Washington, and members of the Wounded Knee Legal Defense/Offense Committee [WKLDOC]: Fran Olsen, John Keller, Doug Hall, and Ramon Roubideaux, an Oglala Sioux. (Medicine man Leonard Crow Dog and other members of the WKLDOC also helped represent the Independent Oglala Nation in the following days' negotiations.)

Speaking for the United States Government were Assistant Attorneys General Kent Frizzell and Richard Hellstern. They were accompanied by several aides and two members of the Community Relations Service, a liberal agency of the Justice Department that played a go-between role during the confrontation.

Black Elk opened the session with a prayer.

Black Elk: *I want to pray to the powers of the four winds, to our Grandfather the Great Spirit,*

and to our Grandmother.
And I want to pray to all of you here, to bring world peace
here in the Western Hemisphere —
to bring good health and good understanding,
to pave the way for our children,
and our children's children.

After preliminary talks on March 31, the Oglalas returned the next day with a ten-point proposal. This they offered as the basis of the subsequent negotiations, and it was discussed point by point. The preface to the proposal read in part:

"The Fort Laramie Treaty of 1868 between the United States and the Sioux Nation of Indians provided that the Sioux should always live in a state of independence, if not an independent State, but never to be forced to live in a condition of dependency. The Treaty recognized the sovereignty of the Sioux, that being our capacity to govern ourselves consistent with our traditions, heritage, values and beliefs, and to maintain our relationships with our universe and among our people . . . Those promises and purposes of the 1868 Treaty have long been betrayed — and those constant, countless betrayals have returned us to Wounded Knee.

"The 1868 Treaty is basic to our lives. Our armed defense at Wounded Knee is then both defense of life and defense of Treaty. However, it is not a protest born of the hates and hurts of history, as, more immediately, it was made necessary because the present experience of hundreds of Sioux Indian families is too frequently that of fear — while our country and our communities have fallen under a reign of terror . . .

"An end to the armed defense of Wounded Knee can be achieved, if the Fort Laramie Treaty of 1868 is restored in substance to the lives of the Sioux people, and if its standing as being the law of the American land is no longer denied.

"To initiate such a settlement, we propose that certain actions, processes, and commitments be undertaken for completion, or that the appropriate machinery and systems be set in motion to effect the desired or just results. WE DEMAND:

"1. Establishment of Presidential Treaty Commission for the time needed to examine, review, and negotiate Articles and provisions of the 1868 Sioux Treaty and other agreements with the traditional headsmen and chiefs of all the Sioux tribes, bands, or different reservations under the Treaty . . ."

The Oglalas' ten-point proposal specifically demanded that the commission to review the treaty be sent from the White House. It had been Presidential representatives who originally drew up the treaty with the Sioux. But Frizzell's immediate response was that the Executive branch of Government had no power to establish such a commission. He quoted an 1871 Congressional Act to substantiate his position, which had, in the eyes of the U.S., superceded the Sioux Treaty, but which had never been agreed to by the Sioux. After 1871 the U.S. considered Indians to be "wards" of the Government, and no longer sovereign.

Frizzell: It's very doubtful [a treaty commission] would have the authority to implement or negotiate articles and provisions of the 1868 Treaty. Now here's what I'm speaking of, I'm talking now from Citation 25, U.S. Code 71, which is entitled "Future treaties with Indian tribes." "No Indian nation or tribe within the territory of the United States shall be acknowledged or recognized as an independent nation, tribe, or power with whom the United States may contract by treaty. But no obligation of any treaty lawfully made and ratified with any such Indian nation or tribe prior to March 3rd, 1871, shall be hereby invalidated or impaired." Congress would have to amend or repeal that provision before anybody —

Russell Means: No, no, no! We know all about that. I knew about that when I was six years old.

Hank Adams: See, we're not asking for a new treaty, we're talking about the treaty that that law *protects!*

Russell: The 1868 Treaty — that's the one *before* 1871!

Angrily, Russell voiced the feelings of many of the Oglalas.

This is the last chance for the American Indian people to get our treaty rights, not only before the public of the United States and the public of the world, but into your courts, and into substantial discussion with the Federal Government. We want recognition as a people, by the White House. You know, otherwise it's going to come down to a massacre.

Now, this is our last gasp as a sovereign people. And if we don't get these treaty rights recognized, as equal to the Constitution of the United States — as by law they are — then you might as well kill me, because I have no reason for living. And that's why I'm here in Wounded Knee, because nobody is recognizing the Indian people as human beings.

They're laughing it off in *Time Magazine* and *Newsweek,* and the editors in New York and what have you. They're treating this as a silly matter, just as they've treated Indian people throughout history. We're tired of being treated that way. And we're not going to be treated like that any more.

You're going to have to kill us. Because I'm not going to die in some barroom brawl. I'm not going to die in a car wreck on some lonely road on the reservation because I've been drinking to escape the oppression of this goddamn society. I'm not going to die when I walk into Pine Ridge and Dickie's goons feel I should be offed. That's not the way I'm going to die. I'm going to die fighting for my treaty rights. Period.

Ellen Moves Camp, Gladys Bissonette, and other ION negotiators.

Many of the other issues in the ION's ten-point proposal were related to the 1868 Treaty, but dealt more specifically with Pine Ridge Reservation in 1973. The Oglalas in Wounded Knee saw a return to the treaty as eventually meaning a return to government by the elders of the community. They objected to the entire Tribal Government system, saying that the elected Tribal officials were puppets of Washington. But in talking with the Government they limited their demands. Their fourth point asked specifically that the United States Government prosecute those Tribal officials and vigilantes who had committed crimes.

Ramon Roubideaux, Oglala Sioux attorney with WKLDOC: What we're interested in is that the criminal actions start — that there be a complaint, the person arrested, and bond set. This is what's been missing in the past. We haven't been able to get these people arrested for their crime.

Hank Adams: You're obligated to it by law. Yet we don't

APRIL 1: "They brought in the law enforcement agencies to protect buildings rather than protect people's rights out here. And the end result — Wounded Knee."
— Russell Means

see the arrests. / We want to see the crimes committed here *prosecuted.* / The complaints of three days ago [when an attorney from the Civil Rights Division of the Justice Department was allowed into Wounded Knee by the ION to take affidavits], the complaints you heard yesterday here in the tipi — we can verify your commitment when there are arrests for these crimes.

Richard Hellstern, U.S. Assistant Attorney General: There will be an intensive investigative campaign throughout the reservation.

Russell: And prosecution?

Russell Means, Wallace Black Elk, Ramon Roubideaux.

Hellstern: We will do anything and everything that shows hard evidence, and there won't be one of them that we'll turn down. No group will be left out.

Carter Camp: There wouldn't have been a Wounded Knee, had the Government made that commitment sooner. This number 4 is what brought us here.

Gladys Bissonette, Oglala civil rights leader: [If there is a settlement here,] I would suggest that they remove Wilson at the same time, because we are not safe with him around.

Frizzell: What I assume and consent to is a sufficient number of marshals and FBI people would remain on the Pine Ridge Reservation, and there would be no Wilson men, as such, with any authority, other than the BIA police.

Ellen Moves Camp, Oglala civil rights leader: The BIA police is with him.

Frizzell: Well, of course, if the FBI and marshals are here, the BIA police would be very reluctant to take any advantage because they are subjecting themselves to a civil rights complaint.

Ellen: They didn't do it before we came in here.

Frizzell: Well, we didn't have any FBI and marshals on board.

Ellen: There were U.S. Marshals in here since February 14, two weeks before we came in.

Carter: They put the sandbags on top of the BIA office in Pine Ridge.

Gladys: And that Tribal office, upstairs — and I know you know as well as I do — is loaded with ammunition. I seen 'em loading it in. There's ammunition — boxes and boxes.

Frizzell: Well, of course the BIA is going to be under the close eye of the Department of the Interior if an agreement is reached — and the Department of Justice and the marshals and the FBI.

Ellen: But they've been here all this time — since two weeks before we came here, the Justice Department and all was there!

Frizzell: Well then, what would you suggest as an alternative?

Gladys: Throw them all in jail.

Ellen: Throw them all out.

138

Frizzell: We have no authority to do that.

Gladys: You can take your guns back that you gave to the BIA and the goons.

It was late afternoon on April 1 when the negotiators got to point five, the ION request for an audit of Tribal financial records by a source independent of the Bureau of Indian Affairs. Frizzell suggested that he would send the Interior Department in to look things over, but the people expressed some skepticism, as the BIA is an agency of the Interior Department.

Russell: There is time after time that the Department of Interior comes in on various reservations across the country, to investigate an audit, and they always come up with affirmative auditing investigations. They strengthen the position of the agency or local office that they are auditing. So any further knocking your head against a brick wall is sense-

Fran Olsen (rear), and Rachel White Dress.

less — because the Government takes the position that the Interior Department is just. That's like asking the —

Frizzell: — the fox to watch the henhouse.

Russell: Like asking John Mitchell to investigate Watergate.

Hank: See, we've been in the national BIA office seven days last November, and we saw some of the investigations they've done — and ignored. We've seen $60,000 embezzlement on the Navajo Reservation and recommendations that nothing be done. $6,000 embezzled on Devil's Lake in North Dakota under [BIA Area Director Wyman] Babby — and no recommendation for action.

Russell: And a million dollars at Fort Yates, the farm agriculture program. And it was under the administration of the Area Office of Wyman Babby. And no explanation or recommendation.

Hank: And $375,000 in a housing project in Fort Berthold expended on no houses. The Bureau and Interior become defenders of their own administration of funds and programing. They become defenders of the things they've ignored that have been happening wrongly and criminally. Ultimately, the people have to be in there to make some judgement.

Russell: And the people don't have that. Like in the village of Porcupine. The people voted down cluster housing 12 times because it makes a ghetto. But we're getting it anyway. They're shoving it down our throats.

Ramon: You know, I used to work for Congressman Case 25 years ago, and when we got a complaint from Indian people what we would do is write a letter to the Department of Interior, asking for a report, and this is all that was done. Of course, they'd write back a letter saying that everything was all right. And this is what radicalized a lot of Indian people over the years. You just can't get anything done.

Russell: You see, we are also trying to adjust ourselves to a shake-up of the BIA bureaucracy. So that it can respond and not permit any of these abuses or illegal actions by "Tribal governing authority." We shook up the bureaucracy in Washington, D.C., and still these things are permitted to happen. In fact, the result was that it got worse and more repressive at the Agency level. In fact, they started closing off any redress of grievances that individual Indians had, hoping to insulate themselves from anything happening like what happened in Washington, D.C., in terms of takeovers of buildings. They brought in the law enforcement agencies to

138
138

138

protect buildings rather than protect people's rights out here. And the end result — Wounded Knee.

We haven't demanded any radical changes here, only that the United States Government live up to its own laws. It is precedent-setting that a group of "radicals", who in the

Hank Adams, Kent Frizzell, Richard Hellstern.

minds of some are acting outside the law, are just in turn asking the law to live up to its own. We're not asking for any radical changes. We're just asking for the law to be equitably applied — to all.

Why wasn't a Grand Jury called to look into the allegations against the Tribal Government? This is what we are asking for. There is no functioning Tribal Council and Dick Wilson is making all the decisions. His goon squad has liquor which is on this reservation illegally. They raped two of our women last Thursday. Wilson is using [U.S.] Revenue Sharing money to pay his goons $8 an hour.

Frizzell: We'll investigate all this. I'm sending six FBI men out here to do it. *We'll* impose the law and protect Wilson's men and the anti-Wilson men *impartially*.

During the negotiations, Wounded Knee continued to receive occasional gunfire from the military positions on the hills. The Oglalas explained to Frizzell that this made it difficult for them to take seriously the Government's "impartiality."

Clyde Bellecourt: There are people concerned about the APCs that have moved in. They're concerned about the sniping that continues each night.

Frizzell: I understand that early this morning there was a movement forward of an APC. It was done without our authorization. That happened to be one of the BIA roadblocks.

At this point, there was a general uproar in the tipi, as people learned with consternation that the BIA police had been given APCs and other sophisticated equipment.

Carter: Do the BIA have APCs?!

Frizzell: That was their APC.

Carter: Who supplied them with an APC? I want to know that!!

Hellstern: This is part of the [Federal] Cooperative Training Program

Frizzell: To my knowledge, there are two BIA roadblocks, and each of them has an APC.

Fran Olsen, attorney with WKLDOC: Do you have the power to take away the APCs you gave to the BIA?

Frizzell: I won't promise you anything.

The next day, April 2, the people from Wounded Knee arrived for the third negotiating session, angry at what they felt was the Government's continuing bad faith in the talks. The new medical team, which had been trying to get into the village for several days, had again been denied entry. Up until this time these volunteer teams had been permitted in each week on a rotating basis. The people questioned Frizzell on this latest move.

Frizzell: The medical team — the first time I had any contact with it was with the CRS man. There's the CRS man. When was the first time you contacted me about it?

CRS Agent: When we were advised that a new medical team was here. It was first brought to your office and referred to Mr. Clear in Interior. Mr. Clear attempted to clear this through, and he advised then that it was turned down.

Frizzell: By whom?

CRS: By the chief.

Frizzell: You don't mean the chief, you mean Mr. Wilson.

CRS: Mr. Wilson, excuse me.

Russell: Wilson is not a chief.

CRS: Mr. Wilson refused them entry.

Frizzell: Let me tell you about my experience with the medical team. The first I knew of it was yesterday morning when Ramon called me from Rapid City. I said, "Certainly, send them down." During that conversation, Ramon, neither you nor I ever discussed the problem of the Tribal road-block. It didn't even occur to me. The original medical team went in before the Tribal roadblock was set up — they encountered no trouble that way.

After telling you to send them down, they appeared last evening. Wilson came by in the BIA Building where I was talking to these five, six, seven people. I motioned him over and I explained to him that this was the relief team for the medical team that would be coming out. Did he have any objection? He said, "Yes." I said, "Mr. Wilson, this is not going to add or detract from the population in Wounded Knee, it's just going to be an exchange." "No." "Mr. Wilson, there are sick children and people in there, I desire

that they go in." "No!" My response was, "Well, I disagree with you strongly." Then I tried with the medical team to try and explain what happened, and I know they think I was in bad faith, but I wasn't.

Mark Lane, attorney with WKLDOC: Well, I saw you yesterday morning about 9:30, as you recall, and at that time you said, "I have some good news for you. I talked to Ramon about the medical team and they will get in this afternoon. And if Wilson gives us a problem, we'll bring them in through one of the other roadblocks."

Frizzell: No, I did not say that.

Mark: You said that to me yesterday.

Frizzell: I have never in my life even given any inference to that effect, and if you say that I said that, I say you are lying.

APRIL 2: ". . . Then I tried to explain, and I know they think I was in bad faith, but I wasn't." — Frizzell

---

Mark: Well, I say that you are lying if you deny it.

Frizzell, to Fran Olsen: Did I say that?

Fran: You said that you would get them in this afternoon.

Clyde: Why don't you just fly them in?

Frizzell: All right, I'll say again what I said before. Early last week [at the time of the March 26 and 27 firefights], we were having trouble with Wilson's men behind our lines. At that time, he had established two — and was about to erect a third — roadblocks. I had nothing but a whole day's complaint from my marshals and FBI, saying, "Frizzell, you gotta do something about Wilson's men behind our lines, particularly at night." That was the only problem I could see at the time. To be able to solve this problem, I had to enter this agreement with him: "You remove your men from behind all of our lines, remove all roadblocks but your Roadblock 1, and I'll give you word that I won't run the press in any of our roadblocks. I won't run food in any of our roadblocks, and you can maintain the integrity of your roadblock at One. But I want no more men behind the lines." Now maybe that was a bad agreement on my part,

as I look back on it a week later — I think it was. But the fact is, I made that agreement.

Clyde: You talked about food and the press. *We're* talking about the medical team.

Frizzell: We've been sending in the medical supplies to my knowledge.

Russell: You keep saying *Wilson. Wilson's* doing this and *Wilson's* doing that. He *can not act* without Tribal Council authority and they have not met since February 23. You are taking the dictates of one man, which are illegal — according to Interior [Department] rules, the Indian Reorganization Act, and the Tribal Constitution, and the Constitution of the United States. I can't understand why you keep going to Wilson. When you should be going to the Tribal Council in the first place. The Tribal Council can't meet, so consequently there is no Tribal Government, and you're in total control.

Frizzell: May I respond then? I have been before a so-called — quote, unquote — Tribal Council. I don't know if there was a quorum, whether they were all Tribal Council members or not, but that's the audience that I sought, and he claimed he gave me. They purported themselves to be

Eddie White Dress and Reed Bad Cob.

the Tribal Council.

Russell: Fourteen of them?

Frizzell: Well, there were only about 10 or 12 people in the room —

Russell: That's illegal.

Frizzell: The truth is, I have to deal with Mr. Wilson and the Tribal Council same as I have to try and deal with you. And I don't like all the actions of the Tribal Council myself. But I do the best I can with what I got.

(The relief medical team was never allowed to pass Wilson's roadblock and the Government refused to allow them through any of the other four. Eventually they hiked in overland, through a snowstorm.)

A long argument followed on the proposed Presidential Treaty Commission, which was the most difficult point for the Government to agree to because it would open up the issue of all the broken treaties for public discussion. Frizzell would not commit the Government to a commission. Instead, he proposed a meeting to discuss a commission, the meeting to take place some time after the end of the occupation:

Frizzell: The Government will have a meeting with the traditional Sioux chiefs to "outline the need for and workings of a Presidential Treaty Commission to re-examine the 1868 Treaty."

Doug Hall, attorney with WKLDOC: Would it be correct to say that the people in Washington have reservations whether or not the commission should be established?

Frizzell: I think to answer you candidly, I'd have to say yes, they have reservations. But they're willing to hear you out as to the needs and the function and what formalizations of such a commission would be composed of, and its life, financing, etc.

Russell: Your proposal says our chiefs and headmen will "outline the need for and workings of" a treaty commission. All *that* means is that it is a meeting to hear the chiefs state why they think the commission is necessary. There's nowhere where it states that there will *be* one. The wording of this sounds like where they take our chiefs to Washington throughout history. They meet with them, let them get their gripes off their chests, and send them home. And in this century, they try to get them drunk, take them on a fancy tour of Washington, D.C. It's phenomenal how this parallels the centuries.

So we propose a re-examination of the 1868 Sioux Treaty. They can say, "Fine and good — we'll take this

APRIL 3: "You know, the Indian has a long memory." — Russell Means

Gladys Bissonette and Lou Bean.

under consideration. Thank you for coming. Good bye."

Doug: Do we understand that this is the most that could come from the White House?

Frizzell: That is my definite feeling, after exploring it for three hours this morning.

Russell: If we come up with some kind of language that it will state —

Ramon: — that it will be established if the Indians so request.

Russell: Exactly.

Frizzell: I can not sell that.

Russell: That's in the terms of the 1868 Treaty.

The next day, April 3, the process of hammering out the Presidential Treaty Commission continued. The Independent Oglala Nation negotiators did not believe that the Government would voluntarily carry through on a commission once the people inside had disarmed; but they also felt that the Government would not publicly give in to their demand for a guaranteed commission, so they tried to work out some compromise.

In a revised Point 1, the ION proposed a "preliminary meeting" to take place before evacuation of the village, where ION representatives could speak directly with the White House to "insure . . . an examination and review of the articles and provisions of the 1868 Treaty . . . in the third week of May." The ION felt that the White House could be held accountable for any promises made directly, in a way that middle-man Frizzell could not. At the same time, the ION felt that holding the treaty meetings later, after an evacuation, would allow the Government to save face, and was clearly a significant step down from their original demand that the Government commit itself immediately to holding a Presidential Treaty Commission. But Frizzell responded that even this would be too much of a concession on the part of the United States, even though he had often reassured the ION of the Government's seriousness in reconsidering the treaty.

Frizzell: First of all I feel I will have a difficult time selling any agreement, even if point number one weren't in the final agreement — what I'm saying is, I don't think the Government will entertain any visitors as long as somebody's pointing a gun at the head of the United States. That's not the way to bring about good faith and trust.

Russell: The White House did it in Viet Nam, and the White House did it when the treaties were made. The White House seems to be able to do it at their whim when guns are pointed at one another. In this instance, a .22 against an APC, I don't think we're pointing anything at the White House. We're pointing it at our own heads. If those guns happen to go off, so do we — we go off the face of the map. So I don't agree with that line of argument.

Frizzell: May I inquire into the rationale, why, if a good faith agreement is entered into on both sides, why this type of a trip to the White House — why it has to occur before the dispossession of arms? Are you afraid that we won't keep that agreement and allow that meeting to take place?

Gladys: That's right! They never do keep agreements.

Russell: You know, the Indian has a long memory. Time and again, our traditional chiefs and headmen, they went to Washington, D.C. and things got worse.

With Frizzell refusing to arrange even a preliminary meeting with the White House before a disarmament, Carter proposed another compromise. He suggested that while the ION representatives were meeting with the White House, leaders of the ION Security force would hold talks in Wounded Knee with the U.S. Marshals to plan a stand-down of arms.

At all times the ION regarded the disarmament as a purely tactical matter, subordinate to the political question of whether their demands had been sufficiently met. The stand-down itself was conditional on the Government's following through on their part of the agreement, convincing the Oglalas that they were serious about the meetings to take place in May. Frizzell did not respond directly to Carter's suggestion:

Carter: If Russ and Chief Bad Cob and Crow Dog go to Washington, D.C. and we have communication from them that things were proceeding at pace, then we would get to-gether — [Wounded Knee security chief] Stan [Holder] and myself — with [head] Marshal Colburn, and begin a complete and detailed system of standing down all the arms here. It's already been recognized that you can't just jump in the APCs and split. We'll have to work out the specifics of the protec-tion of our people on this reservation. As soon as they get to Washington and give us a phone call that things are pro-ceeding — I'd be willing.

Frizzell: If I were in your shoes and working for the same cause as you are, and a good faith agreement were signed and delivered, and that agreement was made public, you would have the greatest cause to pursue for the next gene-ration if in fact the White House did not comply with the straightforward commitment of that nature. There is no way the White House can renege, when it is set forth in straight-forward language. Your position would be better off if the Government *did* renege, so far as a cause for the next 20 or 30 years.

Carter: Well, see, the thing is, we don't need a cause for the next 20 or 30 years. We viewed Wounded Knee as some-thing that would accomplish something for our people. If we have to go into generations, we might as well just fight it out here. We're not looking forward to that type of thing.

Frizzell: I guess it's just the basic feeling that I have. We both bat around the term, the phraseology, "good faith and trust." And we both profess to enter into this agreement with that frame of mind. Well, if that's true, why does my good faith and trust have to be tested, and not yours?

Carter: Ours is tested throughout this whole agreement. At each point, we're taking on good faith that your investigation will show the malfeasance of the Department of Interior and the Bureau of Indian Affairs, and they'll be removed and no longer effective on Indian land. That includes people like Dick Wilson, Stan Lyman, and Wyman Babby. Those people are what we came here to get rid of. We ask you to enforce the laws that you should have been enforcing ten years ago. We're taking it on good faith that you will. Everything is good faith by the Indians — only this one point would be good faith by the U.S. Government.

". . . Just a little beyond Porcupine Butte we were coming this way when we were met by the soldiers . . . This officer asked Big Foot — "Are you the man that is named Big Foot? . . . I want you to turn over your guns." Big Foot answered, "Yes, I am a man of that kind." The officer wanted to know what he meant by that, so the inter-preter told him that he was a peaceful man. He says, "You have requested that I give you my guns, but I am going to a certain place and when I get there I will lay down my arms.

"Now, you meet us out here on the prairie and expect me to give you my guns out here. I am a little bit afraid that there might be something crooked about it, some-thing that may occur that wouldn't be fair. There are a lot of children here."

— Dewey Beard, a survivor of the 1890 massacre.

By the end of the day, Frizzell had basically agreed to the ION's ten-point proposal, including the requests for Government audits and in-vestigations of the Tribal Government, and prosecutions of the criminal and civil complaints against the vigilantes and the Tribal officials. The only unresolved issue was the site for the preliminary meeting.

The next day, April 4, the Independent Oglala Nation negotiators returned angrily to the meetings. The Government's aggressiveness in the field had been increasing, and the ION questioned Frizzell's good faith in negotiating a peaceful settlement of the issues.

Carter: You guys are talking peace with us — but all this time you people are getting closer and closer. Just before you guys came in [today], one of your APCs came down that hill. That would have precipitated a hell of a firefight if they'd come down. CRS called them up and told them to go back and they went back.

Frizzell: Who was it? Which — who was manning that APC? I want to know, because I'm going to —

Carter: RB-5.

Frizzell: Where did it come from?

Gladys: It came from the west. And pulled up right over the trailer houses, right in the community here.

Carter: Stan Holder talked to Marshal Colburn about the possibility of getting your people out of rifle range. You would still have a ring around us — but there wouldn't be a chance of anybody getting shot. We think that would be a hell of a good gesture on your part, to easing tensions. Because on the Porcupine Road they got a new bunker — where that yellow dump truck is parked on the road — that is sitting right on top of one of our bunkers. See, they were on the slope side of that hill over there. By bringing themselves over the top, they're right down on our bunker.

Frizzell: Like you say — it could blow the whole thing.

Carter: Ever since this has started you guys have had agreements with us and you said that you're not going to move in

Negotiations in the round church, April 4. Bedrolls are stacked on the shelves to make room for the meeting.

and you're constantly moving in. We put in our positions and we've never changed since the first two or three days that we've been here. You ask us to accept some things from you in good faith, but then you sit here and tell us lie after lie, about the most vital thing — and that's your ability to bring death on us all.

Frizzell: Well, there's no excuse for the APCs coming down. I've been assured daily for the last three days by all the law enforcement personnel that they would not allow this to happen, to spark off an incident. And I will again bring it to their attention.

Carter: Yesterday you asked us if there was going to be any problem with us when it comes to this agreement. There will — if this type of thing keeps coming up. They're now using their flares as an offensive weapon to burn our houses and burn our fields. I have seen them shoot ten or fifteen times at the same target. We know that you guys are committing offensive actions. It's only by great restraint of our warriors that they haven't gone out — cause you know we have the military capability of taking any one of these roadblocks. But we haven't made the aggressive actions that you have.

You guys asked us to believe that the North Vietnamese are violating their treaty agreements over there, that they're violating the cease-fire. Right now we can see that that's a bullshit lie because you guys can't even keep your treaty agreements or your cease-fire here.

You shoot each other and blame the Indians. You report incoming tracers on the radio — our people don't have tracer bullets. You say we fire out of a church where we know we don't have any weapons. And that's the kind of excuse you're using for returning fire and putting "suppressing fire" on our bunkers and streets. This is a constant and everyday thing.

By the end of the April 4th session, Frizzell had basically agreed to the Independent Oglala Nation's ten-point proposal, including the requests for Government audits and investigations of the Tribal Government, prosecutions of vigilantes and Tribal officials for criminal and civil violations, and a preliminary meeting to take place the following Saturday with the White House to plan for the later May meetings between the White House and the Teton Sioux chiefs. Frizzell wanted to hold the preliminary meeting in Rapid City. But the ION objected, commenting that it was one of the most racist cities in the nation. They insisted on meeting in one of the capitals of the negotiating parties, Washington or Wounded Knee.

The most difficult point to agree on had been the preliminary meeting, and at the end of the day Assistant Attorney General Hellstern reiterated his understanding of the sequence of events that had been agreed to. Several days later, the timing of the disarmament would be the point on which the agreement would break down, when the Government officials would claim they had a different interpretation than the following one that Hellstern had outlined:

Hellstern: One point on clarification — we contemplate a signed agreement with everyone here. And then the next immediate step would be a preliminary meeting with the White House and Means, Chief Bad Cob, and Crow Dog. And then the discussions will begin between Colburn [head of the U.S. Marshal force] and your people on how we're going to resolve the arms situation. We're on the same wavelength, aren't we?

Russell: Right. I thought we cleared that up yesterday.

Chief Tom Bad Cob and medicine man Leonard Crow Dog.

APRIL 4: "We're on the same wavelength, aren't we?" — Hellstern

Brief negotiations were held on Thursday, April 5. Frizzell announced that White House officials refused to come to Wounded Knee, so the preliminary meeting would be held in Washington on the coming Saturday. Then the negotiations adjourned while Frizzell went to Pine Ridge to bring some members of the press back with him to witness the signing of the agreement. At 2 p.m. the Oglalas and the Government officials returned to the tipi to smoke the pipe together.

Crow Dog: *So many hundred years ago
the white man and Indians smoke the pipe.
Now, today, they're going to smoke the pipe again.
Before they smoke the pipe,*

*I will blow the whistle that been given to the
American Indian people.
(He blows the whistle in the four directions and prays in Lakota.)*

*At this time, Great Spirit,
many, many things that we ask.
Many, many days that we're here in Wounded Knee
at this sacred altar,
this sacred holy circle.
At this time Grandfather, I ask you to take care
of my Indian people, my red man.*

APRIL 5: "Sacred kind of words never die . . ."

*I ask you to take care of my generations,
my relations that's throughout the United States.
The sacred pipe that we're gonna smoke —
the white man ain't gonna lie
and the Indian ain't gonna lie.
This will be known by the Great Spirit
and the mother earth,
the Grandmother.
HO!*

*Mr. Means will smoke the pipe,
the white brother will smoke the pipe,
my sister will smoke the pipe,
Banks will smoke the pipe,
Carter and the national leaders
of the American Indian Movement —
and the Oglala people will smoke the pipe.
(As the people pass the pipe, Crow Dog chants.)*

*Many, many tribes sign treaties, promises,
sacred kind of words never die.
We been waiting for long time
but now the American red man is back where he's
supposed to belong.
Anything we do in Washington, D.C., we always gonna
remember the sacred things that we been doing —
months, weeks here.*

Gladys, in Lakota, translated by Black Elk: *We smoke
the sacred pipe here
with our white brothers,
and we hope this will bring peace.
Because in the past there were a lot of violations
of the sacred treaties and honors.
This is real.
We're not playing here.
So now all the people that go to Washington —
think real good,
because our lives are at stake.
It concerns our children's children,
the unborn.*
Metakuyeayasi *— hear me, all my relations.*

Frizzell: *I pray to our Father in Heaven, as you do to your
spirit, that the treaty we are — the agreement we are about
to sign is not full of empty words, and that men of good
faith have entered into it. And I commit myself and my
government to the extent that those promises are fulfilled.*

Crow Dog, giving his eagle-bone whistle to Pedro Bissonette:
*Pedro gonna watch this whistle for me.
Anything through your mouth brother, at this time,
only good things.
Till we come back,
wear this, take care of it.
HO!*

After the ceremony, the group went outside the tipi to sign the agreement, and community members beat the drum and sang. Then Russell Means, Leonard Crow Dog, and Tom Bad Cob, the three Independent Oglala Nation representatives, left for Rapid City, where Russell was arraigned and bailed out, then proceeded to Washington.

The agreement began:

"1. a. The parties agree to effect meetings between representatives of the White House and the traditional chiefs and headmen of the Teton Sioux tribes, bands, or different reservations so that these Sioux representatives may outline the need for, and workings of, a Presidential Treaty Commission, which they propose as a method of reexamination of the 1868 Treaty. These meetings will be held during the third week of May. . .

It went on to give the broad outline of a disarmament, and provide for investigations of the Tribal Government, with prosecutions where appropriate.

But the Oglalas learned quickly that — as in many treaties in the past — the understanding reached in the tipi did not match the terms of the signed agreement. There, all had concurred that the preliminary meeting in Washington would be simultaneous with a meeting at Wounded Knee between the ION security forces and head Marshal Colburn, to plan the details of a mutual disarmament. But, in fact, the legal jargon of the agreement's point 1.b. read, "To effect a meaningful agenda for the meetings [in May] a preliminary planning meeting will be held in Washington, D.C., by a limited number of representatives while the details of the dispossession of arms and the accomplishing of this agreements objectives are being implemented." The Independent Oglala Nation, in line with their understanding of the agreement, expected that the Government would hold the meeting in Washington on the coming Saturday, April 7. Instead of waiting until then to begin the talks with Colburn, they called for the meeting a day early. Colburn himself had not attended any of the negotiations, and had only the text of the agreement to follow. When he received the radioed request to meet, he replied that there was no need to, since he planned to move into Wounded Knee at 7 o'clock the next morning with a force of 180 marshals for a "sweep" of the village.

The people in Wounded Knee were shocked and angered by Colburn's message. They called a meeting with Frizzell to resolved the two contradictory interpretations of the pact. That evening, and again the next morning, Carter and several of the Oglalas met with Frizzell and Hellstern. Meanwhile, Frizzell had contacted his superiors in Washington to postpone the Saturday meeting there until the situation at Wounded Knee was settled.

The ION representatives explained that the disarmament had always been understood to be a mutual disarmament — where the APCs would pull back and the marshals return home, as the ION Security forces took their hunting rifles and shotguns and returned to their homes. At no time did they envisage the Federal forces sweeping down through the village.

Carter Camp began the meeting in the DMZ on the evening of April 6:

Carter: Colburn had a plan where he would come in tomorrow morning at 7 o'clock, after Russ gave us his phone call. Our understanding is that tomorrow morning, talks between Colburn and our security chief, Stan, and myself and probably two of the squad leaders, would begin. We were to talk about the implementation of the dispossession of weapons and also the protection of our people throughout the Pine Ridge Reservation — not only by the Department of Justice, but by people from the American Indian Movement. We said that simultaneous with talks in Washington, Stan and I would begin talks with Colburn. Dispossession takes a lot of planning . . .

Colburn just said, "If you don't do this, there'll be no fucking talks in Washington." That's his exact words. And we have to be careful when he starts talking like that. He said, "We're moving in. We're coming into town at 7 tomorrow morning."

Ellen Moves Camp: People are so anxious for the Indians to disarm!

Clyde Bellecourt: It's like 1890.

Hellstern: Do I understand that you're not ready to make any moves towards dispossession until Means and company come back?

Carter: There'll be a lot of moves toward dispossession — in the talks about how you'll be dispossessed, how our people will be protected, how the goon squad is going to be nullified. All those things are substantial moves on dispossession and have to be taken care of first.

Hellstern: What is the dispossession of arms conditioned on?

Carter: Plans for it will begin tomorrow.

Hellstern: Even if everything Russ brings up on his agenda in Washington has not been adequately resolved to his satisfaction?

Clyde: Do you have any doubts that it would be?

Hellstern: No, I don't — but —

Clyde: You keep sounding like you have doubts. If Carter didn't call this meeting, Colburn would have been marching in here tomorrow.

APRIL 6: "People are so anxious for the Indians to disarm." — Ellen Moves Camp

After the signing of the agreement on April 5. Back row from left: Florine Hollow Horn, Karen White Butterfly, Gladys Bissonette, Clyde Bellecourt, Carter Camp, Russell Means, Hank Adams, and U.S. Government aides. Front row from left: Ellen Moves Camp, Ramon Roubideaux, Lou Beane, Tom Bad Cob, Wallace Black Elk, Pedro Bissonette, Kent Frizzell, and Richard Hellstern.

150

Carter: He has the Great White Father syndrome. He thought he could come in here and deal with his inferiors as they should be dealt with. He was taking a pretty hard line. He said he'd come in and I said, "You're gonna have a hell of a fight, brother."

Frizzell: My understanding is different from yours.

Ellen: I don't see how you can misunderstand it when they explained it.

Frizzell: I've got to reassess the Government's position with regard to the agreement.

Lou: Mr. Frizzell, yesterday we smoked the pipe with you — and we trusted you.

Frizzell: Well, I'm sorry if you feel that way.

The meeting resumed at 10 a.m. the next morning, April 7.

Frizzell: Your important point is the [treaty] meeting the third week in May. Our important point is to end the confrontation. The entire purpose of the Government was to end the confrontation and go about the daily tasks of what we agree to do in that agreement of assuring the civil rights of everybody on the Oglala Reservation, of assuring the unlawful criminal acts will be prosecuted, of assuring that bad practices within the BIA, tribal government, will be investigated and audited. But we can't do any of that until the armed confrontation ends.

Stan Holder, head of Wounded Knee security forces: There have been countless times when our people have been asked to stack their arms.

Frizzell: I see your hang-up. But either you trust me today or you do not.

Stan: I know that five minutes before we signed that agreement I had to go to that hill over there [to meet with Colburn] and find out why an automatic weapon was fired, and the minute I got there a 12-guage shotgun was put in my face no more than two inches from my nose. When you were signing that agreement.

Finally the two sides gave up trying to convince each other that their own interpretations of the agreement had been the correct one, and instead began discussions for a fresh solution to the disarmament problem. At 10 p.m. that night, Carter and Stan met with head Marshal Colburn and Assistant Attorney General Stanley Pottinger, another newcomer to the negotiations. Pottinger read his plan for disarmament.

Pottinger: "Phase I: The bunkers and roadblocks come down mutually and simultaneously, with inspection and pictures on both sides at that point." The next part would be immediately after this part. "With helicopter assistance, a transfer of marshals to the three pre-arranged areas." These would be the tipi church, trading post, and the white church. These would be the places where the business of dispossession would take place — where the FBI can conduct their

---

APRIL 7: "Your important point is the meeting. Our important point is to end the confrontation." — Frizzell

---

questioning and search. I would rather do it in three than one because if you do it in one, one confrontation becomes a total confrontation. If you do it in three separate ones, one confrontation becomes an involvement of a third and you can put that down without serious danger to anybody.

Colburn: We just want to neutralize and sanitize the area. The marshals will appear in their blue uniforms with a sidearm — no rifles or anything like that. This is strictly a business transaction.

Stan: When my people are disarmed in Wounded Knee, I feel that a simultaneous disarming of your people —

Colburn: Now wait a minute! You don't want that to happen.

Stan: During the time that people are being processed, I feel that nobody in Wounded Knee should have a weapon.

Colburn: I couldn't do that. I don't even think that we could even arbitrate that because I couldn't operate without the normal sidearm. You know what that is — just a police belt with a revolver.

Frizzell: There we go — trying to impose our form of government on them again.

Pottinger: "Phase II: Agents in sufficient number will report to each of the three areas. First they will interview. Second they will process those with warrants outstanding." This will include bracelets, but only plastic bracelets, and they will be sent for arraignment.

APRIL 8: "We're at an impasse. We have abided by the agreement, and we're in Washington, D.C., waiting. We're stuck in a hotel that the Justice Department got for us, that we can't afford — I apologize for being short tempered, but there's over 200 men, women and children down there that at any time could be ripped off, and I'm sitting here in a goddamned bourgeois hotel room getting fucked over by the White House . . ."   — Russell Means

---

Stan: I don't think the people should be handcuffed inside the village.

Colburn: I have already said no waist chains, no metal handcuffs, no leg irons. I think I'm a helluva guy.

The Government's proposal was unanimously rejected by the community that night, on the basis that it was a call for a surrender. It would have allowed the Government to come in after a lay-down of arms, seize the weaponry of the ION — including those guns which were legal — and maintain absolute control over the area and the people.

The Oglalas met all that day and telephoned their people in Washington. Crow Dog related a vision he'd had that a solution could be achieved if there would be a pullback by the Government positions and the ION warriors would stack their arms in the sacred tipi, placing the peace pipe before it to assure they would not be removed. This was incorporated into a seven-point proposal which the ION negotiators presented to the U.S. side the following day:

Clyde: The proposals you made night before last were taken back, tapes of them played. There was wide discussion among all people down there, and that proposal was totally thrown out the window. The people are pretty uptight about the fact that there would be marshals coming in with handguns and they would be totally unarmed. And they still envision what happened to Big Foot and his band in 1890, and they totally distrust the United States Government at this point. And when they're told we're running low on food, they made the statement that they would eat horses, dogs, cats, mice, or dirt before they surrendered under those terms. Since then, the Oglalas have gotten together — 58 of them met and worked out an agreement on their own. They presented this to the general assembly. There was wide discussion and they accepted it:

"1. The traditional Sioux chiefs and headmen be allowed in and out of Wounded Knee, to help settle the dispute.

2. That six passenger carloads of food daily shall immediately be allowed into Wounded Knee, together with the necessary medical supplies, propane and butane fuel for both heating and cooking purposes. Telephone service will continue and not be interrupted, and AIM will install their own phones. 3. That the U.S. Government armored personnel carriers and all troops

---

APRIL 9: "Whichever you treasure the most, your dollar bill or your Bible, put it in front of your APCs."
      — Lou Beane

---

and bunkers surrounding Wounded Knee will move back to their original perimeter. 4. All weapons inside Wounded Knee will be tagged with numbers and placed in the tipi outside the Security building with the peace pipe placed in front of it. 5. Community Relations Service of the Department of Justice personnel and AIM shall monitor all of the above. 6. The meetings in Washington, D.C., as per the agreement of April 5, shall commence immediately and the delegates of the Oglala Sioux shall be allowed to return to Wounded Knee immediately following such meetings. 7. Seventy-two hours from the time that paragraphs 1 — 5 are effectuated, all the terms of the agreement of April 5 shall be promptly implemented."

Frizzell: What bothers me is your demand that we give you the meeting in Washington, D.C., prior to the implementation of any dispossession of arms.

Beverly Axelrod, lawyer with WKLDOC: You will have your CRS people monitoring the placing of all weapons inside the tipi with the peace pipe in front, which is a very sacred thing. And these people are not going to violate that. So

APRIL 11: "Why play their game? They're playing with paper. Meanwhile our lives and our children's lives and our generations are at stake." — Roger Iron Cloud, Oglala warrior

there will be no guns pointed anywhere. I would like someone to explain to Mr. Frizzell what the meaning is, of placing the peace pipe there.

Wallace Black Elk: This is a sacred pipe and we dedicate our life to it. We're sworn in to the Great Spirit. And that is why all these guns will be stashed here and this sacred pipe will be there. So the Great Spirit is there, that no man-made law cannot go in front of this.

But I never have the chance to sit down you law enforcement officers of the United States Government to explain this. We want you to lay down the arms and vice-versa — you have to lay down the arms and we have to come together and talk in a sense of humanity.

. . .

Gladys Bissonette: We want you to move your APCs back to the original perimeter.

Frizzell: If we move back to the original perimeter, there will be no perimeter. You can leave at will.

Hellstern: We can do a much better job protecting you folks in the village if we stay in our present perimeter.

Lou Beane: One thing too, Mr. Frizzell. Whenever you pull back your APCs, whichever you treasure the most, your dollar bill or your Bible, put it in front of your APCs.

The Independent Oglala Nation was informed that Washington had unilaterally cancelled the preliminary meeting until there was a disarmament. Relations between the United States and the ION were frozen. Two days later, on April 11, the Government finally issued a counter-proposal, and instead of sending in a negotiator to discuss it, sent a written copy into Wounded Knee.

This new version represented a hardening of the Government's position. While it accepted putting the "legal" weapons in the tipi during disarmament, it cancelled the preliminary meeting in Washington, calling instead for an agenda to be submitted by the ION for the later treaty talks.

Although people in Wounded Knee were prepared to leave at this point, there was a general feeling that their medicine man's vision should not be altered, and a growing frustration with the process of negotiations altogether. One Oglala warrior said, "Why play their game? They're playing with paper. Meanwhile our lives and our children's lives and our generations are at stake."

The Oglalas decided to reject this proposal. Dennis Banks announced their decision late that night to the general Wounded Knee community at meeting in the trading post:

They still want us to lay down our weapons. Not only that, they want all of us to identify ourselves to the FBI and the marshals. They wanted the stacking of arms to take place starting at nine Saturday morning. Then *after* that, they will pull back the APCs, the bunkers, to their original positions. So the Oglala Sioux have completely rejected this document. They have said that the April 9 [Crow Dog's vision] proposal will stand. There will be no more changing it around.

Now — number one announcement. A baby was born to Mary Ellen Moore today, 7½ pounds. I got another announcement from Cheryl Petite. Her baby was 7 pounds, 14½ ounces and already he's spoiled. She sends her love to all of us — and to Mary. So to Mary Moore, there's going to be a naming ceremony when Crow Dog gets back. We want to make sure that everybody that's going to be in the ceremony, go to the sweat lodge.

Number two announcement — "To the residents of Wounded Knee, from the Department of Health. Subject: spring clean-up." Now, this is not to be confused with the FBI's promise that they're going to come in and sweep this area. On April 12, beginning at 1 p.m., everyone is asked to join in an attempt to clean up Wounded Knee. We are asking all residents to aid this project. All able-bodied men, women, and children are asked to report to the store at 1 o'clock with shovels, picks, axes, wheelbarrows, hammers, and nails, ready to work.

So much for the sour announcements. While we're working, some will prepare a barbeque. Our cattle is dwindling fast. ∎

9. THE WOUNDED KNEE COMMUNITY

"First time you ever met somebody in your life, and you say 'Hi, brother.' Then you know what your cause is and what you're fighting for. And that's how close your ties are."

— Richard, an Oglala

Big Foot's band assembled for a Ghost Dance in August, 1890.

WOUNDED KNEE:

Grace Black Elk, an Oglala, was brought up in the reservation community of Allen, and came to know Wounded Knee as a child when she went with her parents to sell handmade crafts to the white family who had owned the Wounded Knee trading post since 1929. Inside the liberated store one afternoon, she spoke about the history of the massacre site.

People abroad and even here in the United States — they never thought there was a Wounded Knee. Even though they killed some people here all they thought of was tourists coming in, making money off these dead people here. Them dead people have bullets in them. Still. Nobody dug their bullets out. They just took them up and dumped them there in that trench.

The people were doing a ghost dance, a spiritual dance, a strengthening dance. Right where that church is, that's where that Hotchkiss gun was, the big gun that killed all these people, our ancestors.

And then this Catholic, Episcopal and Presbyterian, they saw a good thing, to gather a lot of sheep in the name of these dead people. They put up their church here and never thought nothing, not one bit, of those dead people up there. Them people are not baptized at all. They're not Catholics, they're not Episcopals, they're not Presbyterians at all. They followed

the Original Ways, the Sacred Pipe Ceremonies. Yet the church is there and there is a cross on top of those graves.

Then this Gildersleeves comes along and sees a good thing where he could make a lot of money — "Let's put a trading post and a museum and make some money from the tourists who will come here." See, they are all making money off our dead people. To them nothing is sacred at all. What if we go up to John F. Kennedy and pitch our tent there and start making money off that president that got killed?

And all the people that's been living here — they get monthly check, like ADC, pension. Some of them have no transportation so they have to come here to buy groceries. So he holds their check and sometimes never gives it back. And when they can't afford to buy food, they come over here selling their valuable Indian work, moccasins and all that stuff. He buys stuff off of people real cheap. And when he sells it, boy, it's sky-high.

So actually the tourists are spending money in the name of our dead people. And from now on, this Sioux Nation, this Sioux Independent Nation, doesn't want no more tourists things here anymore. People don't like to be used. Especially our dead people.

A MEMORY OF 1890

Wounded Knee massacre site, December, 1890.

Wounded Knee massacre victims being buried in the mass grave.

"Why did you stay in Wounded Knee the whole time?"

"Because I have a wound that was never healed. Back in 1890 my grandfather was in that massacre. And my dad's three older brothers were shot and killed. My grandfather escaped with wounds. He died later. I wasn't actually in the fighting but I stayed because I didn't want to see them die alone. 'If they are going to be wiped out,' I said, 'I want to be one of them.' "

— Rachel Hollow Horn,
Wounded Knee resident

Three Oglalas, Florine Hollow Horn, Karen White Butterfly, and Eddie White Dress, who had lived in Wounded Knee all their lives, and stayed there with their families throughout the siege, described the village before and after February 27.

WOUNDED KNEE:

Are your children here with you in Wounded Knee?

Florine: Yes, and my younger brother – he's 16.

How do you get your food now, and how do you take care of them?

Florine: We're getting these rations from the store – the trading post, it used to be. It was rationed out to the local residents and the people that came in.

How did you get your food before Feb. 27 when the trading post was run by Czywzcynski and the Gildersleeves?

Florine: That was the only near store and we had no choice but to go there. Their prices were really high.

Eddie: Czywzcynski's a lot of trouble to the people at Wounded Knee, especially when we're trading with him. He threatens them, these people that get monthly checks. They won't be able to trade there or have no credit unless they sign their whole check to him. He wants to keep their whole check and they don't make a power of attorney, so it's not legal, but still he does it.

What would people like to see here instead?

Eddie: We'd like to see a trading post being operated by Indians, not by a white man. Because there is a lot of beadwork and stuff that we want to sell. Like in Kyle they have that co-op business going, that's mostly run by Indians now. But this way Czywzcynski makes it all for himself.

Did any Indians work in the store?

Florine: One man did – he was working there because he had credit there of $300.

A COLONY
UNDER THE BIA

Right: Wounded Knee residents.
Below: The post office in the
Wounded Knee trading post.

How much did he get paid to work there?

Florine: Something like $8 a day, and half of it — half he owes and half is his take-home pay.

Are there any other places in Wounded Knee where people can work?

Karen: At the Head Start nursery school there's a teacher aid and a bus driver and the cook.

Florine: And they have a NYC — that's the Neighborhood Youth Corps. You have to be 16-21 years old to work there.

What about other jobs on the reservation? You were telling me me that you had worked in the moccasin factory in Pine Ridge.

Karen: Close to 90 people work there. You get $1.60 an hour, and to make more you have to do piecework. Like they'll time you and — like I was doing silk screen and I was doing 12 dozen per day, at $1.60 an hour, but if I want to make more I have to make more than 12 dozen. And then I think it's about 50 cents per dozen. So if you make 14 dozen you get a dollar extra. They run a doll factory, too.

Sally Hat, life-long resident of Wounded Knee,
talking to one of the warriors.

Did they sell them in the trading post here in Wounded Knee?

Karen: Yeah, they sell them all over.

Who buys them?

Karen: Tourists. Some tourists tour in the factory, and it's
funny, because Indians can't do that. They probably don't
trust us.

This church we're talking in, you were never in here before?

Florine: The minister that watched this place never allowed
us here. That lady didn't want us in here. She keeps the
doors locked and says we can't go in because we don't go to
church. The minister, Mr. Lansbury, he's got a station wagon,
he picks up all the Indian kids, he goes house to house.

There's two churches here where the ministers are white
people and two that the ministers are Indian people — just
their relatives go. And the white ones, just a few Indians go
there, because they were raised to go. About six cars of white
people go to them, they don't even live near here. Some are
white ranchers and they come from Denby.

Eddie: I don't hardly see anybody going to the churches.

Why did the ministers come here to start churches?

Florine: They get funds, church funds and private funds.
They use the Indians to get clothing and when the clothes get
here, they don't give it to the Indians — she puts prices on it
and sells it to them. I remember one morning when I came
into the house where she usually sells clothing. Some white
people brought in some big boxes of clothing. The address on
the boxes was from Indiana.

Who owns most of the land in Wounded Knee village?

Eddie: That belongs to the Gildersleeves. They got 40 acres
there in the "downtown." I think the Episcopal Church owns
about 80 acres. They just said they would put that church on
this ground here — "We'll just leave our church here." That's
the way some of these churches are being run on this reservation. [The Tribal Government] says, "We'll put the church
here and we'll donate so and so acres for church grounds."

There's been a lot of churches moving into South Dakota,
and I don't know which one to believe. Every church you go
to they say, "Well, you better come to my church, it's better
than that other one." They even bring you to church, they
even go after you. The churches run each other down, too,
especially the one Lansbury's running. He came in from
Brazil — said that they'd been about 10 or 15 years in South
America.

Florine: Around here, only the church runs the schools. Holy
Rosary was the first school I went to, in '52. I don't know
why I ever wanted to go there — cause my aunt was going to
school there and my mother used to tell me I'm real young,
but I wanted to go to school. I was four years old, but anyone
could go to school, so all of a sudden they took me over there.

I didn't understand white — you know, English — but I went there and half the time I didn't understand what they were saying, so I'd just shake my head, and if these nuns would ask me something, I didn't know what they were saying. So one time a nun really slapped me. I didn't know what she was saying. We weren't even supposed to speak our own language. They punished us.

Karen: And they made us go to church in the morning, before seven. Before breakfast you had to go to mass.

Florine: I didn't understand why all this was going on, but I'd just go along with it because I was little. And it was *cold* in that church, kneeling there.

How long did you go to school there?

Florine: Four months.

You didn't last very long.

Florine: No. I didn't want to go — I just spent a long time crying. I stayed there one month without seeing my folks, and then one night they came up and they said, "Hi, Florine." They greeted me in Indian and I didn't know who they were! I wondered how they knew my name. And all the time they were my folks. They said they were going to take me home.

Wounded Knee residents helping to dig bunkers near the housing project.

WOUNDED KNEE:

The first child born to the Independent Oglala Nation.
Grandma Wawasick, midwife, holding Mary Moore's son several hours after he was born on April 11.

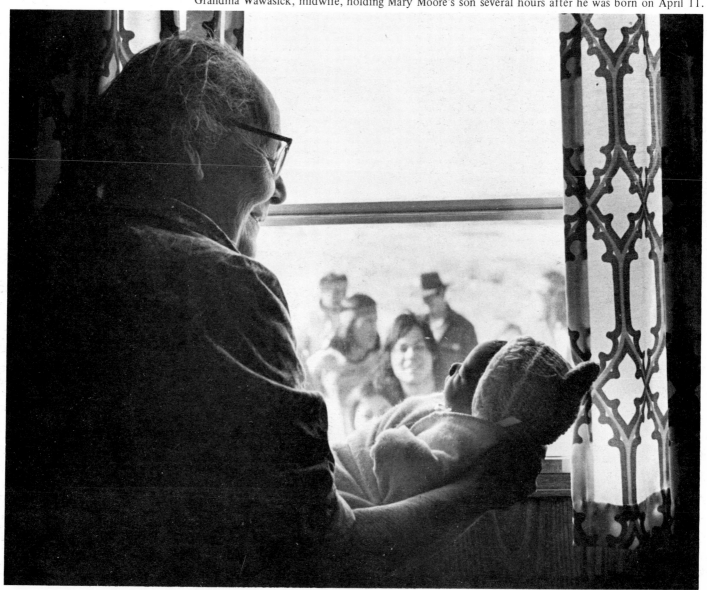

THE INDEPENDENT OGLALA NATION

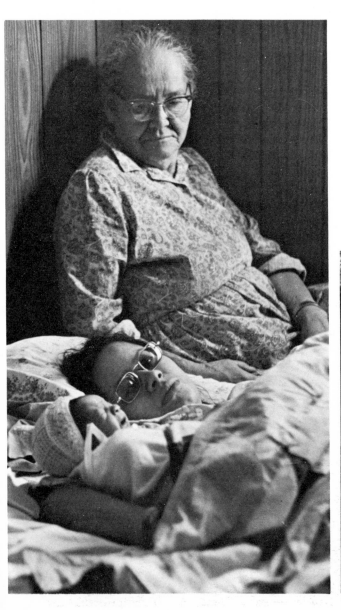

One woman, Barbara, a member of the underground media, kept a journal during the siege. She wrote this description of life inside the liberated village during the second month:

April 11 A beautiful spring day. Up early and out for a walk to Little California bunker and around Wounded Knee creek . . . Mary Moore just had her baby. Will finish this later. Everyone is going out to her trailer to sing . . . Sporadic gunfire this afternoon. Army jeeps and APCs came down to our Manderson roadblock, driving real close to trailers and housing project. The pigs are being very provocative . . . Too damn many people have been leaving in the last couple days.

April 12 The government is trying to isolate us from the outside world more than ever. But the isolation is bringing people closer — all we have is each other to depend on. Everyone's working real hard — the older women running the kitchens and the younger men and women out on bunker duty and roving patrol. Judy and Anita come back from Denby bunker at 6 in the morning to cook and wash clothes.

Clyde Bellecourt left today to do organizing and fundraising on the outside, and Russell still isn't back from

Left: Grandma Wawasik, Mary Moore, and her son.
Below: Eve, a medic, with a calf born several hours after Mary's child.

Chief Fools Crow speaking to a group in the trading post when he and Matthew King came into Wounded Knee on April 9.

Washington. The AIM leadership isn't as visible as it was a month ago — the nightly meetings they led in the trading post are less frequent now. The Oglalas meet often — some are the original residents of Wounded Knee and some from other parts of the reservation. They're the ones who make the major political decisions. Their meetings are usually in the round church where they sit in a circle and everyone participates — none of this face the front and listen to the speaker at the podium business. I go a lot of times just to listen, and each time I'm more amazed at how much they have it together . . .

People also look to the traditional chiefs for direction. After the declaration of independence some of them left to go to the U.N. and on a speaking tour around the country. When they got back — just a few days ago — Chief Fools Crow and Matthew King came in here to talk to everyone. Then they left to meet with the 11 other chiefs on the reservation. They're all supposed to come back in together in a few days. Everyone looks to them to decide on whether to come to an agreement with the Government and go out and organize in other places, or if everyone should stay . . .

Saw the house the feds burned with flares and all the burned land around it. Sickening. Went out to the bunker on the road to Porcupine. The feds' bunker across from here is so close — I could walk from one to the other in five minutes. They're so ridiculous! What the hell are they doing up there?! And there are so many pigs out there we don't even see. Last night Beverly, one of the lawyers, went from town to town around here looking for a motel room and almost didn't find one, because of all the marshals and FBI staying in them. A gas station attendant told her something about 400 Air Force men nearby and the weapons in here aren't anything compared to what they've got out there. . . Snuck up around the creek to get up close to the feds' bunker to take some pictures. I wish I had a long lens on my camera. . .

April 13 This little adventure has cost the government more than 2½ million dollars so far . . . Finally found a hot shower — after two weeks! . . Talking to Tiger this afternoon. He told me about a guy who walked out towards Porcupine last night — past the government bunkers, APCs, jeeps, goons — and then looked back and decided he couldn't leave Wounded Knee, so he turned around and came back! . . .

April 14, 8:30 p.m. A general meeting — only about 50 people turned out in the storm. Banks — "We're at a critical stage now — between wars." . . . It's raining after three days of beautiful weather, so there will be lots of pack trains going out

tonight while the feds are off guard and don't want to get wet — . . . Security is working long, hard hours these days . . . There will be no negotiations with the government until the chiefs, and Means, Crow Dog, and Bad Cob come back in and decide it's necessary. Carter no longer thinks this will be negotiated to a close in the near future. "It looks like Wounded Knee is going to be a rather long occupation." . . . Now the feds are using dogs to patrol the perimeter — and trip flares. Carter gave a pep talk to get people to stay. He said, "I wish we could set up R&R but the pigs won't cooperate."

April 15 The chiefs haven't come in yet, and I was afraid the goons stopped them, but Dennis said they're still meeting in Porcupine. . . It snowed last night and still is pretty cold out. Shots fired around noon — people think it was the goons.

Eating at the clinic now — there's no more feeding at the trading post kitchen. For the past week it's been pretty empty.

Mark Lane came in today — feds flew him over goons' roadblock to their roadblock and told him to walk in from there. He heard from a CRS man out there that a man, knowing about the goon squad roadblock, and thinking tl feds were the only obstacle, went up to the Tribal roadbl and said he was AIM and they really beat him up.

Just overheard a CRS man telling another he was late getting here because they had to drive around till their gas got down to ¼ of a tank. They must have been told not to come in here with more than that so people here won't siphon it off.

Tomorrow in Pierre, S.D. the lawyers are bringing up two Temporary Restraining Orders — against the goons and the feds — to let in food and supplies. . . Carter said, "Someday we'll reestablish the museum here — with an APC, a jeep, and a pig."

April 16 14 people walked in at 6 a.m.!!!! People are really starting to come back now!

One of the first events in the community during April was a wedding.
Notices went up that read, "On this evening, the twelfth day of April,
the forty-fifth day of freedom for the residents of Wounded Knee,
Independent Oglala Nation, the first ceremony of matrimony, between a
man, Noo-ge-shik, and a woman, Annie Mae, will take place in the trading
post." Oscar Bear Runner, an Oglala from Porcupine, spoke to the young
couple during the marriage ceremony:

My brother, my sister —
the greatest happening
the first marriage ever performed within the premises of the Wounded Knee
under the Independent Oglala Nation.
The first marriage ever performed here and I'm just proud,
and I want to thank the sisters and brothers of all nations
who have witnessed this marriage.
From here on out you're going to have a long journey ahead of you.
It's going to be hard. It's not going to be easy,
and you are going to take the lead, in your tribe.

You have come to this place
to aid the Oglala Sioux of the Pine Ridge Indian Reservation,
in this South Dakota,
and we want to thank you for coming to our aid in time of trouble,
in time of everything that's so uncertain here.
But you, with your initiative and with your power and willingness,
have come to aid in our trouble here
and now you are in our family.
This is a great family, the American Indian Movement.
We are gathered here all from different tribes
within this Western Hemisphere.

So keep on, travel,
keep on and look ahead.
Don't look back, but look around you.
The people on all sides are looking for your help
and for your aid.
We're really proud of you,
and may the joy of the Great Spirit be your strength —
is my prayer.

The marriage ceremony.

Others described the ION community. Martina White Bear, a Winnebago:

We had a marriage ceremony. That was pretty neat to see. I took part in it. I was the one that burned the cedar. And then they sang the AIM song, about five verses, and Black Elk, he smoked a peace pipe. Four guys and four women made flesh offerings. When they were doing that I was cedaring the whole place, all way around. It was pretty neat. I'd like to get married that way.

As much as I know about the peace pipe, I learned in Wounded Knee. Where I'm from we don't have nothing spiritual like that at all. It's really interesting to me. I'm learning more about it as I go along — Mrs. Black Elk tells me each thing.

Everybody's doing something — there's nobody just sitting there. Like that day they had the shooting — they told me to start an IV [intravenous feeding] and I mean I was scared. I

didn't know what to do. I helped my brother — he got shot. They were firing at us — they had us pinned down when I went out to get him.

At first I didn't really want to do anything. I thought I was just going to lay around in here. But this one lady said that I could be a head cook, cause I cooked once and everybody liked my cooking. I had shifts for kitchen work, two or three girls on a shift. And I'd be on all day or night with them, if I had to. There's five main stations that have their own cooks, that feed the people that live there.

For a while we had potato salad, beans, chicken, but now we are cooking beans three times a day, beans and beans and beans. Two nights ago we had barbeque cow — that was really good. We had bread till we ran out of baking powder and flour. And we had coffee and tea, but now we have no coffee and no tea. For the kids they got evaporated milk and the little kids usually feed first to make sure they get their nourishment. There's quite a few kids, from ten on down, and a few older ones. They're mostly [local residents] from the housing [project].

I'm also on police security and I go out and patrol from four in the morning till eight in the morning. We're usually worried about Mr. and Mrs. Black Elk cause they're older and they need their rest. And those teenagers were really raising hell. So we had to put a stop to it. I made a rule that if they don't want to work they can move out of that store. One night I had four girls mopping that hallway in the trading post — if they wanted to stay up all night — we were going to put them to work. So we did and finally they buckled down and most of them went to bed.

After police duty I would go around to each bunker to see if they have everything they need. And then check around again. And for two weeks I been going out on bunker duty. We take my hand drum and talk and sing — just to get the APCs so they won't be sleeping. Cause one time I went trucking and there were APCs sleeping — we went right by them. And it's really amazing — you'd think they're on duty.

The marshals started fires out there, cause one time I had to come in when they were burning. We had to go right through that fire. We ran through it. There happened to be a little creek. We just wet our clothes and run right through and then the APC spotted us and started firing on us.

One time I came out of Wounded Knee, there was six of us, four girls and two guys. We got lost up there on the hill someplace. We didn't know which way to go and we were sit-

ting there deciding. So finally, I heard an owl, and I remembered what Black Elk said, "If you hear an owl, follow it and it will lead you out." So I kept telling them, "We have to follow the owl." We followed that owl about four miles and we made it to safety. It was really something to me, the first time I ever knew anything like that. It seems like it would be right there when you got there, then it would fly off again, until you get there and then he would go again. Really something.

Martina White Bear (center) with two young Oglalas.

Kathy and Richard are two young Sioux who stayed in Wounded Knee for most of the 71-day siege. About a month after it ended, they described how it had been to live in the village:

Kathy: It was our nation inside there — we just felt like we were building our new nation.

Richard: We felt freedom while we were inside — but outside, man, the tension — you can just feel the tension.

Kathy: The enemy's all around — it's entirely different.

Richard: Like in Rapid City — you had to walk around and have a look over your shoulder. But once we got back into Wounded Knee, it was just freedom. You *know* you're free. That was our land — that was *ours* — our nation.

Kathy: That's the first time I ever felt like I was fighting for something —

Richard: We're fighting for our rights.

Kathy: Most of us are nonviolent people, but if we're forced to fight, we will. It's a last resort.

Richard: I went there because Wesley Bad Heart Bull was my first cousin. And a lot of my relatives were in that massacre. I used to live in Wounded Knee. As a matter of fact we own land there in Wounded Knee — right near the massacre site.

Kathy: You have to have something that's worth dying for, or else life isn't worth it. If you're living and you're afraid of everything, you're just half alive. But if you feel you can die for something you believe in, you're totally alive.

Richard: We weren't afraid to die — we just didn't *want* to! Just to freak out the cops during firefights some guys on our squad would be poking our heads from one hill to another till one time they said over the radio, "What the hell are we fighting? gophers?" Truck up one end, pop a few rounds off, run down the ravine, run up another one, popping his head up at every other place — freak them out!

Kathy: They really started getting uptight.

Richard: One guy over their communications system said, "Hey, I quit. We're not going to fight those crazy Indians down there." A lot of them quit their jobs, just walked off the job. Up there — they didn't know how to handle the situation, which made us feel good.

Kathy: They couldn't understand how us Indians could be so close. It's something they'll never understand — how much we care for each other — as a family.

Richard: They say, "Wow, this guy never knew that guy." But shit, first time you ever met somebody in your life and you say, "Hi, brother," then you know what your cause is and what you're fighting for. And that's how close your ties are. Whoever came in, we had no prejudice in there, cause if you had any prejudice, it wouldn't be worth it. If I was prejudiced against one guy, during a firefight, I'd just blow him away. But none of that happened. And whenever we got down there

and started singing, sing the AIM song, then we'd feel really good. I was singing all the time.

Kathy: If we see each other again we're always going to feel close to those people. It's just a feeling of sharing everything, when you don't have anything. Any time you have a cigarette, you'll tell somebody, "I've got a cigarette, if you need one," or they'll tell you. An Indian automatically, will have something, won't even think about it, you just take it and share it, light up a cigarette and it will go around to everybody. That's another thing that the marshals and the people on the outside couldn't understand — the head of the marshals said, "We're going to change their lifestyle." But they didn't change nothing. They just made it more like we're used to living. It didn't make it that much harder, cause we're used to surviving anyway.

Richard: It made it just as simple for us. They're used to the comforts of society —

Kathy: — so-called civilization —

Richard: — but we adapt to anything that comes up. Like the sleeping situation — on security we'd be taking turns, waking up the other guys in your bunker. There'd be a change of shift, so you'd take over their bed, it didn't matter. You found sleeping quarters wherever you went to sleep at. You found food — we had our supply points. They'd constantly cook — till we started running out of supplies — and then we had to start cutting down on rations. And some would fast a day and eat the next day and fast a day.

Kathy: In there we had our own laws set up. You could do things you felt like doing instead of by somebody's clock or

time schedule. You didn't have to eat three meals a day at certain hours — get up when somebody told you to get up. You go on bunker duty because you want to. You're fighting for yourself instead of everybody else —

Richard: — you're fighting for your life —

Kathy: — yours and everybody's —

Richard: — but then you're fighting for every oppressed person in the United States —

Kathy: — in the world.

Richard: And you know this is what you're doing, so you feel good about it. Even though they have indictments on a lot of us, everybody feels it was worth it. I think that everybody that was in there had a taste of freedom — what freedom is really about. And that put a deep impression on everybody that was in there. Throughout their life they'll al-

ways remember this, that "I was *free*," at one time.

Kathy: For one thing, Wounded Knee united Indians everywhere.

Richard: There'll be more Wounded Knees. But it depends on how the Government handles this situation, the treaties here. We still have a lot of oppression around the United States, and if the treaties here don't go through, everybody that was in Wounded Knee will be hitting these other places.

Kathy: It's just the beginning. The war's not over.

Richard: The war has just begun.

In anticipation that the April 5th agreement would be carried out, many defenders had left Wounded Knee, taking their weapons with them. But by mid-April, many of these people began to return, and new supporters joined them. Their early morning arrivals became a daily celebration in the village. On April 16, fourteen people hiked in — the largest group so far to make it in safely. One of the women in that group described their experiences:

We left on Friday night, pulled out of Rapid City in two cars and headed south towards the reservation. Going through Scenic, a drinking town just off the reservation, we slumped down in our seats and sped through to avoid being seen by the goons. We were supposed to pull over and coordinate with the other car behind us, but our driver, a local woman, said, "Are you crazy? This is the worst road on the reservation. People get raped or robbed here all the time."

An hour past Scenic we found the house near Porcupine, seven miles outside of Wounded Knee. Other people were already there waiting. The kitchen was stocked with food donated for Wounded Knee — cans of fruit and vegetables, and rice and lentils from a health food co-op — most of it too heavy to pack in. By the time the other car and our guides arrived it was almost midnight. The moon was full and the sky clear, and we decided it was too bright to truck. So ten of us bedded down in the tiny two-room house, spreading out our sleeping bags and blankets.

The next day was like spring, and we spent it hauling wood and water,

One of the trails that people hiked in on. "If you are in with the land and close to it, you can look down a valley and see where they are probably going to have a bunker or one of their patrols positioned to try to stop you coming through. You begin to think like a bird, you look all around."

eating frybread and keeping watch. The nearest house was a quarter-mile away, but we stayed inside to keep out of sight of the occasional cars on the road and the Government helicopters that flew by to survey the area.

By night the wind was blowing and the sky cloudy — a perfect night to walk right past the feds. So we started out for Wounded Knee. But around two in the morning we ran into a blizzard and couldn't see ten feet in front of us. Another three hours through the freezing snow and we saw lights on either side. "That's Wounded Knee!" someone said, "Watch out, those lights are APCs." A car drove by and we dove into the snow to avoid being seen. But a few minutes walk and we realized that we were back in Porcupine, at the back door of a house that we knew was a

stop-off point for people like us, trucking in. Our local guides had gotten turned around in the snow, and walked in a circle all night. We stopped at the house, and spent the rest of the night drying off by the woodstove, laughing at ourselves.

The next day it rained and we waited out the day, hoping the sky would stay cloudy. In the afternoon we had a scare — four BIA police-cars pulled up the road, a few hundred yards from the house. It seemed like we were surrounded. We turned off all the lights and covered the windows with blankets. Those who had guns picked them up, some kept watch through the cracks in the curtains, and some stood by the door ready to shoot if attacked. We knew that if it came to a shoot-out we were trapped in a

cardboard box with much less powerful weapons than the M-16s the BIA police were now carrying. But we also knew that the BIA police were not anxious to attack such a large armed group, although we had heard stories of beatings and shootings by the police and goons of smaller groups. It turned out to be a false alarm. Fifteen or twenty minutes later the cars pulled out and left.

By evening more people had arrived and we now numbered 14, six women and eight men. A few had been in Wounded Knee before and were used to the hills and the cold — one of the women who ran the Wounded Knee military radio, a couple of young Oglalas who had been out to visit their family, and a few warriors who had gone to Rapid City for supplies. And some of the people were new, like

Frank and Morningstar Clearwater who had hitch-hiked 2000 miles from North Carolina.

So that evening, Sunday, we started out again. We had to move fast to reach Wounded Knee by morning. Many, especially the new people, had trouble during the nine-hour hike and had to leave their packs behind to keep up.

The night was perfectly clear and it seemed like we could see shadows on the hills for miles. About a mile south of Porcupine, six miles from Wounded Knee, we heard APC motors, three or four of them roaming the roads and nearby hills. Our two guides went out to scout, leaving the rest of us flattened in a gully, hidden by the trees. We laid there, perfectly still because the dry, freezing air carried sound clearly. One man who kept coughing finally picked up his

"We're always at the hospital. We have to have somebody up all the time — 24 hours a day. So most of the time I'm a night-owl. People truck in and they come to the hospital cause they want to drink some coffee. So I find out the outside news. And it's crazy to find out how people trucked in and out. What happened to one guy — he was coming in and a woman in his crew kept falling and stumbling. They were all getting disgusted with her — but they just kept bringing her. But when they got in they found out that she was carrying dynamite on her all that time!"

— Lorelei DeCora

In the kitchen of the clinic.

"The sacred hoop is round. We're sitting in this tipi — it's round. The cycle of life — it's round. It's all part of the Great Spirit — nothing's ahead or behind. Like you can walk into the trading post — which is square — built by a white man — but the people in the room — Indian people — are sitting in a circle. The drum is round — and the drum in the center — all these different tribes here to support this one band of Sioux."
— Lorelei DeCora

rifle and pack and walked the mile back to the house, so his coughing wouldn't give us away. For two hours we laid there, then we moved on.

Again our long single file of people headed south along the sides of the hills. Wounded Knee lay far over the ridges of the hills, but we could guide in on the stars and on the flares which shot up periodically over the village, lighting up the quiet countryside for miles around. We had heard there were sensor and trip flares planted in the gullies and stream beds near Wounded Knee, but weren't sure how far out they were. As we got closer we often had to hit the ground and shield our faces to keep the light from the flares from reflecting off our skin and giving our position away to the marshals with their powerful scopes. Finally we came over the last ridge and could see down into the village. There were Government positions all around and we could hear APC

motors running. Our guide looked at the night sky, then said, "Well, we might as well just go ahead." The sun was rising as we walked straight over an open field between two Government bunkers and a roadblock. No one tried to stop us.

We were through their perimeter and then ours. As we came across the creek and up to the back of the Catholic church, the bunkers emptied out and everyone came running to greet us, grabbing our packs, hugging us. "Welcome home," they said. "It's good to be home." ■

10. TEN DAYS OF WAR

"Try and flush 'em out of that bunker and you'll have good targets."
— Red Arrow, U.S. Govt. command post.

"We have this tendency to over-estimate the power of the enemy, and to under-estimate ourselves. But with a little courage and strength on our part, and a little knowledge of what we are up against, they can be defeated."

— Bob, a warrior

APRIL 17 / AIR DROP — GOVERNMENT ATTACK — FOUR PEOPLE WOUNDED

On April 17 an all-day firefight broke out. Frank Clearwater, who had hiked into Wounded Knee the day before, was fatally wounded when a burst of gunfire from RB-4 ripped through the wall of the room where he was resting. He never regained consciousness and died ten days later.

A cease-fire had been maintained since the beginning of the April negotiations, broken only by occasional fire into the village by over-eager FBI agents and angry Wilson supporters. The Federal forces spent the period enlarging their positions, stockpiling supplies, and bringing in personnel from different posts around the country for field experience. The people in Wounded Knee fortified their community, and their defenses, though still expecting negotiations on the treaty and disarmament to resume once their head negotiators returned from Washington.

Then, on April 17, the Government attacked again in full force. At dawn Wounded Knee's night-shift roving patrol spotted three small planes coming in low over the hills, and woke up their friends to greet a long-awaited airdrop. The planes dropped ten parachutes and flew off. The FBI helicopter "Snoopy" opened fire on some of the families from the housing project who began to gather up the bundles which were dropped near their homes. Wounded Knee warriors fired back to drive the helicopter out of range, and the firefight raged on till four in the afternoon. The press at this point had access only to Government press conferences in Pine Ridge and reported the Government's story that their helicopter had been fired upon without provocation and that they had refrained from firing for two hours after that.

Each of the parachute bundles contained a printed message which said, "The delivery of these packages of food to the courageous people in Wounded Knee is being carried out by a large number of Americans who have worked and continue to work to end American aggression in Indochina. Wounded Knee shows us that the just struggles can not be stopped by any President or any policy." One of the pilots described the drop:

The whole thing was done by a large number of people who contributed either money or food or skills or parachutes or packing materials. One night we were putting all the gear together, and one of the neighbor women in the house next door and her two daughters stayed up all night sewing parachute packs for us to use. They knew where this stuff was going. There was a very wide spectrum of people involved in the whole thing.

Seven people were aboard the aircraft when they went in. There were three planes, all large single-engine planes, brand-name "Cherokees." The planes took off from a Midwestern city hours before dawn, and timed the flight to arrive over Wounded Knee at sunrise so that everyone would be sleeping and there would be a minimum danger of shooting. We'd been told a couple of days before of rumors that the vigilantes had .50 caliber machine guns — so we didn't want to provoke a firefight on the ground, so we thought it would be best to come in with the minimal amount of light we needed to accurately make the drop.

From what we could see from the air, all of our parachutes landed down within the Wounded Knee perimeter. I saw five of them hit directly on the main road and as soon as they were down, 40 or 50 people ran out from both sides of the road and took the food in. There was no activity at all in the vigilante or Federal bunkers when we flew over them. APCs were parked all around, but they seemed to be deserted.

It was a milk-run for us. We just went in and did a slow 180-degree pass around one-half of the perimeter, flying at about 90 miles an hour and 500 feet off the ground. The parachutes opened up at about 150 feet and floated the other 350 feet. Then we split in three directions, each of us flying a different way at 500 feet to avoid radar detection from Ellsworth Air Force Base which is about 70 miles northwest of Wounded Knee.

A woman from the Hawk Eye bunker squad described what happened that day:

We heard three Cesna planes in the distance. They flew low and many of us thought they were going to bomb or gas us. Ten bundles were pushed from the planes and floated down on colorful parachutes. Some of us joked that it might be poisoned flour or blankets infected with smallpox, as had been given to our people in the past. But it turned

out to be food airlifted to us by people from the anti-war movement who enclosed a letter of support and praise. We gathered the bundles and took them to Security where the letter was read and the food was distributed, with laughter and tears, eating cashews, prunes, chocolate, and ham — it was the first fresh food we had seen in a long time.

As we walked back to our bunker to sack out, we heard shots from the APCs on the surrounding hills. Apparently they thought the bundles contained rifles and ammo so they broke the cease-fire and started a firefight. All around us bullets were hitting the ground and we flattened. We were right out in the open, so we got up and ran like hell to our bunker, the one-room church by the creek. We laid down, thinking that a cease-fire would soon be called, and intending to get some sleep.

All of sudden, three bullets ripped through the east wall and someone cried, "Frank's hit!" Frank was an Apache from North Carolina and had just woken up when he was shot. I grabbed a clean T-shirt and pressed it to his head, laying down next to him so as not to be hit myself. I tried to comfort him, not realizing that he was unconscious. The bullet had ripped his skull and blown out the back of his head. Soon a lake of blood surrounded us. Meanwhile, Richard was trying to radio Security to send a doctor and tell us what to do. But the batteries were half-dead, so for about 20 minutes we hardly had any communication.

After about 45 minutes a stretcher crew arrived, three women and three men. The nurse told us to continue pressure on the wound, carefully load him on a cot stretcher, and take him to the clinic about a half-mile away in the center of the village. They had a truce flag and it was obvious that they were carrying a body, but against all rules of "honor in war" the snipers continued to fire at the stretcher crew. That firefight lasted all day.

The medics and warriors finally managed to bring Clearwater through the gunfire to the clinic. Several hours later, Government forces ceased firing long enough for Clearwater to be taken to RB-1 where he was flown to a Rapid City hospital by helicopter.

As the people in Wounded Knee were taken by surprise in the early morning, the bunkers were not on full alert and three people were hit while running out to their positions. It was almost impossible to move outside without being shot at.

When the Government positions began firing on the local residents who

Medics and warriors carry Frank Clearwater out of the Episcopal church where he was shot, using a mop handle to raise a make-shift truce flag.

"We were shot at all the way up the hill and all the way into the house. He had a bad injury in the back of his head, and he was taken out under two white flags, held very high, and we were shot at all the way back to the clinic area."
— Anne, a medic

were gathering up the food dropped in the parachutes in front of their houses, a Wounded Knee roving patrol was sent out to help them. Later in the day, one member of the patrol explained what happened:

We were in Security and they were sorting out the food. We got a call on the radio that somebody was shooting down at our Manderson roadblock. So a bunch of us jumped in a car and went out there. Everybody was scattered up on the hill on the west side of the road. We were taking fire to the southwest and to the west.

We drove up to the top of the hill and then we parked and we all got out. Everybody started going to the south. We had a busted window and I was cleaning out the glass in the back of the car. Everybody started hollering, "Hit the deck!" and I looked around and I heard a zing over my head, and then

I got down too. There was five of us pinned down right next to the car. They opened up on us from the south and from the west. They had us at a 90-degree angle.

On the south was an APC and what appeared to be one jeep. To the west we could see real clearly — they were up on the second ridge with an APC and two or three jeeps. The position south of us looked about 600 yards away. Right from the start we were taking automatic fire from both positions.

We tried to go over the top, the way we came, but they had us pinned down — we couldn't go nowhere. There was a helicopter directly above us, and it was directing fire from the south. So we had to go down into a gully. I led the guys north, up the creek, behind the cemetery, and then we came over the back of the cemetery and walked down into the housing. The firing went on a long time, all day.

"Part of Clearwater's neck was torn, but I didn't know if it went in his skull. I see the flesh is torn off, and he was bleeding profusely, and going into convulsions. Three other people were brought in. The second man they brought in, he was shot four times. And this other man, he got shot in the heel.

"We had local anesthesia, and then we cleaned the wounds. The foot wound went right through, a little below the toe. This other man, in the right arm, there was three wounds. Two of them are still lodged deep. The other just went in and came right out. This is about the worst I've ever seen people get shot. We'll need other surgery to get the other bullets out."
— Wallace Black Elk, medicine man

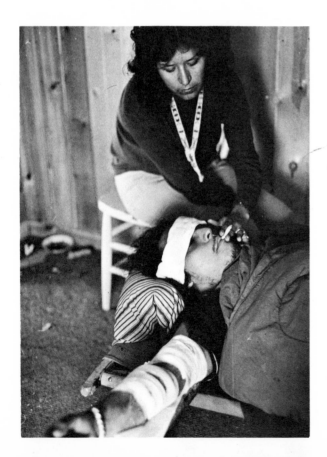

Sitting on the blood-covered floor where Clearwater was shot, Richard tries to fix the radio to contact Security.

Morningstar Clearwater did not leave Wounded Knee with her husband, as she said she was afraid of being arrested at the Government roadblock. Two days later, when word came in that Frank was dying, she decided to go out to Rapid City to be with him. Federal officials told Morningstar that they would take her to Rapid City where Frank was in the hospital. But as she feared, she was arrested by the FBI at the roadblock. When she got out of jail several days later, she made the following statement at a press conference in Rapid City:

I was in Wounded Knee when my husband got shot — I had gone to get some food at the church. He was at the little white church, laying down on a mattress. And the shot came on the right hand side of the big white church and the next thing I knowed, my husband was shot in the head, laying on the mattress, and he was almost dead.

My husband's dying, and people in there are starving. They don't even have cover, they don't have no food, they don't have nothing. The federals said they were going to take me to see my husband, and I had to walk up to the roadblock. When I got there they got me in the car and then they took me to jail, and the lawyers had a hard time getting me out to see my husband. I just got to see my husband yesterday evening. I stayed up all night with him. The doctor said he has a 50-50 chance.

APRIL 18 / SOME RESIDENTS COME HOME

When word of Clearwater's fatal injury reached the outside, more people started turning toward Wounded Knee. Many of the original defenders who had hiked out when the April 5th agreement was signed returned with more supplies and weapons.

Many of the Wounded Knee residents who were kept out by the Federal roadblocks were growing impatient. They demonstrated in Pine Ridge, demanding that the siege be lifted so they could return. Many of these refugees made daily visits to the BIA building, requesting permission to go home, but were turned away. So on the morning of April 18, thirty-five Oglala women and children drove up to the Government's Roadblock 5 and demanded to be allowed through. When the marshals refused, some of the women walked right around the roadblock. This was the first time anyone had successfully come straight through a Government roadblock in broad daylight. Fourteen made it – the rest were arrested.

As one of the women who made it through told the story, "We just walked right on past the marshals. They were really caught off guard. One of them got so upset he just dropped his radio and kept right on talking into his hand! He started jumping around, yelling, 'Don't move, you might get hurt.' We just laughed and walked right on through."

At the time that the Wounded Knee residents were walking in, Wounded Knee Security monitored the following Government radio transmissions calling for gas and reinforcements to send to Roadblock 5. (Red Arrow was the marshals' field command on a hill on the eastern perimeter. Headquarters 2 was the second-in-command and was located at the command post in the BIA building in Pine Ridge, 15 miles west of Wounded Knee. Government transmissions begin in the left margin; Wounded Knee transmissions are indented, with conversations in the Security building in italic.)

Red Arrow to Roadblock 5: Headquarters 2 wants those people headed off, trying to come through to Wounded Knee.

> ***Warrior, listening in Security building:*** *Thirty-five people are walking in through the roadblocks!*

Red Arrow: They're still violating the perimeter.

> ***Warrior:*** *We're violating the perimeter?!*

Red Arrow: . . . We have people [Government reinforcements] coming in from Zebra and X-ray. And we have at least four over here waiting to be airlifted over and we have some coming over from Apple . . . Where do you want that chopper down with the manpower?

Red Arrow to Headquarters 2: That's 10-4, sir. We'll get that gas [CS-2 tear gas] for you and we have the men standing by

Wounded Knee residents at RB 5 on April 18.

here for you at Red Arrow. Unable to make contact with Wounded Knee as of yet.
. . .

Red Arrow to Headquarters 2: See if they have any plastic cuffs with them. They're going to need plastic cuffs over there.

Red Arrow to Wounded Knee: Be advised there are several people attempting and have attempted to sneak into Wounded Knee by flanking RB-5. They will be arrested and will be detained. And you violate our perimeter.

Wounded Knee to Red Arrow: Is it your perimeter or ours they are violating? I don't think they are violating yours. Your perimeter is outside. If they are coming into our perimeter they are not violating our perimeter. Wounded Knee out.

Red Arrow to Headquarters 2: Sir, be advised, I finally made contact with Wounded Knee and advised them of the situation and they got very perturbed and shut me off.

Red Arrow to RB-5: You need a bus over there to take 10-15s [prisoners], is that 10-4? How many 10-15s you got over there?

RB-5 to Red Arrow: Between 20 and 30.

When Red Arrow told Wounded Knee Security that they were violating the perimeter, warriors went to man the bunkers, expecting the Government to use the demonstration as a pretext for an attack. The marshals began pinpointing people inside the village for targets. Some of their transmissions are as follows:

Red Arrow to Headquarters 2: Be advised that they are starting to man that bunker in front of RB-6. They're moving people up there that are armed. And the one van with the AK-47 is back up there in that vicinity again . . .

X-ray to RB-4: That station wagon that came into that bunker down there in front of you has been picking up cement blocks from the construction and they are rebuilding that bunker.

RB-6 to Red Arrow: We got one guy with that red shirt that we think was a sniper yesterday — he's on top of that water tower. I think that is from where he was shooting at us yesterday. We been watching him.

Red Arrow to all RBs: Be advised there is increased activity, stand by, be alert. 10-4.

Red Arrow to RB-5: Be advised from RB-6 that there are two men heading toward your 10-20 [location] along the ridge line, and they are armed.

RB-6 to Red Arrow: Be advised that there are about four more people up on the water tower.

Red Arrow to RB-6: 10-4. If it starts you know where he's at now.

RB-6 to Red Arrow: We have them under observation and there are four other people going along the road into the village. And that Volkswagon that has been disabled has been manned by two people.

Warriors sitting around the Security office radio listening to the Government radio and mimicing Red Arrow's Brooklyn accent: Oh, those no-good dirty Indians are going to do it again, they're going to sneak up and assault them.

Jim Fennerty, a lawyer with the Wounded Knee Legal Defense/Offense Committee, who was with the Oglalas at the roadblock, described what happened as some of them left the area, "As we were leaving the area of the roadblock we were surrounded. Some were assaulted — I was assaulted. We were handcuffed and taken to the station. Some people were thrown against the wall and kicked. Then we were interrogated by the FBI and thrown in the cell. The jail there is one of the worst I've ever seen. In my experience practicing in Chicago, I haven't seen anything worse than that. People have no rights in there."

AN OGLALA WOMAN TALKS

One of the women who broke through the lines on April 18 was Irma Rooks, from the reservation community of Wanblee. A little later, when the excitement died down some, she talked with the two reporters left in the village, women from the underground press:

Even little kids know about the treaty, because our grandparents handed down what they know from generation to generation. And we all know what the Government promised the Indians, and that they never kept the promises.

So that was a big thing before Wounded Knee was taken over?

It always has been. People always has been bringing that up, that they should go back to the old ways, so we can have something better and make the Government live up to its promises. They were supposed to help the Indians develop themselves, but they never give them the chance. If we go and try to make a loan, for instance, to make a start, we are not accepted because we are a "ward of the Government." This ward of the Government is something really terrible because you can't make a bank loan, you can't do anything. You have to get permission from the Tribal Council; then your Tribal Council don't approve it and then you can't get anything. Mostly the people that are part Indian and part white get the best, but not the fullbloods. Fullbloods never get anything.

The mixedbloods benefit from the system?

Just the small number of the family that are related to the Tribal Council, or to whoever the Tribal President is at the time, are the only ones that benefit from it.

How do they benefit?

By getting jobs and getting loans, things like that. I think it's high time the white people think of the fullbloods, instead of each individual doing things for themselves and not thinking of the other aspects. It's really bad. They're the ones that's supposed to be representing us. And I think what the AIM are doing is really beautiful because for a change somebody is really fighting for the people. They're going to try and make the Government live up to its promises and I think that's really neat.

Do the people in Wanblee and the other districts on the reservation agree with that?

Sure. They're the silent majority. They're scared. How would you like it if I beat you up every time you said something? Would you go around voicing what you want to say? Would you be able to stand up and say, "I want this done?" And if nobody hears you, would you be able to stand up and fight?

Has this been happening for a long time?

It's been going on for quite a while. But it really got bad since Wilson got in. He's dividing homes, friends — and everybody's threatened. If he's such a good leader this wouldn't have happened. They would have been united. But he's a dictator.

Have people been beat up in Wanblee?

Sure. People has got threats. If they don't do what Wilson says they get beat up. Some of our Tribal Representatives are hiding out because they're scared. They're speaking out for the Indians, now they're hiding out. They can't live in fear for the rest of their lives. Something has got to give. I think it's really important that the Government start waking up and

Lou Beane (left) and Irma Rooks.

listening to the people. Because what the people want in here is what other people need too, to have a better form of government. Not being scared and hiding at nights. That just don't go with a lot of people.

Outside, there's just a few people that are bought off by Dick Wilson. A lot of people are in the dark to what's really happening, because like I said, they don't want to get too involved because they might get hurt. And they're scared to voice their opinion.

But when I hear they're going to beat me up, I'll run. And I'll run to the nearest person that I know that could help me. I'm not going to sit around and let them come and beat me up. Because they mean what they say, the goon squad. A lot of us Indians are safer in here, even though the marshals are shooting at us. But if the marshals get out of here, we can fight our own battle.

Do you think things have gotten worse or better over the past two months?

I don't know exactly. Dick Wilson is trying to do something out there which is not succeeding. I wish the Government would open their eyes to what's happening instead of sitting on their butt and getting paid for nothing. They're not helping the original American Indians. They can't keep their promises, and now they're trying to make promises to other countries, signing the Indochina peace treaty, saying they're trying to help them. How can they help them when they can't even help the people they made treaties with here?

You know, when they had this massacre a lot of our relatives were killed here. And a lot of people are more forgiving, so they let their kids go into the service and they take part in it. And when they come back they still don't have anything.

Do people really remember the massacre?

Sure. One of my grandfathers got killed here and that's

one reason I get down on whites. We know all the stories about it because we were told exactly how it happened. It's been handed down throughout the reservation, like I said about the treaties, handed down to the children as they were growing up. The older people talk about it, and they talk about a lot of things that they used to have, the way they lived long ago, before the white man came. They were kind to each other, helping each other, watching out for each other. They were all related. But after the white man came they started teaching them the white man's way. We learned to hate one another.

'Cause the white people are always fighting. The United States is always trying to help other people fight over someplace, putting their nose in where it doesn't belong. And they tell the Indian boys they're fighting for their country — but they're not fighting for their country. It might belong to you people. You do your own fighting. And then we can all stay and defend our own reservations. Because they made it so that Indians are fighting against each other. And that's what the Government wants all along.

The white people that are rich and higher up think they can rule the ones that are lower than they are. But the only thing they have that they worship is their money, the dollar sign. The minority groups, the poor people, know that there is a god, because that's the only thing that they have. And they don't have any other thing.

See, Dick Wilson's fighting two gods. He's fighting the white man's god and he's fighting our Indian god. He's violating all kinds of civil rights, kicking the press out, kicking all the Indians off the reservation that are not enrolled members. Then he said non-residents are supposed to get out. Why in the hell are those marshals and feds still here? They're not enrolled members, and they're not residents of here. They should be kicked out too. It's too much.

Maybe I shouldn't talk so much. I quit.

"And I think what the AIM are doing is really beautiful because for a change somebody is really fighting for the people. They're going to try and make the Government live up to its promises and I think that's really neat."

AN "ILLEGAL ARMY"

Since the breakdown of the April negotiations, the U.S. Government had been refusing to allow any food, medical supplies, or lawyers through their roadblocks. At the same time they tightened their blockade, adding APCs and foot patrol manned by the U.S. Border patrol. They tried to stop anyone from bringing supplies in at night. By the third week in April, the food in the trading post had run out and medical supplies were critically low. In mid-April a team of medical workers who had come to South Dakota to volunteer in the Wounded Knee clinic, released the following statement to the press:

We are a group of health workers who have exhausted every possible legal means to enter Wounded Knee for the purpose of providing medical care . . .

There are now approximately 300 people in Wounded Knee who have been subjected to systematic starvation during the past several weeks. In addition, running water has been shut off and on in an arbitrary way, forcing the men, women and children inside to use contaminated water sources. Fuel for heat is gone and sanitation facilities are breaking down. The medical problems follow inevitably from the above conditions: older people, children and infants have pneumonia; over 100 people have influenza or bronchitis; an epidemic of diarrhea is breaking out among the children, and the threat of both typhoid fever and hepatitis hangs over the entire village.

One Government official has described the situation in Wounded Knee as being a "war." If it is a war, then we must demand that the U.S. Government conduct itself appropriately — siege warfare has long been regarded as inhumane and illegal . . .

Joe Alkana, medic
Barbara Bell, R.N.
Alan Berkman, M.D.
Adraenne Bernstein, R.N.
Barbara Zeller, M.D.

In the early part of April the Wounded Knee Legal Defense/Offense Committee was attempting to bring a legal counter-offensive to halt the Government's undeclared war against the people of the Independent Oglala Nation and their supporters on the reservation. On April 16 the Committee filed two suits in Federal Court on behalf of the Oglala Sioux Civil Rights Organization and numerous individuals on the reservation.

Their first suit sought a temporary injunction against the activities of the Federal Government, naming as defendants the Bureau of Indian Affairs,

and the Departments of Interior and Justice. "This case," they asserted, ". . . involves the right to life itself. The United States Government has established a military siege of the village. It proposes to starve the people into submission by depriving them of food and necessities of life. It proposes to reduce them to a state of disease and ill health. . . [and] to deprive them of their right to counsel by keeping attorneys out of Wounded Knee.

"In effect, it has arrested, punished, and imprisoned the entire population without due process. . ." The brief went on to charge that in an effort to avoid using the Armed Forces, which would make this war within

America's borders highly visible, the Government had encircled the village with what it termed an "illegal army." "Nothing in the law," it stated, "suggests that United States Marshals can be converted into an army operating at the whim of unnamed personnel. . . [or] that the FBI can raise or man an army. . . The use of Marshals, FBI agents, and others to perform a military function such as the imposition of a siege upon a village is a usurpation of power which brings us frighteningly close to the creation of a police state."

Another suit filed by the WKLDOC sought a temporary injunction against the activities of Richard Wilson, his "goon squad," and the officials of the Oglala Sioux Tribe. Count One charged Wilson with conspiring to organize a volunteer armed force to "terrorize, harass, intimidate, assault, threaten, and maintain surveillance upon" those who voiced opposition to his administration or support for the American Indian Movement. Count Two charged the officials of the Oglala Sioux Tribe with passing ordinances to deny people the constitutionally guaranteed civil rights of free assembly and free speech, and equal protection under the law.

A thick stack of affidavits were filed with the suit, including statements by Geraldine Janis and others who had been fired for participating in peaceful demonstrations against Wilson; statements against "goon squad" members by Oglalas who had been threatened or beaten because of their support for AIM; and statements against BIA police for working with the "goon squad" in various ways. Both motions were denied in District Court, and the WKLDOC then put them into the lengthy process of appeal.

APRIL 20-22 / THE HARD LINE AGAIN

Following the firefight on April 17, Marshal Colburn, head of all Federal forces in the Pine Ridge area, and Wounded Knee Security chief Stan Holder made a cease-fire agreement. Both sides promised not to move from their present positions and to alert the other if fired upon, in order to resolve the conflicts over the radio instead of in battle.

But the Government was upset at the numbers of people hiking into Wounded Knee, and on April 21 Colburn requested a meeting with Stan in the DMZ. Colburn told Stan that he wanted to move his Roadblock 5 three hundred yards closer to Wounded Knee to "better secure the area." Stan told Colburn that Wounded Knee would regard this as a violation of the cease-fire agreement, to which Colburn replied, "I am sorry if you see it that way, but my men are moving the roadblock right now." This was the last meeting between the military leaders for a time, and the Government's aggressiveness in the field increased, with intermittent shooting coming from the hills day and night.

For almost two weeks following the breakdown of the April 5th agreement, there had been no direct contact between negotiators from the two sides, despite the Independent Oglala Nation's requests for discussions. A series of different Federal negotiators were put in charge, and the Government's negotiating position got tougher. Kent Frizzell, chief spokesman for the Government, returned to Washington on April 10, leaving in charge Assistant Attorney General Stanley Pottinger, a moderate. Pottinger was recalled on April 20, and left saying, "I am concerned that the option I represent – to negotiate a settlement not involving force – has come to an end. The U.S. is in control of the situation, but not in control of the people." Pottinger left in charge assistant Attorney General Richard Hellstern, known to be a "hard-liner" among Government officials. Hellstern told the press that a "police solution might be necessary." The Government was attempting to force the defenders into a position where surrender would be the topic of any negotiations.

The Oglalas had been waiting for Leonard Crow Dog and Russell Means to return from Washington before resuming negotiations. On April 20 Crow Dog hiked in over the hills, after being turned back at the Government roadblocks, and the Oglalas immediately requested talks with the Government. Hellstern replied that they must first present an agenda he could agree to. He said he didn't want to "rehash old talks" – in other words, talk about the treaty.

On April 21 the ION again asked for a meeting. The Government again stalled, saying they were waiting for the Indian "leadership" to get back, even though all the Oglalas who had participated in the early April negotiations, with the exception of Russell Means, who was organizing support on the outside, were still in Wounded Knee.

Finally, on Easter Sunday, April 22, Hellstern sent the Justice Department's Community Relations Service representatives into the village. Many people met with them in the round tipi church, and Carter Camp took this opportunity to explain to the CRS how the Government had returned to overt warfare as a way of ending the confrontation, stalling on Wounded Knee's requests for negotiations:

Those FBI people are saying that their function is to investigate, to ferret out crimes and criminals, but they can't do much investigation from an APC and a bunker. Those of us who have been on Security and facing those marshals and FBI everyday know that it's always the FBI bunkers that start the firing. See, Colburn hears tapes of everything that comes over his radios, and so in order to make that tape sound good for Colburn, the FBI will call in and say, "We're taking incoming rounds," when there hasn't been a shot fired. And they'll call their command post and say, "Can we return fire?" And the command post will say, "Permission denied." And they'll do that about three times when there are no rounds being fired at all.

The last time Roadblock 6 was firing their weapons, but we weren't taking any incoming rounds. They were just making noise so someone could hear the firing. And then we heard these transmissions from two FBI bunkers asking for permission to fire back and permission was denied. I got on the radio to alert our people and to tell them to get in their bunkers, because I knew that they were trying to create an incident. And when Colburn came back from Washington and listened to the tapes, it sounded to him like the Indians have been firing for an hour and a half, I think he said, and he said his people showed extreme restraint.

"And on your way back, tell them marshals not to be shooting at those crackerboxes we live in, cause those bullets go right through."
— woman resident speaking to the CRS

Yesterday they moved in 300 yards on the Manderson Road. That's an obvious violation of the cease-fire. Pottinger, Frizzell, Wood, and the other negotiators who are supposedly the top men in charge here have never had any control over what's happening.

Last Tuesday, [during the April 17 firefight] I heard them over the radio saying, "All positions cease your fire," telling them that there were going to be some medics out in the field. Our medics wore big white arm bands. Yet they shot at them with automatic weapons. We're not protesting the fact that we took injuries during a battle, but it's the fact that they called three cease-fires that day and every time they were broken by [their] automatic weapons fire, and all three cease-fires were for the medics to go out.

Graffiti in the trading post.

Tribal Roadblock: Turn your fucking ass over, you think over. Who is the radio operator of Pawnee? I'd like to know. Give me your fucking name, Pawnee, so I can kick your ass when you get out of there. [pause] Pawnee, [tauntingly] this is roving patrol. Will you give me a time check?
. . .

Tribal Patrol to Tribal Roadblock: We need some help up here. We got twelve guys here, hippies. Some of 'em are not Indian. Can you send some help up here?

Tribal Roadblock: Someone's on their way. Cut their goddamn hair for 'em. We got two vans coming — 'bout a dozen men in 'em. [A new voice comes on, speaking with authority.] You hold them sons-a-bitches and shoot 'em if they try to run. Over.

Tribal Patrol: They ain't got no fight left in 'em. Fuck 'em in the face. Twelve hippies we got and they got about eight women in there and we gonna let the women go. You want we should stand by or what?
. . . Who in the hell is Crow Dog? They said they come from Crow Dog's camp . . . Corn Dog's beating his tom-tom.

Roadblock: What?

Patrol: Corn Dog — I mean Crow Dog is beating his tom-tom . . . I heard Dennis Banks never rode a horse in his life up until the press got there . . . We caught two women coming into Wounded Knee. What should we do with them?

Roadblock: Cut their hair off.

Red Arrow to all Roadblocks: So far it appears they have some people in custody behind the roadblocks. There's a lot of talk about weapons and shooting people and so on and so forth. Everybody be alert to the rear till we get a better location to where they are and what is going on . . . Search units be alert on the west perimeter. [He directs the search patrol to the vicinity of Baker 26, a BIA patrol unit working with the marshals.]

Red Arrow to Search Patrol: Okay — get on that road from RB-1 — between RB-1 and RB-6 — you'll hit that gap in the fence — the post is wired down. He's just a little ways to the right of there. There's a lot of flashlight activity in there and this may be the place where they have these people under this sort of arrest. Need to check that out before somebody gets hurt.

Tribal Roadblock: I'm reading you . . . send a flare up . . . Boys down below you there so be careful. Don't

shoot each other. Let her rip . . . [flare goes up] . . . looks kinda pretty.

Tribal Patrol: Tell 'em boys to slow down — my horse fell with me. Hey, they got twelve hippies and one loosy here.

Tribal Roadblock [to a vehicle, probably an APC]: You might get stuck — come straight ahead here. . . . What did I tell you! That's the fucking bunker you run over.

"I represent 12,000 — good Indians."
— Dick Wilson

The vigilantes were about to confront the BIA Unit 26 sent out by the marshals:

Red Arrow to Command Post [in Pine Ridge]: These people are getting close to 26 [BIA patrol] . . . It's going to get a little touchy, looks like. They have somebody with a strong station on channel 11 called Roadblock Control. I might be able to raise them if you want me to try. . . We got a bad situation here, 26 is taking some rounds. Better get some men over there!

Red Arrow to Baker 26: Why don't you fall back until you find out what is going on over there.

Red Arrow: Search 3 and 4 and all Baker units — get on over there to 26. He is surrounded. He don't know who these people are. Go ahead, 23. Better shake a leg.

Tribal Roadblock: Get the fuckin' weapons ready. Here comes a car. They're shooting!

"There's never one Federal Government, there's a lot of Federal Governments. When you get into a situation like Wounded Knee, you recognize rapidly that the Department of Interior is in conflict with the Department of Justice. And that within the Department of Justice, of course, the marshals might take this tack and the FBI that tack. Then there were the bureaucrats of the Bureau of Indian Affairs who were in collusion with the elected Tribal Government, which felt there was only one answer — an armed confrontation."

— John Adams of the
National Council of Churches

193

Finally Red Arrow contacted the Tribal Roadblock, after monitoring them for over an hour:

Red Arrow: Red Arrow to Roadblock Control. Red Arrow to Roadblock Control. Please answer! . . . Red Arrow to Oglala Roadblock Control. Red Arrow to the Oglala Roadblock Control. Please answer.

[long pause]

Tribal Roadblock to Red Arrow: Go ahead. [long pause — trying to get it together] This is the Roadblock. Go ahead.

Red Arrow: Okay, Roadblock. Do you have some people out on foot with flashlights on the western perimeter?

Tribal Roadblock: Negative.

Red Arrow: 10-4, Roadblock Control. I think we're about to get into a bad situation over there and if you have some people out on foot, you better get 'em back.

Tribal Roadblock: 10-4. We don't have anybody. [sounding sober now] Are you south of us here? Is that you on the hill? . . . Is that you blinking your lights?

Red Arrow to Roadblock: There's several units over in there moving around. Can you see them, Roadblock?

Tribal Roadblock: That's negative, but we'll check it out. We don't have anybody on foot patrol.

Red Arrow to Roadblock: Now everybody hold your positions over there! We're trying to prevent shooting is what we're trying to do. Now if you got somebody on foot you're fixin' to get shot. So stay where you are until we find out what is going on.

Tribal Roadblock: We have no one on foot patrol.

Red Arrow to Roadblock: Ah, does some of your people have a bunch of hippies in custody over there?

Tribal Roadblock to Red Arrow: Not here. Negative.

Red Arrow to Roadblock: 10-4.

Tribal Roadblock: You on top of the hill — why don't you come on down?

Red Arrow to Baker 26: 26, you have some other units there with you? . . . Well, stand by. Don't go into that goddamn canyon until you have somebody there with you. This guy up there is lying to me, and I don't know who those people are.

Tribal Roadblock: You in the car to the south of us — you the FBI or marshals? Identify yourself.

Red Arrow to Roadblock: Okay — this is the U.S. Marshals. Now do you have some people on foot in a canyon with flashlights? If you do, tell me, dammit, because these people are going down in there right now.

Tribal Roadblock to Red Arrow: That's negative. I've told you three times now, we don't have anybody on foot!

Red Arrow: Roadblock Control, are you on the Big Foot Trail?

Tribal Roadblock to Red Arrow: That's 10-4. One mile from Big Foot Trail. One mile north. Are you south of us? Is that you on the hill?

Red Arrow to Roadblock: That's negative. Stand by.

Red Arrow to Wounded Knee: Are you monitoring my transmission to this Roadblock Control?

Wounded Knee to Red Arrow: Roger, sure are.

Red Arrow: All right. They claim it's not their people up there in that canyon. Are you sure you don't have anybody up there? Ah, it's going to be a bad situation here shortly.

Wounded Knee: We have no one out in that direction and besides, our people don't use flashlights and build fires.

No one ever heard what happened to the 12 people captured that night, but rumors of graves found in the hills circulated the reservation for many weeks. Also, no one in Wounded Knee ever heard if marshals or vigilantes were injured, as the Government kept such reports secret.

Once again during the night the marshals removed the Tribal Roadblock from the Big Foot Trail. But the next day Richard Wilson led a group of supporters back to the site where they encountered the marshals again. The Marshals' logs report, "10:05 . . . instructions from Mr. Hellstern is that gas may be used to prevent the establishment of any new non-Federal positions." As Wilson and Colburn confronted each other, FBI Special Agent in Charge Richard Held arrived by helicopter to inform the marshals that word had come from a high Washington source to let the roadblock stand. The Marshals' logs report the end of the confrontation as follows, ". . . Have agreed upon a peaceful demonstration . . . Wilson feels this is being resolved at the DOJ [Department of Justice] – D.C. level." Marvin Franklin, acting Director of the BIA, came to Pine Ridge to trouble-shoot the problems. As a result, the marshals were forced to allow several of Wilson's people to be stationed at their Roadblock 1 and to participate in official patrols around the village.

WARRIORS IN WOUNDED KNEE

With the tempo of the confrontation increasing, the Independent Oglala Nation began to reinforce its defense bunkers and to construct thick earthen walls around the clinic, some of the living quarters, and the kitchens. The work was hard, but pleasant in the warm spring weather. The cooking was all done outside now, and a huge bucket was set on a fire outside the little white church near Denby bunker for heating creek water to wash clothes in.

On one calm afternoon while the cease-fire prevailed, four warriors — all of them Vietnam veterans — talked with one of the women from the underground press about how they had come to Wounded Knee. They were sitting down near the creek, while people walked by carrying buckets of water for the outdoor laundry. Some of the kids were riding their ponies, galloping back and forth across the fields. The Oglalas were meeting in the round church, discussing the Government's lack of response to their last negotiating agenda. . . A couple of dogs kept nosing around, looking for food.

Bob: I was in the Air Force in Thailand in 1968. I saw the Viet Nam war from that point of view and from covert operations in Laos with the U.S. Air Force and the CIA.

Tiger: I spent four years in the Marine Corps and ten months in Viet Nam. I got there in '65 and I was in helicopters. I saw it build up from nothing — very little, no ground troops at all, into what it's turned out to be, a pretty big war.

Tony: I was in the Air Force. I spent a year there as part of a support squadron to the Marines and the Army. Most of my time was spent up north — Quang Tri and Da Nang.

Bobby: I was in the Air Force but I mainly worked for the Army in the Special Operations unit, better known as combat control teams. Our job was calling in air strikes. I served in Viet Nam in '70 through '71. I've been in prisoner of war raids — plus, I was a prisoner for three weeks.

Do you feel that your experience in Viet Nam has something to do with your being here?

Bob: Yes, very much so. A lot of us went to Viet Nam not knowing the political situation of the war. I myself as a white person began to read and question why we were there and what the war was all about. The more I did, the more parallels I began to draw with the militaristic adventures of the United States since its conception and I began to see how the picture fits a pattern that was developed in this country with the genocide they attempted on the American Indians.

In front of the Security building.

Tiger: I went over there in '64 and '65 and I saw the big build-up. Like I say, there weren't no ground troops, a lot of advisors and the Air Force was there, the squadron I was in from the Marines was there. I didn't see it too much as political then, though certainly there was a lot of similarities between here and there. I saw the Government come in and strong-arm everything right from the start.

Tony: What got me started was that my father got killed in the Korean War. At that time I was really afraid of death, I thought that life was the most important thing. But I thought it would be the thing to do — go and serve my country. And when I got in the military, I found out what a bunch of bullshit it really was. Being part Indian, but mostly white, I seen a lot of shit come down on my brothers that were darker than me, the ones that got all those weird little dirty details. That always made me angry. Then they sent me to California and it was about the time Berkeley was exploding with riots and the hippies were down in Haight-Ashbury. I used to spend a lot of time down there talking to people and trying to really find out why I was doing the thing I was doing. When the orders came that a bunch of us were going to Nam, I didn't want to go.

The condition of the first Vietnamese people that we met was just sickening, and I wanted to cry, and scream and a lot of other things. This big guy comes up to me — he was in the Army and he had all this ammo and shit strung all over him — he says, "You got to come with me; come on let's go." So I went down and saw my commander and he said, just kind of jokingly, "You finally made it here. Help us get rid of some of these gooks." I really freaked out. Then he threw a gun at me and I looked at it a second and I threw it back at him. I says, "No." I says, "I don't know what the hell I'm doing here but I'm not going to help kill these people . . ." He got really angry. So they put me on truck detail, thought they would keep me out of trouble that way.

I spent a lot of time talking to the people — the farmers, the people that were working for the government in the different stores, and helping to load my truck. Most of what we talked about was the old days, you know, before the French came and started all this shit. And to me, this is where the relationship to Wounded Knee comes in, because the old people here, they told me experiences about what it used to be like in the old days before the white man came.

And to me it's a struggle of people who just want to be left alone and do the simple things in life that they enjoy, which are very non-profitable, you know, like the Vietnamese are mostly just farmers. All along, in Viet Nam, in Korea, here at Wounded Knee, the white man has just given us a lot of shit. And he told us that he's our friend, like, "We want to help you." So we say, "Okay, give us back our land, give us back our rights, let us go back to the old ways." "Oh, no, we don't want to help you that much."

Do you think this is a war here?

Tiger: Definitely, yes.

Is it the same kind of war the United States is fighting in Viet Nam?

Bob: I think it is. All you have to do is look around the hills here and you can see about 12 armored personnel carriers that are nothing but APCs that didn't make it to Viet Nam. The men carry the same weapons that are used in Viet Nam — the M-16, the M-79 grenade launcher is here, they have starlight scopes that were used for spotting people in the jungle at night time, they have infra-red sensors, trip-flares out here in the woods to prevent our foot patrols from coming in. They use helicopters. So the similarities are more than just obvious.

Some of us in the Air Force went into Laos in civilian

Reinforcing the clinic.

clothes to do operations of a military nature for the CIA. And we always hid from the American public and the press what was going on. The people back home did not know when incidents had been provoked by the CIA just so that we could call in an air strike or go in and hit a village or knock out a section of the Ho Chi Minh Trail. The same pattern appears here. The FBI is sending patrols down from their bunker RB-6. They fire on our roadblocks to provoke firefights so the marshals will open up on the other side of the village.

And the attitudes of the people running the negotiations are the same too. It's like in Viet Nam the U.S. Government has to support the "legitimately elected" puppet, Thieu. They have to support Wilson here. In Viet Nam the CIA had the Phoenix Program, where all the grassroots leaders who opposed Thieu were tortured or assassinated. Here the job falls to the FBI. Their covert operations center around provoking firefights, because a military solution will save the Government from facing the political issues raised by this action.

Bobby: These marshals out there, they're here for the dollar sign, they're getting paid for it. And we're down here for a reason and we're fighting back for that reason and if we have to fight and die for that reason, that's why we're here. But the marshals are down here for that dollar sign. Otherwise you wouldn't find any volunteers to work for that.

Tiger, as an Indian, what did you think about fighting in a white man's army against non-white people?

Tiger: People used to ask about it when I was over there. I figured the communists might come and try and take our land here. I was fighting for the land — I wasn't fighting for the Government. I knew this land was ours and always will be. I never thought it was a personal war against the Vietnamese. To me it always seemed like it was against the communists.

What do you think of that justification now?

Tiger: Oh well, it doesn't matter because I'm still here at Wounded Knee fighting whoever is out there trying to take it away from me. And right now it is the American forces trying to take it away. That's who I'm fighting.

What do you mean by the land?

Tiger: The land itself, our land.

Indian land?

Tiger: Indian land. It was always Indian land.

What does the land mean to Indian people?

Tiger: To the Indian people the land is life. It's not, "How many acres is mine," or, "How much can I take from it, how much stuff can I grow to make more money?" It's the land as it is itself, in its most basic way, the way nature had it. The Indian lived off the land. Everything he had he got from the land in one way or another. It supplied the food the buf-

falo ate, so why tear up the land and starve yourself? Everything rotated in a circle. The land supported the food the Indian needed to live, and in turn the Indian prayed to the land, worshiped it. Without it he wouldn't be anything. He never thought it was his. He thought he was sent here to help take care of the land, not use it to his own advantage.

What about the Vietnamese? What do you think their relationship to the land is?

Tiger: I saw a lot of farmers, growing crops, even while shooting was going on. In fact, the first man I shot was a farmer. He was plowing a field. I could tell they like their land, too. Otherwise they wouldn't be out there during a war working on it. It was theirs and they wanted to keep it.

Bobby: They are fighting for a cause, too. Like when I first got there I wasn't sure what the hell was going on. There was a time when I was out in the boonies and it was "kill or be killed." I realized then that I was killing my same color of people, same kind of skin and color of hair, but yet they are smaller. I found out they were fighting for something they believe in too. It's always belonged to them and they are going to hold it. Course, the Government don't understand, cause they are getting their ass kicked.

Is there anything you learned from the Vietnamese fighters?

Bobby: I learned survival, that's one thing I learned off the Vietnamese. And the guerilla warfare training, that's come into my use a lot. For instance, one time we was out on patrol here in Wounded Knee, and we was sitting down there by the creek, just observing, recon, and about five of this group they call the SOG, Special Operations Group, they come trucking down through there in front of us without even seeing us. We asked for permission to knock 'em out and we were told, "Don't fire." They come right dead in front of us, like an ambush. We could have wiped every one of those suckers out and they would of never knew what hit 'em. But they said, "Just let them go," so we let 'em truck on by.

Bob: Something else the Vietnamese taught us, something that we don't have, and that's that you've got to have patience. We came in here, and we had to take a defensive position. This is really an undefendable valley. It's like Dien Bien Phu or Khe Sanh. You can't hold this against a superior military force on the outside. But we've been using our heads and getting our food and supplies in here overland at night time, using guerilla warfare tactics. We come through there — right through their

lines, past their bunkers — they never see us. We put this training to good use.

How is it that people can walk out through the countryside right past the APCs and not get caught?

Bob: People here are not afraid of the land and nature. Like when a snowstorm comes we realize that it is a part of the earth's cycle — the snow is going to be water for the grass in the spring, and we don't look at it as something cold and hard. The marshals get in their APCs and try to stay warm until the snow melts. And we go out there and just walk all around them.

The night time is our best friend here. They do have their super-sensitive weapons, sniper scopes and sensing devices, but they haven't been able to spot us yet. They catch some of our people, of course. But if you are in with the land, and close to it, you can look down a valley and see where they are probably going to have a bunker or one of their patrols positioned to try and spot you coming through. You begin to think like a bird — you look all around.

Most of us warriors carry our whole supply of ammo in a pouch on our belt. And it's sort of neat to hear over the fed's radio how they have to use helicopters to re-supply with ammo several times during a firefight. We try not to engage in heavy battles bunker-to-bunker. Our main force of warriors is mobile, always on the move within the perimeter from tree to ravine to house to creek to bunker. For every round we fire, the Federal mercenaries must throw in a thousand, because

they can't find us to pin us down.

Something else we learned from the Viet Nam war is about technology and machinery — that the stuff is vulnerable, it is fallible, and it does not always work right. A man can sit in a machine and think he is superior when he's actually not. All it takes is one guy sitting out there with a little bit more ingenuity and he can defeat an APC. We know this here. I think this is what the struggle here at Wounded Knee is going to show the people on the outside. We have this tendency to over-estimate the power of the enemy, and to under-estimate ourselves and what we can do. But with a little courage and strength on our part and a little knowledge of what we are up against, it can be defeated. There's nothing but people sitting in those machines and behind those guns. And we're people down here.

Do you think Wounded Knee will change a lot of Indian people?

Tiger: I think Wounded Knee shows Indian people what kind of a government they were fighting for in Viet Nam. Maybe how their parents and grandparents were treated and mistreated. I think a lot of them will change once they realize why we're here.

Bobby: These so-called "apples" — red on the outside, white on the inside — just haven't realized what's going on. The white society has washed their minds so bad they don't want to wake up. They're going to realize what's going on after it's all over, that they were wrong.

Bob: We see that every day with the roadblock that's manned by goons, Wilson's people. The U.S. Government would like nothing more than to see Indians turn against Indians down here, and supply them with weaponry as they have done on that roadblock. They did the same thing in Viet Nam. This is a tactic of the Special Forces groups some of my friends were on. They would take people who were non-Anglo, that looked maybe to be Oriental or darker skin — they would send them out dressed as North Vietnamese to attack Laotian villages.

Bobby: Several times — hell, I had to do that bullshit, dressing up as a North Vietnamese. I was the biggest one around that crowd but they would dress my ass up and send me out there.

Can you think of any other tactics that were used in Viet Nam that they are using here against you?

Bobby: One is propaganda, the news media. They are not

really telling the truth. And they never will tell the truth because they know that Uncle Sam will take another slap in the face if they do.

Bob: Two times now in the past three weeks we have had indiscriminate firepower unleashed on this little village from these 12 APCs positioned around us. The marshals don't care where they are shooting. It's the same policy as in Viet Nam — if you can't handle the situation, you just go mad and unleash all the firepower you got on it, like they did with the B-52s and saturation bombing. You try to destroy it before it gets too big.

I'd love for some of those people in those APCs out there to come out of their skins just enough to come down here and sit with us in a peyote ceremony one night. To feel what it is to get to know some people. And not feel you have to destroy them just because they are different.

How do you feel sitting down in this valley surrounded by APCs and machine guns?

Bobby, laughing: Scared shitless!

Do you feel caged in?

Tiger: Not really. We're free to move around. There's nobody here telling people that they have to stay. People can leave any time they want to, go up to the gate and tell them they want to go out, or walk out over the hills.

Bob: It's a very uncomfortable feeling to walk out of your bunker every morning and look and see that you are on the wrong end of about 50 barrels pointed down at you. But you get used to it after a while.

You don't have too many of the comforts of life. How do you feel about that?

Tony: Well, I'm not eating three huge square meals a day —

Tiger: — but nobody's starving.

Tony: I wouldn't mind a glass of ice tea.

Tiger: Cold beer. A shot of whiskey.

Tony: I'm warm when I sleep at night.

Tiger: Wasn't anybody starve or freeze to death — I come close a couple of times —

Tony: We've all been through a few exciting moments. I mean, the way they got the place covered, there's no way you can go without catching some kind of shit. But people still go, still live — they still laugh and sing and dance —

Tiger: We still go about our daily lives. People over there are playing ball right now —

Bob: Those APCs are sitting up on the hills around us, watching us. The FBIs over on Roadblock 6 are probably sighting in on us with their sniper rifles.

Tiger: There's a lot of peace and tranquillity inside the village. We've been here 58 days and there's been no real dissension against one another. There have been no fights. Everybody is carrying a rifle, but there's been no gunfights, nobody has shot one another. There have been no fist fights, none of that here.

Bob: When you return to the land — it's like the water flows through this creek over here every day and it takes a little bit of the banks with it as it goes, and there's change involved. There's change in people involved. Outside, in the United States, especially in the cities, change occurs so fast that people don't have time to adjust to it. They wake up and find themselves doing things that they didn't really want to do because it just happened that there's a new commercial on TV and you find you've got a new kind of headache or a new way of looking at a woman because she's selling a body deodorant product. And when you get away from that, when you've had some time to think, and you work with people and get down and do some of the basic chores of life, like carrying water, or sitting out here on this hillside, you begin to know people. I don't say that a return to the land will end racism and imperialism, but it will help people to clear their heads and find that there are some ways of living in this world that are different from what's going on in the United States of America — and maybe we can find these and spread them around. You know, we control here approximately one square mile of land, not very much —

Tiger: But it's ours.

Tony: It's a start.

Tiger: Each person here is rich in the spirit. And out there they want to see how much you have in your wallet first.

Do you think the people here are going to win?

Tiger: I don't think we will all be wiped out. If we are, there are others who will come take our place. This issue won't die here. I think it will spread. I hope it does. I will stay here and help it. I left school to come here and I don't think I'll go back.

Bobby: The first night we came in here I knew it was going to mount up to something. And I'm ready, if I have to, to die here at Wounded Knee for the Indian people. All of us here right now are dedicated to die — to show the white society that we are tired of his bullshitting. They thought they could wipe us out a long time ago, but they found out they can't kill the Indians.

Bob: I have a feeling — solidarity, I guess. There are many people in this country struggling for their own liberation, and the right to determine their own lives. I think maybe Wounded Knee will be a spark for that. And we just hope other people will take this up and some will come to our aid here and other people will get it on elsewhere. Because Wounded Knee is not an isolated event. The Indians have been struggling, like the Vietnamese, for many years. The white man thought they were finally about down, but it's beginning to change. The tide's gonna turn on 'em.

A few months after the occupation was over, Kathy, a member of Hawk Eye bunker's squad, wrote about the experiences of women in Wounded Knee.

Being in Wounded Knee taught us a new kind of bravery: being shot at as you sit in a bunker — bullets and tracers whizzing and zinging by — or dodging from foxhole to foxhole, or running out with a stretcher to bring back the wounded, or manning — womanning — a bunker all day or night. Some of us wanted to, recalling the fierce warrior women of the Nez Perce and of Central and South America, and some did not. But most of us were prepared to handle the fear of firefights, having experienced death, violence, and fighting in both city and reservation life.

You never overcome that fear but you act in spite of it. There were many people in Wounded Knee, men as well as women, who were afraid. Each of us knew we might expect to die; many of us expected to be wiped out the first week.

And there were many women who were heroes. There were Sara and Diane, who handled the radio constantly. Day and night you could hear their voices over the security radio, They worked twelve and eighteen hour shifts, during the long quiet times and firefights. Sara and another woman, Stephanie, helped put out a newsletter, "The Wounded Knee Message," for as many days as the paper lasted, collecting and writing stories, announcements and jokes, and printing it all on an ancient ditto machine.

Several teenaged Oglala women who were familiar with the land often snuck out to backpack in food, medicine, and other supplies. There was Gwen, a Navajo, who was off duty when a firefight began. She located her own bunker through a scope, and dashed off, bullets hitting all around her. Women trained as stretcher crews, practicing over and over in drills with six of them running out to the "victim" and placing the person on a stretcher, and then running back to the hospital. And when the battles came, they would make it out to the bunkers, under fire, to be there if they were needed. One woman medic was pinned in a shallow gully all day; every time she raised her head to look, she would draw sniper fire.

Most of the underground work was handled by local reservation women, hiding people, feeding them, hiding rifles, hiding and packing supplies. When our group was trying to get back into Wounded Knee one night, we stopped at three different women's homes. We got directions, found the way was clear, had coffee, and departed — as their children sat through it all.

APRIL 25 / CLEARWATER DIES

When Wounded Knee faded from the newspapers in early April with the breakdown of negotiations, Vern Bellecourt, National Director of the American Indian Movement and a fundraiser on the outside, issued a call for people to come to South Dakota to show their support. People from around the country gathered at Crow Dog's camp on the Rosebud Reservation, and on April 23, several hundred set out from there to march the hundred miles to Wounded Knee. They carried with them food and medical supplies, and called their journey a "March for Survival." Their reception by the Brule Sioux people of the Rosebud Reservation was friendly, but when they approached the border of Bennett County — a predominately white area which lies between the Rosebud and Pine Ridge Reservations — they were turned back by a road-block of 80 BIA police and Federal Marshals who stood across U.S. Highway 18. Then Chief Frank Fools Crow offered them the use of his land for a campsite. The marchers tried to make it to his place at Kyle, but BIA police arrested many of them and escorted them off Pine Ridge Reservation.

Frank Clearwater died in Rapid City on April 25 from the severe head wound he received in the April 17 firefight. The ION offered a plot of land for his burial in Wounded Knee, and his wife, Morningstar, asked that he be buried there.

But Richard Wilson forbade his burial on the Pine Ridge Reservation, giving as his reason that Clearwater was not Oglala — even though many whites have been buried on reservation land. The FBI at this time was adding to the confusion by telling the press that the fallen warrior's name was "Frank Clear," and that he was a white man. This was an apparent attempt to cool the anger of Indian people around the country towards

the killing, and to add to the myth that it was non-Indians who held Wounded Knee. Medicine men Black Elk and Crow Dog sent out a taped call to Indian people to come to Wounded Knee for the burial of their Apache brother. Crow Dog said:

At this time we make this release throughout the various tribes.
Our brother Frank Clearwater was wounded.
Early this morning our brother left us for
the happy hunting grounds.
Our sister want our brother to be buried in Wounded Knee.
Our brothers in Wounded Knee are mourning.

I want you people to know —
we are red men, we're fighting for our rights.
Many, many years we been mistreat.
So our brothers and our relations throughout the United States,
various tribes, the four winds of the earth —
pray for our brother that deceased.
He been here 12 hours.
He himself never reached the bunkers.
He had intentions to come to Wounded Knee, to help support.
My relations of the American Indian people,
I'm asking you to come to Wounded Knee, the burial.
The reason why is, his companion said,
"Anything happen, he will be buried in Wounded Knee,
in the grave of Big Foot and our loved ones
that been buried here in this sacred holy ground."
About a year ago we buried Raymond Yellow Thunder.
We told white America, "This will be the American Indian

The Rosebud-Wounded Knee march.

Movement's way to bury our brothers."
At that time I thought it would not happen in Wounded Knee.
It's hard to take, what happened to the red man.
The red man and the white man got to understand
the attitude of the Government at this time.
One of our brothers been massacred.
I use massacred because when he got shot he wasn't armed.
He was inside the house.
So all my brothers of various tribes that believe Indian ways —
if you can't attend, you must pray.
You must pray for our people in Wounded Knee.
We will have mourning for four days and four nights.

Wounded Knee began a four-day period of mourning for Clearwater. Soon afterwards, the chief Government negotiator, Kent Frizzell, returned from Washington where he had left his previous post as an Assistant Attorney General to take the position of Solicitor General of the Interior Department, that agency's highest legal counsel. He began almost at once to meet with the traditional Oglala chiefs and headmen at Fools Crow's land near Kyle. The ION representatives had made it clear that they must consult with their chiefs in order to hold further negotiations with the Government. But rather than let the chiefs into Wounded Knee, Frizzell chose to meet with them separately. At the same time he refused to meet directly with ION representatives at Wounded Knee.

APRIL 26-27 / TWENTY-FOUR HOURS OF BATTLE — ANOTHER WARRIOR IS KILLED

In recent days, sniping from the hills had been increasing. Wounded Knee Security daily requested meetings with Marshal Colburn to try and cool the situation down and maintain the cease-fire. Colburn repeatedly refused to meet with Wounded Knee. Finally, on April 26, the longest — and last — firefight broke out. Barbara, a member of the underground press, described it in her journal. Here she relates the events from that afternoon through late evening.

. . . Since Sunday the feds have gone through their little routine every morning — firing at us, then reporting to Red Arrow that they are receiving shots and asking to "return the fire." Today they did a variation and started in the middle of the afternoon, which is strange because more people are awake and on the alert, and we can see the snipers better. If it wasn't the feds themselves, it was the goons, whom they are allowing to patrol around out there. Someone got hit, but I haven't been out to see who it was. On the radio we heard them order in more M-79 gas grenade launchers, and M-319s and 321s — whatever those are.

In the last couple of days some people noticed .50 caliber machine guns — the big ones — mounted on the APCs. They're moving some APCs around there now. You can hear a clanking racket when they move — and they're firing some flares down at an empty house, trying to burn it. The goons have been jamming our radio all afternoon, so we can't understand the bunkers when they call in, and a roving patrol saw some people in the abandoned farmhouse on the southern edge of our border.

After the shooting this afternoon I went down to the white church kitchen and did a pile of laundry and some dishes. I came over to Security around 9 p.m. About an hour later all hell broke loose — must be the heaviest firefight yet. We sort of expected something tonight and most people were in their bunkers when it started, so we didn't get all shot up like before.

Grace and Wallace ran through a storm of bullets to the Security building and we got down into the bunker dug beneath the floor. We were really scared for awhile. The rounds were hitting the building with loud, crashing sounds. Our radios were going and I could hear the guys in the bunkers talking sometimes and also the feds talking on their radio. I could look out the door and see tracers going past, and when they would stop some people would rush in, pick up something or talk awhile and run out again, hitting the dirt or ducking behind a car when the rounds hit close.

Once I heard the Government call a cease-fire and got up to look out the window; just as I did the whole side of the hill was lit up by a solid stream of red tracers coming from RB-4 toward Denby bunker. They fired a huge amount of rounds into the bunker and then acknowledged the cease-fire.

5 p.m. to midnight

The following radio transmissions and conversations were recorded inside the Wounded Knee Security building. The Wounded Knee Security headquarters and bunkers frequently changed their radio code names for greater security. This night, headquarters was called "Lozen." In communicating with Red Arrow, they always identified themselves as "Wounded Knee."

When a warrior had been injured by sniper fire that afternoon, Wounded Knee had again attempted to contact Marshal Colburn, thinking that since he was not in the field, he was perhaps unaware of his men's violations of the cease-fire. Colburn would not meet with Wounded Knee, and sent in officials from the Justice Department's Community Relations Service instead:

Wounded Knee: Red Arrow, Red Arrow.

Red Arrow: Go ahead, Wounded Knee.

Wounded Knee; Roger. We would like to have a meeting with Marshal Colburn at the earliest possible moment, if he is not still giving us the cold shoulder.

Red Arrow: This is from Marshal Colburn. He has been willing to meet with you, but he is observing your mourning period.

Wounded Knee: Roger. Is he willing to meet with us this afternoon?

Red Arrow: Standby a minute.

Last Stand bunker to Lozen: Want to report some gunfire to the left of us. Sounds like it is coming from behind them. Maybe it is the goons attacking some of our people coming in.

Red Arrow to Wounded Knee: Be advised Marshal Colburn will attempt to work out a meeting with you first thing in the morning.

Wounded Knee to Red Arrow: Ask him if he understands the gravity of the situation here. We're trying to talk to him and not shoot all the time. We think that is a much more reasonable approach and to delay matters like that is not conciliatory.

Red Arrow: 10-4.

RB-4 to Red Arrow: About six people just entered the bunker in front of us. We have a pretty full house down there.

Red Arrow to RB-4: 10-4. Just keep 'em close together when you use that 79 [M-79 gas grenade launcher].

RB-4 to Red Arrow: There was a small caliber round from the bunker in front of us.

Red Arrow to RB-4: Aimed in which direction?

RB-4: We didn't take a hit, you know. We heard the round go. It must have gone over us — it didn't hit the bunker or in front of us.

Red Arrow: That's 10-4.

Red Arrow to Wounded Knee: Be advised that RB-4 has received a shot and apparently it went over their heads.

> **Wounded Knee to Red Arrow:** Okay — I'll check on that and get back to you.

Red Arrow: Headquarters 2 has asked me to advise you that the next round — repeat, the next round — that any of our bunkers receive, we will open fire. 10-4?

> **Wounded Knee:** We checked with our bunker down there across from you RB-4. They state they have not fired a round, but they are doing construction work around there. If you have been here for any length of time at all, you know your people don't know the

sound of a guy chopping wood from a rifle round going off, because we have had cease-fires broken for that reason before. Over.

Red Arrow: 10-4. I've been here for some weeks.

Red Arrow to Headquarters 2: Wounded Knee advises that they are building up that bunker in front of RB-4 — construction . . . they state they are breaking wood, sawing wood, hammering and state that our people can't tell the difference between chopping wood and a round. 10-4.

RB-4 to Red Arrow: There isn't anybody outside the bunker to do anything like that. They're all in the bunker. Those were rounds!

Red Arrow: That's 10-4.

RB-4: I get a little worked up when they start that stuff.

Red Arrow: That's 10-4.

Red Arrow to Wounded Knee: Be advised it might be good for you to advise your locations to quit construction so we can determine which are and which are not gunshots. 10-4?

> **Wounded Knee:** That would be good if we could, but

it is necessary to chop firewood for the camp. Plus we have construction going on all over. In this valley, sound really travels well, as I guess you know. But I repeat again in all sincerity, our people say they have not fired a round down there. We would like to resolve this situation somehow. Over.

Red Arrow: That's 10-4.

Red Arrow to Command Post: . . . They are not going to stop their construction. They are taking defensive positions and beefing up. They claim they have not fired a round. I repeat: they claim they have not fired a round. 10-4.

Wounded Knee to Red Arrow: We were wondering if there has been any reply from Marshal Colburn? If he would be willing to talk with us this afternoon?

Red Arrow to Wounded Knee: Message from Marshal Colburn: that is negative on a meeting this afternoon.

Wounded Knee: Tell him I just personally wonder what he gets paid for if it is not to try and calm down situations like this. It seems to me that is the very function of his job.

Red Arrow: I'll relay the message . . . Message from Marshal Colburn: "I have arranged to have two CRS people meet with you within the hour if I can be assured from you the cease-fire is in effect."

Wounded Knee: Roger. That will be okay with us. We are trying to maintain the cease-fire. We're not out to violate it. If we were, we wouldn't lie to you — we'd just go ahead and it wouldn't just be small sniping. Yes, CRS people will be guaranteed safe conduct down here if they wish to enter.

Red Arrow: I was not finished with the message. "These people will be instrumental in arranging the meeting between you and the senior Justice Department officials."
. . .

Red Arrow to Command Post: They have disclaimed any firing at all. And acknowledging this last message they said if they were going to violate the cease-fire, they would open up all the way around instead of sniper firing. 10-4.

Command Post to Red Arrow: 10-4. You tell them that is the same with us. It won't be one shot when they get it from us.

Red Arrow: That's 10-4. I already did tell them that, sir.

Lozen [Wounded Knee Security] to all bunkers: Maintain a strict cease-fire and go to a 50% alert.

During this time two CRS representatives drove into the village and began meeting with Security.
2000 hours . . .

Lozen to all bunkers: Remember our overall plan. Our plan is to stay cool and observe our mourning period. And please report to us when you hear these shots — make a record of it.

Red Arrow to all roadblocks: Message from Headquarters 2: "The same rules apply. All squad leaders — the same rules apply. Play it cool and if you take confirmed shots, repeat, confirmed shots, take the necessary action." Headquarters 2 says that you will be backed up.

Approximately 2130 hours . . .

RB-4 to Red Arrow: If we see one of them long-haired hippie dudes jump out of that bunker in front of us with long black hair with pigtails, we got a Search 4 [search party] out there, and if we capture him, first off we're gonna cut his hair.

Red Arrow to RB-4: That's 10-4, RB-4. Use caution in it.

RB-4: Okay, we'll watch it. One night he's gonna walk right into our arms.

Red Arrow: That's 10-4.

Bruno [Government bunker] to RB-4: We don't see him — advise us which way he is walking so we can put our strobe [light] on him. Advise us where that Yahoo is.

RB-4: You stand by, Bruno.
. . .

At 2200 hours Wounded Knee was startled by a countdown over Red Arrow radio. Then, the sky was lit by about 50 aerial flares, fired from all Government positions. At almost the same time, someone opened fire on Wounded Knee's Little Big Horn bunker — the one opposite RB-4 and Bruno. At this time, too, third-party forces opened fire on Government RBs 2 and 5 from behind.

Red Arrow: . . . 4 . . . 3 . . . 2 . . . 1 . . . GO! *WaaHooo!*

Little Big Horn: They're coming in on us!

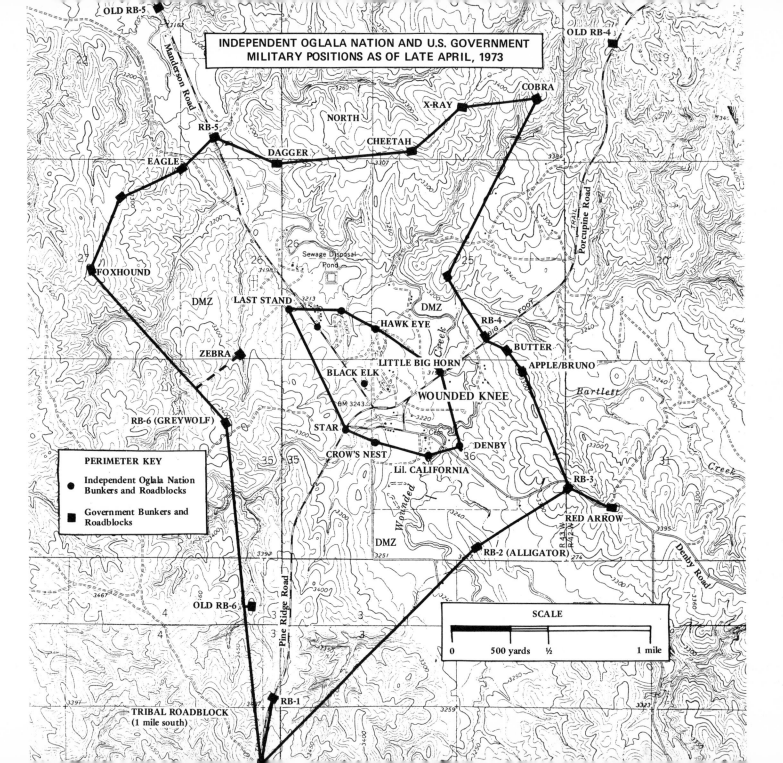

INDEPENDENT OGLALA NATION AND U.S. GOVERNMENT
MILITARY POSITIONS AS OF LATE APRIL, 1973

PERIMETER KEY

● Independent Oglala Nation
Bunkers and Roadblocks

■ Government Bunkers and
Roadblocks

SCALE

0   500 yards   ½   1 mile

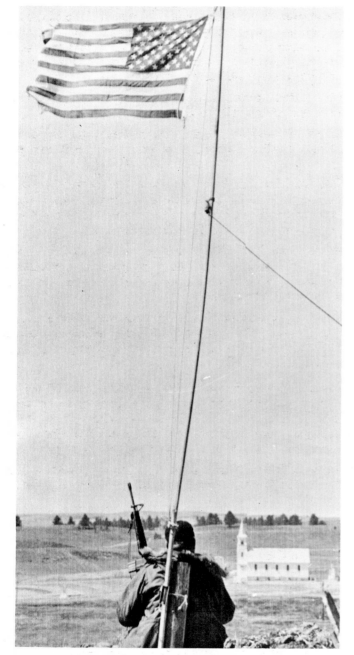

U.S. Marshal at RB-4 watching Wounded Knee. Off the photo, 400 yards to the lower right, is Little Big Horn bunker. The trading post area is to the left of the church.

Red Arrow to Command Post: Confirming all fire. Squad leaders have been advised to use discretion. These are confirmed hits aimed at our bunkers.

Red Arrow: All RBs, all RBs. CP advises confirmed hits being received your RBs. You pin-point targets, start with controlled return fire at targets. Pin-point targets first.

Lozen: All units: we are now on 100% alert!

Red Arrow: . . . pin-point the targets. Use controlled firing.

Little Big Horn: We are now under fire. Over.

Lozen: That was not an order to fire. Over.

Little Big Horn: I know that, but we are under heavy fire.

Lozen: 10-4. Go ahead and return fire. Over.

Red Arrow to all RBs: Pin-point your targets and return controlled fire.

Warriors in Security building: *Everybody going out — go in pairs. Don't go out in groups. Go to your areas . . . you all get down there! Get down there!*

Denby bunker to Lozen: We are under heavy fire. Over.

Lozen to Denby: Return fire if you are being fired upon.

Looking towards RB-4 from Little Big Horn. The burned-out trailer is behind Government lines.

Denby: Roger. I read you loud and clear.

Lozen: All units. This is Lozen. We are now under 100% alert. If you are fired upon by any APC, please return fire. Over.

The Tribal roadblock radio contacted Lozen, pretending to be Wounded Knee's Hawk Eye bunker. They said that an APC was on top of their position, that they had scattered in a field and needed help. Although this was a false message, in the confusion it was believed. Ten warriors went out of the Security building under heavy fire to help the warriors in Hawk Eye.

Wounded Knee Security was still trying to re-establish a cease-fire. They knew that relations between the vigilantes and the marshals had been bad for weeks, and they contacted Red Arrow, hoping that it was mainly vigilantes who were provoking the firefight, and that Red Arrow would cooperate in getting it stopped. Security was also hoping to get more information on the vigilantes' positions.

Security could see that the marshals' Alligator bunker was receiving automatic-weapons fire from vigilantes behind them, and could hear the marshals discussing it on the radio. But even Alligator, the bunker under fire, continued to return all their fire into the village.

2230 hours . . .

Red Arrow to Alligator [RB-2]: Be advised there is a vehicle moving along the tree line toward your 10-20 . . . over to your left flank, Eddie, in that tree line to the rear of you.

Wounded Knee: Red Arrow, Red Arrow. This is Wounded Knee.

Red Arrow to Alligator: We have no idea — we just spotted it, Eddie.

Red Arrow to Wounded Knee: Go ahead, Wounded Knee.

Wounded Knee: Be advised, this is what we found out. The report of an APC in our perimeter was false message transmitted by the goons sitting in that farmhouse down below your RB-2. Now, somebody is going to have to get them out of there, cause they started this firefight tonight — either you're going to do it or we're going to do it . . . did you copy?

Red Arrow: That's a 10-4.

Wounded Knee: Can you relay that to your headquarters and get this firefight stopped before somebody gets killed?

Red Arrow to Alligator: Have you seen any movement to the

farmhouse over to the left of you? Wounded Knee advises — claims — quote — that the goons are down in that farmhouse with a CB radio making erroneous reports and that they started the firefight. I want to confirm if you have seen any movement around that farmhouse at all.

Alligator to Red Arrow: 10-4. Be advised that the first burst of gunfire was at this RB from Wounded Knee. 10-4.

Red Arrow to Alligator: 10-4. You pin-point the targets over there, Ed? . . . All right, try and get those muzzle flashes and lay 'em in . . .

CRS-2 to Red Arrow: Would it be worth a try to, if we could, hold off the Federal fire for just a few minutes to see if we can get word to the AIM bunkers to hold theirs, to see if we could slow down the firing for a little bit more.

Red Arrow to CRS-2: 10-4. I can pass that word but be advised that if our bunkers continue to be fired on they will return fire under controlled conditions. But I will request that they all cease-fire at this time.

Red Arrow to all Roadblocks: If you can, cease-fire at this time, but if you continue to be fired upon, defend yourselves.

Lozen to all bunkers: Hold your fire! Hold your fire. Cease fire. Cease fire.

Red Arrow to Command Post: . . . negative on the 30-06, we're low on the .30 caliber but in good shape on the other. . . . Be advised I have told all RBs to cease-fire by request of CRS. They're going to attempt to calm down the AIM bunkers. But I have told them to defend themselves anyway.

Red Arrow to RB-4: That's 10-4. Try and hold it off a little bit longer, but I'm not telling you to stop entirely — defend yourselves.

RB-4 to Red Arrow: Bruno is out in front of us here. If we have to return fire, he's going to foul us up.

Red Arrow to Greywolf: Don't take any chances. Defend yourself. That's up to your judgement as per Headquarters 2. Squad leader's judgement.

Wounded Knee to Red Arrow: We're trying to find out if there's a third party on your RB-6 on the hill above our Pine Ridge Roadblock that's firing upon us. We're taking automatic weapons fire from up there.

Red Arrow to Wounded Knee: Stand by.

Inside the Security building: a map showing Wounded Knee and Government bunkers hangs above the radio headquarters.

Red Arrow to Command Post: Be advised RB-5 reports receiving fire from pin-point location. They are now receiving fire — they are trying to pin-point location. RB-6 is still under fire. RB-4 is under continuous fire. Bruno is receiving fire.

Red Arrow to Alligator: RB-3 is really laying it into that bunker [Denby] — see if you can help him.

> **Denby to Lozen:** We're being fired upon tremendously. Can you get us any back-up help? Over.

> **Lozen to Denby:** Keep your head down and hold on. Don't waste any ammo . . . they would like to drive you out of that bunker — it is an important position.

Throughout the night the marshals never moved to arrest or apprehend the vigilantes. Red Arrow falsified radio reports to their headquarters in Pine Ridge, never mentioning being fired upon by a third party or by vigilantes, only by Wounded Knee. Although Red Arrow may have communicated the vigilantes' attacks by land telephone or courier, they avoided stating it over the radio, which was being taped and logged at Headquarters. Wounded Knee Security speculated that it would have been politically dangerous for the marshals to keep a public record of their de facto approval of the vigilantes' illegal operations.

Finally Red Arrow admitted in conversation with Wounded Knee that a "third party" was firing on the marshals and on Wounded Knee, but they continued to pour heavy fire into the village.

Red Arrow to Wounded Knee: Be advised our RB-6 held fire for three or four minutes and they are still receiving fire from the bunker in front of them.

> **Wounded Knee to Red Arrow:** Our people report taking almost continuous automatic weapons fire from that hill over by RB-6.

Red Arrow to Wounded Knee: 10-4. A couple of our RBs have reported firing and they don't know who is over in those positions. They report that it is being fired into Wounded Knee.

> **Wounded Knee to Red Arrow:** Roger. You think you're pretty sure we got a third party out there firing on us with automatic weapons?

Red Arrow to Wounded Knee: That's what it sounds like.

> **Wounded Knee to Red Arrow:** Okay — somebody is going to have to get those guys.

Red Arrow to Wounded Knee: 10-4.

> **Wounded Knee to Red Arrow:** Can you help us on the location where that third-party fire is coming from?

Red Arrow to Wounded Knee: One that we definitely know is to the left front of RB-2, over in the wooded area. He's north of the farmhouse a little bit south of the yellow house.

> **Wounded Knee to Red Arrow:** Roger, we've observed some drunken people in that farmhouse earlier tonight, so we know somebody is down there.

Red Arrow to RB-4: You still receiving fire from that bunker in front of RB-3? Have you tried using that M-79? Use caution — that wind is blowing right across to Greywolf.

It became clear that the marshals were using the vigilantes' attacks as an excuse to pour fire on Wounded Knee, which received an estimated 20,000 rounds that night. Because of the intensity of the fire, Security felt that the marshals might attempt to take over the village, and bunker squads kept shooting back to keep Federal forces from moving in.

Hawk Eye to Lozen: Tell somebody to knock out that spotlight. They're zeroing in on us with a .50 caliber and we can't even get up. The spotlight is right on our shit. Over.

Lozen to Hawk Eye: We want you to hold your fire out there. We're trying to get a cease-fire going here. Don't fire unless you got a definite body within your perimeter. If you can get a bead on that guy down the hill there trying to zap you — zap him. Over.

Hawk Eye: What do you mean by the bead on the guy down the hill? Whereabouts is he? Over.

Lozen: I thought you had somebody down the hill trying to zero in on you while that spotlight was on you. If there is nobody there, hold your fire.

Hawk Eye: It's not them — it's the APC. Over.

Lozen: Roger — he's too far away anyway. You can't penetrate him, so save your ammo.

Hawk Eye: He's not that far away. He's down inside the perimeter. Over.

Lozen: Can you tell me how far down the hill he is?

Hawk Eye: Three-quarters.

Lozen: Okay. Just keep an eye on him to make sure he don't come in on you.

Hawk Eye: That I will do, believe me!

Midnight to 1 a.m. — More fire

In her journal, Barbara made the following entry describing the events which took place between midnight and 1 a.m. on Friday, April 27:

Spent most of the time in Security listening to the radio — heard the feds calling for more ammo. They used a lot of gas on Little Big Horn — gassed them out and they escaped into the trench they dug this morning — just in time. Feds are really out for those guys — it's the closest bunker to them. Little Big Horn's yelling up to RB-4 that they better surrender cause they're going to get it, like Custer, and RB-4 yells back all kinds of racist things.

Feds' radio said the AK-47 was in the church firing tracers — they're really seeing things — we don't have any tracers for any guns! It was *their* tracers, coming across from their RB-6 on the opposite hill, aimed too high. They keep trying to pin down the AK — so uptight that anyone else might have an automatic weapon, when they have bunkers full of them.

All night they've been calling cease-fires — but you can tell they don't mean it by their tone on the radio — it's always "if you can" or "but defend yourself." They don't even notify us that they've called it, and then a few minutes later they start up again. When their superiors read the recordings in their logs, it will look like we were doing the attacking.

Shortly after midnight the vigilantes again opened fire on Wounded Knee and the Government forces, in an effort to keep them firing at each other.

Denby to Lozen: Lozen! Lozen! This is Denby. Somebody's starting to shoot at us heavy again. Over.

Lozen to Denby: Okay. They probably got M-79s and light artillery up there, but be advised there are goons all down in that area too with M-16s. They're down in that area somewhere along the creek. We figure they are down in that farmhouse or in that bunker on that hill away from you there. But be careful — when it starts the feds think it's you firing on them.

Denby to Lozen: Roger. I read you loud and clear.

RB-4 to Red Arrow: I got that M-79 zeroed in down there [on Little Big Horn bunker].

Denby bunker reported taking rounds from snipers.

Lozen to Denby: Give me a distance and direction on those snipers.

Denby to Lozen: I figure they are at least 150 to 200 yards down. Ah, I think one is down around the creek area to our side. And another is on the ridge between the two APCs.

Lozen: Okay — that guy down in the creek: was it one of our people firing?

Denby: I doubt it. The shots are coming in over our heads and they are coming in pretty accurate. Over.

Lozen: Okay — if you can get a bead on him, you better wipe him out.

Denby: Roger. Will do.

On the eastern perimeter, the aggressive Government bunkers RB-4 and Bruno were trying to get close enough to capture Little Big Horn, the Wounded Knee bunker most isolated from the downtown area. The winding creek and darkness provided excellent cover for both sides to maneuver. Meanwhile, RB-6 on the western perimeter wanted RB-4 to light up Star bunker for them from the back:

Red Arrow to RB-4: Have you tried your 79 down there? Is that wind blowing the wrong way? . . . You can't get it to the other side of them so it will cover them first? . . . RB-6 wants you to put that light on the bunker in front of them on Big Foot Trail.

RB-4 to Red Arrow: We can't keep anybody out there on that light. [A man has to expose himself to operate the light which is mounted on their APC.] We're taking rounds directly. They haven't hit the light yet, but they're hitting short.

Red Arrow to RB-4: That's 10-4. Shut it down. Shut it down.

Bruno to RB-4: We're getting it from the creek bed, direct to the right of the bridge. Put that light down on the creek bed by the bridge . . . a little more to the right, 4.

RB-4 to Bruno: We can't be around it all day!

Bruno One to RB-4: Just a hair to the right. You're good there — he's right by the telephone pole.

Bruno to RB-4: We got smoke down there. Looks like we got 'em running. Get some more gas grenades and put 'em in that creek bed.

Last Stand to Lozen [in between music that is jamming the radio]: We need some more men and ammo out here. Can you send some men out?

Lozen: I wish I could accomodate you. Over.

Bruno One, Bruno's squad leader, was on foot patrol in the DMZ with a SOG squad coordinating fire from Bruno and RB-4. He had moved in close enough to the village for Wounded Knee Security to clearly monitor his small pocket radio as he continued to direct fire on Little Big Horn.

Red Arrow to Command Post: Greywolf, Alligator, Bruno, and RB-4 are all still receiving fire. Cheetah is also receiving fire, sporadic. RB-3 is now taking fire. Confirmed fire tonight started at 2205 on RB-6 and Alligator.

Bruno One to Bruno: Can you help us with some flares in the creek?

Bruno: We don't need any flares — you're lighting us up like a Christmas tree.

Bruno One [urgently]: That was a while ago. I couldn't help it. Give me a flare in that creek bed.

Bruno: I don't think we can reach it. It ain't going to do you any good.

Bruno One [in a commanding voice]: I said get a flare in that creek bed. Everytime one of those goes out, put another one down there so we can see . . . Did you see where that flare hit?

Bruno: 10-4. Right down there behind the white car.

Bruno One: 10-4. I see it smoking. . . Give us another flare.

Bruno: It looked good. It should be right behind the house in the creek bed.

Bruno One: You're right on, Don.

Bruno: 10-4. We thought we heard a round come out of that creek bed.

RB-4: I saw a flash, but I couldn't tell.

Bruno: 10-4. I got another one on the way. Watch it.
. . .

Bruno One to Red Arrow: From my location, it looks like they're firing tracers out of the steeple of the big church.

Red Arrow: 10-4. Do we have anyone who can zero in on the the steeple of the big church?

Red Arrow to Command Post: We need some .300 magnum ammo. [Ammunition for the high-powered rifles that the SOG snipers used.]

To the north, vigilantes and marshals were engaged in a firefight:

Hawk Eye to Lozen: Be advised that there is a force that is attacking the Government from behind. The bunker straight in front of us may have been knocked out. How are you copying me? Over.

Lozen: Not too well. We're being jammed. Over.

Hawk Eye: It is Cheetah. [U.S. bunker] They are being fired on with automatic weapons from behind. Cheetah turned and fired back on them and now they haven't fired for more than five minutes. Over.

Lozen: 10-4. Be advised we can't always copy what is going on out there. The same with you, Denby.

The Government again called one of their routine cease-fires, waited a couple of minutes without notifying Wounded Knee, and then resumed the firing.

Red Arrow to Command Post: Be advised the RBs attempted a cease-fire and they are still taking fire from the bunkers in front of them.

Bruno to Red Arrow: We just took two right over our head.

Bruno One to RB-4: Can you get a 79 [gas grenade] down there? A round just popped out of that bunker.

Red Arrow to Greywolf: What kind of view do you have of the trading post? . . . See if you can copy muzzle flashes down there and check the target.

Greywolf to Red Arrow: I'll do my best.

Red Arrow to Greywolf: Can you zero in down there? Anybody zero in there? That AK's firing full automatic.

Bruno One to Red Arrow: That's out of the big church. It's dark now. I just saw a bunch of tracers come out of there. Sounds just like that AK.

Red Arrow to all RBs: That's out of that big church, RBs. That's out of the big church.

RB-3 to RB-4: Light it up for us, 4.

RB-4: We're taking fire on our light right now.

The music jamming the radio stopped for a minute and Security made a radio check of some of the Wounded Knee bunkers coming under the heaviest attack:

Lozen to Denby Bunker: We hear a lot of rounds coming that way. What's the situation?

Denby: At least we're making it. We're all right.

Lozen to Star Bunker: What's your situation down there? A lot of rounds are coming your way.

Star: We're okay.

Headquarter 18 to Red Arrow: Would you ask for a cease-fire and let's see what we get.

Red Arrow: Red Arrow to all RBs. Red Arrow to all RBs. Let's try a cease-fire again. Repeat: let's try a cease-fire again.

RB-4 to Red Arrow: We're taking fire from out of that bunker in front of RB-3. And we're taking fire from in front of the church.

Headquarters 18: Yeah, I'm hearing. Return the fire.

Star to Lozen: Are there any casualties yet? We're holding here. It's a lot of fun watching the tracers go by. Over.

At this point, Headquarters 18 (the field commander) told the Command Post to bring Headquarters 2 up to date. Headquarters 2 was not at the Command Post or in his room in Gordon, Nebraska, during this, the most intense firefight to date:

Red Arrow to Command Post: Contact Headquarters 2 at the Hacienda Motel, Room 31. Advise him of the situation — tell him we have repeatedly attempted to effect a cease-fire.
. . .

Red Arrow to Command Post: Will you make another attempt to locate Headquarters 2?
. . .

Red Arrow to Headquarters 18: Do you have any other place you can contact Headquarters 2?

Headquarters 18: Negative. Tell them to keep trying about every half-hour. Advise him there is no need to come out here. Just advise him of the situation.
. . .

After some minutes, Red Arrow came back with a firm order from Headquarters 1 for the marshals to get back in their bunkers and not commit offensive movements. Headquarters 18, who had expected a more hard-line response from Headquarters 2, questioned the source of the cease-fire order. This incident revealed that the Justice Department command was split on how to handle the firefights. Field personnel would thus try to contact the superior officer who would give the decision they wanted to hear.

Red Arrow to all RBs: Message from Headquarters 1. You are

Cleaning weapons in Security.

to dig in, protect your positions, and cease-fire. Repeat: you are to dig in, protect your positions, and cease-fire.

Alligator [RB-2] to Red Arrow: 10-4.

RB-3: 10-4.

RB-4: 10-4.

Bruno: 10-4.

Cheetah: 10-4.

Dagger: 10-4.

RB-5: 10-4.

Eagle: 10-4.

Foxhound: 10-4.

Greywolf [RB-6]: 10-4.

Headquarters 18 to Red Arrow: Could you check with command post and see if they called Headquarters 1 or Headquarters 2?

Red Arrow to Headquarters 18: Stand by . . . They called Headquarters 2 and Headquarters 1 called back with the order to cease fire.

RB-4 to Red Arrow: We've ceased fire and already we're taking rounds from right in front of us.

Red Arrow to RB-4: That's 10-4. You are to cease fire!

In her journal, Barbara described the cease-fire that held from 1 a.m. to 8 the next morning:

    . . . 1:30 a.m.: The fire was very heavy last night, and more accurate than before. The bunkers really got it. I think they would have come in if we hadn't been firing back. Little Big Horn spotted some armed men sneaking up the hill from the creek and drove them back. The Government's been telling the press that only a few people are left and maybe they believed it themselves.

    Finally ended around 1 this morning. This time they meant it — you could tell by the firm way they said, "cease fire!" But everyone expects that it will start again in the morning.

    . . . 4 a.m.: Just got back from the white church kitchen. Went down there when the firing stopped to get some chow for me and the women running the radio. They had taken a lot of hits down there. Everyone has moved out of the round church too because it is so vulnerable.

    When I got back here five people had just arrived who'd trucked in. They brought guns and lots of ammo, which is always needed. Said they watched the firefight from behind the lines, but didn't fire because they couldn't figure out what was going on out there. They spent a few hours circling the area trying to find a way in. Then came the cease-fire, and they walked up to the church on the hill, knocked, and asked if this was Wounded Knee! They say there's a lot of food stockpiled in Porcupine, if we can just get it together to pack it in.

. . . 8:30 a.m. — A lot of rounds were taken by buildings in the village, but few went through. The walls people built around the clinic and white house a few days ago were just in time!

The tension has kept a lot of us up all night. So I went to hang out laundry out on the line. Stopped down by the kitchen — there was only one woman there with a huge stack of dishes from breakfast, so I stayed to help her out. By this time the exhaustion had really hit me. Figured I could sleep at 8 a.m., and headed back for Security. Stopped at the outhouse on the way and when I was in there the firing started up heavy. Knew I didn't want to get stuck in there, so I ran back through the gunfire, knowing the pigs could see me through their scopes but I couldn't see them — that felt weird!

The AK-47 — the only automatic weapon the Wounded Knee defense forces had.

The John Birch Society circulated photos of this gun as "proof" the AIM was "Communist-backed."

Actually, the weapon was brought home from Viet Nam by a U.S. veteran.

8:30 a.m. — Firing resumes

All during the early morning the Government radio had been full of cryptic messages between their bunkers and talk of a new plan. Nearby, they had an army tank and several helicopters, poised, it seemed, to move into the village.

The following radio transmissions were recorded on the morning of April 27; the marshals at RB-4 suddenly started firing gas grenades into Little Big Horn bunker. Wounded Knee's ammunition supply was nearly exhausted and radio communications were failing due to the constant drain on radio batteries during the night. The sound of rapid-fire weapons from the hills alerted the village and everyone braced for the expected assault. (Security headquarters, called "Lozen" in the previous day's communications, was renamed "Clearwater" to honor the slain warrior.)

Bruno to Red Arrow: We're receiving direct hits.

Red Arrow to Bruno: That's 10-4, Bruno.

Red Arrow to RB-4: Try and use that 79 gas and flush 'em out of that bunker and you'll have good targets.

> **Clearwater to Little California:** Okay — you're coming in all broken up so repeat your transmission twice and tell me if there is anything going on in your area.
>
> **Little California to Clearwater:** The Feds are shooting back and forth in front of us, over.
>
> ***Warriors in Security building:*** *Where's their position over there?*
>
> *I think they're shooting from over on Strawberry Hill. They're heavier than fuck over there, and they're using that helicopter to fire on the guys in Star.*
>
> *Now they're firing gas from the helicopter, too.*
>
> *They got gas on 'em down at Little Big Horn?*
>
> *The wind's blowing pretty strong. It ain't gonna hold. That gas will go on out. The winds are blowing too heavy for it.*

Bruno to RB-4: You're about 30 yards short.

RB-4: 10-4. I'll try and elevate a little.

> *See that red flag down there? There's the gas again down in the creek. Hey — they're getting that right in there. See that yellow truck up on the hill, up there to the right of their bunker? I saw a guy run out there when they gave them permission to fire. That's him right in front of the truck.*
>
> *They're hitting closer to my window.*
>
> *Some rounds just went down the street.*
>
> *Listen to those meadowlarks sing. Don't stand near that window!*
>
> *This is what you call pushing your odds to the limit, standing in the middle of an open doorway during a gunfight. For people who like to live dangerously, this is the place!*

RB-4 to Red Arrow: That 79 just hasn't got enough oomph to 'em here.

Red Arrow to Supply: Send out that .50 caliber.

Although the Government bunkers reported taking continuous fire from Little Big Horn, there were only two warriors, a man and a woman, in the bunker that morning. The main crew had gone to Security for a briefing while things were quiet, and were unable to return through the heavy firing. RB-4 was finally able to get some gas into Little Big Horn, forcing the two people outside, where the man was hit in both legs. His wife helped him back into the bunker and called Security. They in in turn arranged for a ten minute cease-fire with Red Arrow, after some delay, to allow a medic out to the bunker. While the unarmed woman medic walked along the road, the marshals at RB-4 opened up on her and she had to take cover in a ditch.

0900 hours . . .

Red Arrow to Command Post: Wounded Knee advises they have a wounded party in the bunker in front of RB-4. Stated that they were going to send medics in. The man that went to that bunker was carrying a rifle. We will not recognize a medic carrying a rifle.

> **Wounded Knee to Red Arrow:** Red Arrow, this is Wounded Knee. Red Arrow, this is Wounded Knee . . .

Fifteen minutes pass. Red Arrow didn't answer. Finally . . .

Red Arrow to Wounded Knee: Go ahead, Wounded Knee.

> **Wounded Knee:** Be advised that our medic that's going down to that bunker has a helmet on. And we have people all over the place that are trying to move around there and so it would be normal that there would be guys moving around out there with rifles — but the medic you can clearly spot. She has a helmet on with a big cross on it.

Red Arrow to RB-4: Supply's here with all the equipment.

Bruno to Red Arrow: We need some M-16 ammo down here at Bruno.

Red Arrow to Bruno: 10-4. We'll get it down to you.

Bruno: Just hold the .50 caliber up there, and if we start taking more fire, we'll have to use it.

Red Arrow: That's 10-4.

Fifteen minutes pass.

> **Clearwater to Little Big Horn:** Can you tell me if the medic has made it down there to you yet?

> **Little Big Horn:** This is Little Big Horn. The medic hasn't come down here yet!

On the radio in Hawk Eye bunker.

Clearwater: Okay — we saw her come under some gunfire coming down there. So hold on — she will be there shortly.

Several warriors tried to reach the medic, not knowing if she had been hit since she could not be seen in the ditch. They, too, were pinned down before they could reach her.

1015 hours . . .

Little California to Clearwater: They're firing gas to the south of us down here. Over.

Three hours after the warrior had been hit a new radio operator was on duty at Red Arrow and Wounded Knee was finally able to get a response:

Headquarters 2 to Red Arrow: All right — tell them they got ten minutes. One person with a white flag, and no weapons. If they got weapons, we're going to open fire. And if their people open fire during this time — this ten minutes — we're going to return fire and it will be their own responsibility. Ten minutes, starting right now.

Waiting for a lull, medics and warriors take shelter behind a building.

Red Arrow [speaking sharply] to Wounded Knee: Be advised that you have ten minutes with one person with a white flag to move that person out of that area. If there are any weapons or any firing from that area we will fire upon them. Over.

  Wounded Knee to Red Arrow: I'm telling our people here.

  Clearwater: Little Big Horn! Little Big Horn and Denby, and Little California — hold your fire! Last Stand also, hold your fire! We got a man under a white flag that's going down to see if the medic has been hit. Do not open your fire. We have ten minutes with one man with a white flag. If anyone opens fire, this man is dead. So hold your fire!

Red Arrow: Cease fire! Cease fire! Acknowledge, over.

A warrior walked with a white flag to find the medic, who had not been injured. The marshals watched as they walked back to Security.

Bruno to RB-4: That looked like some broad to me.

RB-4 to Bruno: That *is* a broad, I think.

Bruno to RB-4: Right — we're thinking it is, too.

1230 hours . . .

The man injured at Little Big Horn did not get medical aid, as the marshals were now insisting that the medic return directly to the clinic. As soon as she returned to the downtown area they opened fire on Little Big Horn again.

During the lull, a warrior had come in from Last Stand bunker. He brought word that Buddy Lamont had been killed early that morning. He had been hit from behind by a sniper and died instantly. Security notified the Government that Wounded Knee wanted to bring its dead warrior down into the village. At this point the Government agreed to a cease-fire. Gradually the shooting died down, and Buddy's body was brought to the clinic. It was only now, too, that the man injured so many hours before could be brought in by the medics.

Barbara's journal described how she and some others spent the day:

    . . . We all laid on the floor of the white church kitchen from 8:30 a.m. till around 4 in the afternoon. We took a lot of rounds there when the pigs overshot Denby bunker, and some came through the walls. One even went in one wall, across the room, and out the other side. A woman was grazed in the hand. The strongest feeling I have is helplessness,

even though we laugh a lot. With the weakness of the military position we're in, all we can do is lie here. Even the people in the bunkers can hardly move — if they lift their heads, they get zeroed in on.

In the afternoon we heard that Lou Beane's brother, Buddy Lamont, got shot through the heart right outside his bunker. Lou was in the white church with us and everyone felt so awful. Finally, someone came in to tell us there was a 15-minute cease-fire to allow them to bring Buddy's body into the clinic. The firing never did start up again. We all went down there to pay last respects to Buddy. Talking to Lou and other relatives — she said, "If an Oglala had to be killed for things to get fixed up, that's the way it had to be." Everyone mourning, expecially the local people. He was from Pine Ridge and much respected.

And then right after the cease-fire CRS came in — with Frizzell's message that he has agreed to negotiate and approved our agenda. It looks like he was just waiting until someone else got killed so that he could come to us when people are down. We gave him the agenda five days ago . . . Some of the warriors are really angry over Buddy's death, were talking about hitting the Government tonight, but I don't think they will do anything because most of the Oglalas are against it. They had planned to wait to negotiate until Clearwater's mourning period was over, but now people are thinking that if this goes on longer, more people will be killed.

Outside Last Stand bunker on Manderson Road.

22

Preliminary meetings between the United States and the Independent Oglala Nation began the day following the firefight. Dennis Banks and Leonard Crow Dog met with Kent Frizzell in the demilitarized zone to discuss the burials of Clearwater and Lamont, and to arrange for negotiations.

Dick Wilson was still refusing Clearwater's burial on the reservation, on the grounds that he was not Oglala, and Frizzell said he would "leave this matter up to the Indian people." People were highly incensed at both the Tribal and Federal Governments' attempts to use the deaths as a bargaining point. One Oglala woman retorted: "I guess we'll have to dig up all them white ranchers then."

Frizzell told Dennis and Crow Dog what he had told the chiefs a few days earlier in Kyle – "time is running short." He said, "My immediate impression, without even coming down to Wounded Knee, right there in the BIA building between the marshals and the FBI, right there, there's bad feeling. Between the Government and the Wilson people there's bad feeling. Tensions are higher than I've ever seen them." Frizzell implied that all the tensions were pushing him into a tougher negotiating position. He informed the ION negotiators, "All I'm saying – I don't mean this in any way as pressure or threat, but as a practical thing – I'm finding in my phone calls back to Washington that the hardliners are gaining the attention of the authorities. I am almost alone now in saying, 'No, it's not down to the hard options, it's still possible.' "

Dennis reminded Frizzell, "It seems to me you've taken a hard line already – with all the deaths." "Well, yes, I can see that you can interpret it that way," Frizzell responded.

Frizzell also told Dennis, in response to the Oglalas' preconditions for a resumption of formal negotiations, that he did not consider restoration of phone service or attorneys' access "essential." Such "outside influence" had been, in his opinion, "partly responsible for what happened to our April 5th agreement."

On April 29, Barbara wrote this in her journal:

Life here has returned to "normal." Thursday's and Friday's long firefight now seems like a spring storm that's passed over, leaving things very calm, but with a new seriousness after Buddy's death. Food's very short – most of the cooking is done outside now. The electricity was shot out during the firefight, so no lights and no running water. We're using kerosene lamps and hauling water from the old windmill. Not too different from life in the districts here.

Bonfire outside tonight – always brings spirits up.

April 30: The trading post burned down last night. A kerosene lamp caught some curtains, and by the time anyone noticed it, it was burning too fast to stop, especially in the wind. We lost everything in there, even a bunch a ammo which exploded in the blaze. We had about 15 buckets going from the windmill, and managed to save Security by chopping down a wall. It was raining and cold and muddy – an exhausting night!

Frizzell had met with the traditional Oglala leadership in Kyle on April 25, 26, 27, and 29. He had attempted to impress them with his "good faith" on the one hand, and on the other hand, with the imminence of a military assault on Wounded Knee. Finally, on April 30, he allowed them to come into the village.

The chiefs met with the community and affirmed that the negotiations which were to begin the next day would center on the 1868 Treaty. They said that Frizzell had warned them of the danger of more deaths at Wounded Knee if a settlement was not agreed to soon. Frizzell had suggested that Buddy Lamont be buried on Crow Dog's land on the Rosebud Reservation and then reburied by Big Foot's grave, after a disarmament. "If the body goes into Wounded Knee, as things stand now," he told them, "I will predict much more bloodshed and many more bodies to bury, and the chances of negotiating a settlement of Wounded Knee will probably be out the window."

The chiefs also brought news from Pine Ridge. Buddy's death had caused great anger on the reservation. People were blaming Wilson for it, and it was even splitting the Tribal Government's camp, since some of his large family worked in the BIA bureaucracy. Many people were planning to come to Wounded Knee en masse for his funeral. ■

Buddy Lamont (in center) escorting Government negotiator Harlington Wood into Wounded Knee on March 15.

11. THE LAST WEEK

"We have created a problem that the U.S. can't hide. It's like a big black cloud over them. Everybody sees this cloud. So what they're going to try to do is pacify us with words and papers. The whole world is looking at Wounded Knee, not just Indian people. The Government has to save political face. They're more desperate than we are."

— Lance Yellow Hand

NEGOTIATIONS AGAIN . . .

Negotiations finally got under way in Wounded Knee on May 1. These talks were more low key than those in early April, with many in the village skeptical now as to what might be gained, given the Government's demonstrated bad faith. The meetings were held in two school buses in the demilitarized zone, a more difficult setting for serious discussion than the circular tipi, where everyone could face each other. There were separate "military" and "political" discussions, one in each bus.

In the military talks, Dennis Banks and four members of the Wounded Knee Security force met with the Director of the U.S. Marshals, Wayne Colburn, Assistant Attorney General Richard Hellstern, and Marshal Hall. There the AIM Security representatives reiterated that disarmament was a purely tactical matter and could be handled easily, if and when a political settlement satisfactory to the Oglalas was reached.

In the political talks, Leonard Crow Dog, Gladys Bissonette, Vernona Crow Dog, and five other Oglalas met with Assistant Attorney General Kent Frizzell, FBI agent Noel Castleman, and an attorney from the Justice Department's Civil Rights Division, Dennis Ickes. The Oglalas asked that the traditional chiefs and their lawyers be allowed into Wounded Knee for negotiations. They proposed a meeting to take place within a few days between the Independent Oglala Nation and the chiefs on the one side, and White House officials on the other, at which the later May treaty meetings would be arranged and an agenda for them set. The Oglalas stated that they were willing to let this proposed planning session stand as the sole guarantee for the later May meetings, similar to the earlier attempt to secure a guarantee of Federal good faith when their representatives had travelled to Washington, following the signing of the April 5th agreement.

But Frizzell was adamant in insisting that no meeting could take place before a disarmament. He asserted that once the people had given up their weapons and submitted to arrest, the Government would be more than willing to listen to the "grievances." As in previous negotiations, the Government's goal was to end the confrontation before anything else, promising to settle the issues later when they would be in a position of power and the ION would be in no position from which to bargain.

Further, Frizzell threatened that if a disarmament was not arranged soon, more drastic measures would be taken. He told the Oglala negotiators, "I can't keep all the hotheads held off that long. I'm not talking about your side – I'm talking about my side. I'm talking about people on the outside who say, 'Sixty days is too long for them to hold the Government at bay!'" It was not clear whether Frizzell was referring to any specific

new plan on the part of the Government, or if they thought they had to do something before May 4, when the vigilantes had threatened to attack the village. Regardless of where the threat originated, Frizzell used it whenever he could, to try to convince the traditional chiefs, the lawyers, and the Lamont family, all of whom he was meeting with on the outside, as well as those in Wounded Knee, that they should settle for promises now and action later.

To attempt to prove the Government's good faith, Frizzell brought Dennis Ickes to the negotiations to describe the progress of Federal investigation of civil rights complaints. The Oglalas were concerned that some action be taken against Wilson that would protect them when they left Wounded Knee. They questioned Frizzell about the 150 unanswered complaints filed against the Tribal Chairman before the occupation even began, and the many complaints the FBI and Ickes had processed since then.

Frizzell: Now, I'd like for Dennis Ickes to bring you up to date on what's going to happen on some of these civil rights complaints.

Ickes: . . . We have had 42 complaints. Out of those 42 complaints, we have 30 of those which have turned out to have no prosecutive merit. 11 of those 30, we went to the homes of the people who were the alleged victims, people who someone would tell us that, "So and so was beat up in Manderson the other night," or "So and so was raped," or whatever. We went to those victims. We asked them if the events alleged had occurred. And 11 of these people said, "None of the things alleged ever happened to me. I have no complaints to make." I don't know whether those people are afraid to tell us the truth, or whether in fact nothing happened, but as to 11 of those 30 there was no complaint to be made, and if there's no complaint to be made, there's nothing that we can do to prosecute.

Frizzell: We've got to have a complainant and facts and evidence to present to the court.

Ickes: So, out of those 30, 11 had no complaint. The remaining 19, we investigated thoroughly, and in our opinion as lawyers who prosecute these cases, they have no prosecutive merit.

Frizzell: Tell them what you mean by that. You can't win the case?

Ickes: Right, that's what it means. We feel if we took the case before a Grand Jury, either the Grand Jury would not indict the person, or, even if we got an indictment against the person, then we could not succeed in a court of law to find that person guilty of the crime charged and to fine him and imprison him for the crime.

Looking through a bunker port towards Star, the ION roadblock on the Big Foot Trail.

Frizzell: Now, tell us some good news. You've told us about 30. You got anything else?

Ickes: Okay, that's the bad news. Now the good news, if people want to construe it this way. We believe we have two separate instances, two cases that look very good against members of the goon squad. I cannot say what their names are for obvious reasons, but we do have what I think are two real strong cases.

Frizzell: That you're going to take to the Grand Jury —

Ickes: Well, I can't commit the Government —

Frizzell: But you're going to recommend it.

Ickes: There are three others that look very strong but have further investigation to be completed on them.

Frizzell: They look good at this stage —

Ickes: At this stage, they look like they're going to go all the way. But I reserve judgement on them until the investigations are complete. So we have a possibility of five cases. That leaves 7 cases in a position where I can't make any comment be-cause they're just getting under way . . . I can assure you that we're putting forth our best efforts — we have six agents whose sole duty is to work on civil rights complaints — we have insisted, and they are commanded, not to take part in any of this other activity that occurs on this reservation. Their only job is to investigate civil rights complaints. So that sort of brings you up to date with regard to the investigations.

Castleman: As part of the FBI, I'd like to say that we will go anywhere, at any time, under any circumstances to receive a legitimate complaint. We will give you fair and impartial investigation. But we have had a continuing problem in getting people to come forward. We can't give our casework to Mr. Ickes until it is complete. We cannot complete it until we get complete signed and thorough statements that support the charge. That's the one area that we need help in more than anything else. The time for fear is through.

. . .

Gladys: Take a full view of this place. For how many hundred years have they kept us like this? Starving us to death!

Frizzell: Well, what is it that you want out of here so we can all go about our business and do a better job than we've done in the past? I understand —

Gladys: — Reform the whole government.

Frizzell: Well, you can't do that overnight, and we can't allow the confrontation to go on until the whole government is reformed. I know, in my own hometown, we get good and bad politicians. What you have to do is work to get rid of them. But you can't go down and surround city hall with guns and hope to get it done. Because those in city hall control the police guns, and you're going to be met with resistance every time.

Gladys: Well, we have wrote letters, we have sent phone calls — I know, I did myself. We have made statements to our Congressmen. We asked, we begged, that Pine Ridge be investigated. It never was done.

Frizzell: I'm willing to commit, here and now, and in writing, in an agreement to end the confrontation at Wounded Knee, that we'll have a Congressional investigation. We'll have an audit of the Tribal funds.

Gladys: That story's old, "We'll have, we will."

Frizzell: I'm willing to put it down in writing. And the civil rights attorneys will stay here as long as you have any complaints. The FBI will stay here. We'll protect you on this reservation after the guns are laid down.

Vernona Crow Dog: I think that if you want to end this confrontation you would try your best to get these men [White House representatives] out here . . . You'll get the men here if you really want to.

Frizzell: Well, Matthew King indicated to me that you want the Government to have eight treaty commissioners to meet with the headmen and chiefs from the eight reservations. But I don't know — with everything that's going on at the White House, resignations and everything, I don't know if I could get eight people out here. Do you all know what's been going on at the White House the last day or two? Attorney General Kleindienst resigned, and will be replaced by Elliot Richardson, who is now Secretary of Defense. Mr. Erlichman and Mr. Haldeman resigned, on the immediate staff of the President. And John Dean, the attorney or special counsel to the President, resigned. So really I don't know if they can scare up eight bodies around the White House to come out here. Mr. Kissinger has got so many problems over in Viet Nam with that treaty that was signed, that *he* can't possibly come here.

Things are happening so fast back there I can't tell you who they would send or how many.

Gladys: Now if they told the truth and dealt with these things the right way, all this world wouldn't be in this mess it's in. We just can't seem to get through to nobody. Just by sitting here — how long have we sat here? and we wind up with nothing. All we're asking is for our '68 Treaty. Or is the Government afraid that we might sue? No, they wouldn't let us sue because we can't even sign a complaint on Dick Wilson. They'll hold us down one way or another.

Frizzell: You can too sign a complaint on Dick Wilson. I'll take any you've got, right now.

Gladys: Oh, I've heard that story before. . . Intimidation — that is why you cannot get a lot of witnesses. You get denials from people because you still got the goon squad traveling around with their guns. And let anyone say something, they'll get their head caved in. My daughter probably said something. That's why they beat her up. Or maybe they beat her up because I'm in here.

Frizzell: All of these fears that you have, aren't going to be resolved as long as you have the confrontation here at Wounded Knee. Wilson's goons are still roaming, like you said, because all of our Federal troops are down here. If we can end this, *we* will have the guns available to protect you. We'll

keep a residual force of FBI and marshals. We'll set up a police station right down in Wounded Knee. But we can't do it as long as you're down there and all of our officers are engaged in a war-like action. . . I'm willing to give you a meeting in Washington, here, wherever you want it, with representatives of the White House to discuss any and all matters on an agenda regarding the 1868 Treaty . . . but I can't do that as long as the arms are in Wounded Knee.

Gladys: — and as long as we got a Washington.

Frizzell: No — Washington agrees with me on this. The Secretary of Interior, I've talked with him, he agrees with me. The Attorney General of the United States agrees with me, the White House agrees with me, but they're all of one mind: "This thing cannot go on indefinitely. You've got one more chance, Frizzell, and if you don't get it across, then the hard decisions are going to be made." *I don't know how to tell you any plainer.* I don't want that hard decision to be made.

Gladys: Well, why don't they send one of their top men then to us —

Frizzell: Because —

Gladys: — instead of sending just middle men like you that tell us something over and over and over. We are tired. We don't care if we die here . . . We can't even turn in our complaints. We turn in our petitions — there's nothing done. They bring up another tricky —

Frizzell: *You* just heard his report, Gladys. There's going to be something done on some of those complaints you turned in, that are *valid* complaints. You can't do anything about *invalid* complaints —

Gladys: Dick Wilson sits up there and he gives orders, and the *whole Government* listens to him. The Indians, we *never* get listened to.

Frizzell: Does he have his roadblock up there?

Gladys: No, it's down, but he's still in there! And the goons are peeking over — you watch.

Frizzell: And that's a better bargain for the Government — to have two unarmed observers of his, than to have him down there with 15 men running around with rifles. *Sometimes you've got to compromise and you people have got to learn that! Now I'm willing to compromise with you, to avoid bloodshed. But you've got to meet me half-way!*

Gladys: You've got to meet us half-way, too.

Frizzell: *I'm trying to tell you — where is that half-way? You tell me! How can I guarantee you that meeting?*

Gladys: You guaranteed *a lot of things* to us before —

Frizzell: How can —

Gladys: — and you haven't done it.

Frizzell: What haven't I done that I guaranteed?

Gladys: That agreement, for instance.

Frizzell: It doesn't do *any* good to tell you —

Gladys: You got them into Washington, D.C., on their own expense.

Frizzell: I never promised that we'd pay their way —

Gladys: I know, but they went on their own expense.

Frizzell: That's right.

Gladys: Now Dick Wilson, you'll having him flying —

Frizzell: Not on my —

Gladys: Money all over —

Frizzell: No —

Gladys: The Federal Government will.

Frizzell: Well, that's because he happens to be in charge of the Tribal Government.

Gladys: Oh, boy, and see what he got us into. You and I wouldn't be sitting here quarrelling if they listened to our petitions and stuff. The Government is *using* him.

Frizzell: We're trying to do something about these things, Gladys. And in due time we *will,* but it's *not* in time to end the confrontation at Wounded Knee.

Gladys: *Why* the confrontation? We aren't bothering nobody! We're just sitting here waiting for our 1868 Treaty.

Frizzell: There's a lot of lead coming out of Wounded Knee —

Gladys: There's a lot of it come in, too.

Frizzell: I agree. I agree.

Gladys: *More so!*

Frizzell: I agree.

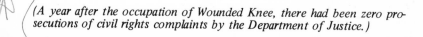

(A year after the occupation of Wounded Knee, there had been zero prosecutions of civil rights complaints by the Department of Justice.)

228

On Wednesday, May 2, the chiefs were allowed into Wounded Knee to advise the Independent Oglala Nation on negotiations. Also allowed through the roadblocks for this meeting were Agnes Lamont, Buddy's mother, and Darlene, his sister. The women told how Frizzell and Castleman had visited them daily since Buddy's death, warning that others might die if the occupation continued.

Members of the Wounded Knee community crowded around the long table in the little white church to hear the advice of the chiefs and the wishes of Agnes and Darlene concerning Buddy's funeral. Frizzell had told Agnes that only eight to ten members of the immediate family would be allowed into Wounded Knee for the funeral, and they could not bring any food for the traditional Sioux feast.

Darlene: [FBI Agent] Castleman came over to the house and talked to Mom about funeral arrangements. And they said that somebody here had said that they would lay down their arms, you know, have a cease-fire. And then he said he would have no objections to anybody coming in for the funeral. And then the negotiations could take place after. It kind of hangs on what you all say today. And another thing, they won't let us bring our food in.

Dennis Banks: One of the dirtiest low-down tricks that a person could ever pull! They're going to use the body of Buddy Lamont —

Darlene: No, Dennis — now before you go on, Mom had understood somebody to say that there would be like a cease-fire or agreement. The way Castleman understood it, there would be negotiations.

Agnes: He asked me when, before or after the funeral, so I said after.

Gladys: He's been lying back and forth to them about us. And he's been lying to us about them.

Darlene: He told us that he was on a timetable, that he only had so many days left to negotiate. I don't know what they're going to do after that. But we don't want you to give your lives because if you do — you people are the backbone, and if you're gone, we have nothing.

Agnes: We will have no leaders.

Darlene: Years from now, our grandchildren will be going through the same thing again and we need you all. And if you die, it's not going to do us any good. So we don't want you to give your lives like that, any one of you. Now this is her request. She's asking you —

Agnes: Now, look at home — you have relatives. Children are waiting for you. [She continues speaking in Lakotah to the Oglalas.]
. . .

Darlene: We want you please to try and come to some kind of peaceful end.

Agnes: I been praying and praying every day for you people. That God will have mercy on us, and give you our demands. Our treaty. We will win out. It's coming. All I want to ask is that we have a wake in Porcupine one night, and one night here. And bring food in.

Darlene: And I told him this [wake ceremony] isn't something we made up off the top of our heads — this has been going on for hundreds of years.

Agnes: It's our tradition.

Dennis: I tried to say earlier that Frizzell is a low-down human being. He's using Buddy's death, now, as a way to end the confrontation. He's not going to allow food in for the wake. The Government is dictating the funeral rights. They dictate from the minute that we're born on the reservation, till the minute that we're dead. Now they want to dictate beyond that. They want to dictate how we're going to be buried.

Henry Wawasik, Ojibway warrior: That treaty's all that's going to protect us. Even if there is a peaceful solution, if we all leave here and go home, they'll pick us off one by one. They won't come to the door knocking — they'll come shooting. They say, "We're going to let you out peacefully." Sure. But for how long? You've read in the papers what happens to people that try to oppose this Government.

We have a spot here. This is the most safest place there is. We know who the enemy is. But when we get out there, we don't know who anybody is. It's a scary place out there. Anybody who's been out even for a short period of time can tell you that. There's a cold feeling there. We have to carry on them traditions.

About this food coming in — they know that it's a tradition to feed during this time. Are they going to deny this man his right? Not letting him be buried the way he lived?

Lance Yellow Hand, Creek warrior: Isn't this what we came for, to save our people, to save our traditions?

Henry: They want to talk about paper? Then deal in with their first amendment. It's *their* paper, not ours. Freedom of that religion. Are they going to deny that man a place to rest? Let them show that good faith they always talk about.

Molotov cocktails.

After the meeting in the village, representatives of the Independent Oglala Nation, along with the chiefs, went up the hill to the DMZ to meet again with Frizzell. This was the first time that the Government negotiators met with the chiefs and representatives of the ION together.

Dennis Banks, to Frizzell: With the advice of the chiefs and after consulting with Mrs. Lamont, we're agreed that the 1868 Treaty must be the continuing foundation for all discussions. After Buddy Lamont's funeral, the chiefs will discuss with you this proposal: "1. The 1868 Treaty has to be reopened and discussed. Set up an agenda immediately for the Treaty Commission during the third week of May. 2. Rescind the 1934 Howard-Wheeler Act. 3. The chiefs and headmen will govern the Teton Sioux." There will be an immediate pull-back of arms when this is guaranteed.

Frizzell: I do have authority to insure that the Government of the United States, certainly the White House, and probably Congress, will discuss anything with your chiefs — anything and everything you want to discuss about the 1868 Treaty. I think there will be Congressional hearings into the 1868 Treaty. I have authority to tell you that any and all criminal violations against you by any outsiders will be prosecuted. I do have the authority to tell you that members of the Tribal Government will be prosecuted.

Gladys: According to the 1868 Treaty, there aren't supposed to be any marshals, any white men, pointing guns at Indians on this reservation. And this is why Mr. Frizzell is so defensive when we start asking for our 1868 Treaty.

Frizzell: I'm trying to bring about a meeting with the White House to examine the 1868 Treaty.

Gladys: And then you turn around and cut us down, say you haven't got the power, you know they won't do it. You never set up the meeting for Crow Dog and Means and Bad Cob.

Frizzell: Well, let's don't look back. Let's look forward. There are very few White House, or Congressional, or people in the white world that know very much about the 1868 Treaty of the Sioux Nation, or of the many other treaties that were entered into by the Government.

Frank Kills Enemy, traditional Oglala elder: I'm a treaty man. There was a treaty in 1851, 1851 Treaty. Sioux observed the treaty. Harney attacked the Sioux. And then he smoked another peace pipe, 1865. Then war in the same year. Then peace, 1866. And in '66 and '67 there was war. See what the Government did?

Frizzell: I can't be responsible for what the Government did a hundred years ago. We're willing to have a treaty commission after the laying down of arms —

Frank Kills Enemy: In '68, a treaty. And in '71, a war. And in '72, another one. The Government is guilty right there — violating these treaties. War plan, 1874. Peace plan, 1874 and '75. Then war in 1875 and '76. That's what he did.

This is a concentration camp. Hundred years confinement. And we're bounded by the military of this nation. And I want to face these who are coming from Washington. I like them to face what laws they have violated.

So, if they want to lay down the arms, they have to do it according to the treaty law of 1868. That law stands firm like the Black Hills. This law can not be moved, like the Black Hills. Only us fullblood Indians, we have a right and we have a power. This is our reservation.

Frizzell: I'm willing to get the opportunity for you to present these treaties.

Frank Kills Enemy: Why don't you do it now?

Frizzell: I can't get the President's representatives to come to Wounded Knee as long as the guns are being pointed at Federal officials. I don't care if it's only symbolic. The Government won't come and discuss the treaty as long as people are shooting at each other.

Gladys: We just want you to show us a little justice. And peace.

Frizzell: The marshals and FBI would stay in as a residual force to restore order.

Vernona Crow Dog: What do you mean by "restore order?" We don't want to be pushed around by your FBI men.

Frizzell: Well, that's why we'll have somebody here that's not connected with the Federal Marshals, or the FBI, to monitor *their* activities as well. That's why we have people here like Dennis Ickes with the Civil Rights Division. He owes no allegiance whatsoever to the U.S. Marshals or the FBI. He is dedicated to enforcing civil rights. And if a U.S. Marshal or an FBI man doesn't treat you according to the law, he will be prosecuted for that act. Can't you do that, Dennis? And will? Have you ever in the past?

Ickes: Our policy in the past has been, in regard to Federal officers — I'm not talking about BIA officers — is that we haven't had an instance arise where we've prosecuted anyone.

Frizzell: Well, all I'm saying is, you have the power and authority to do so if they overstep their bounds.

E SO. DAKOTA
...IONAL HISTORIC SITE
INDIAN MUSEUM -- TRADING POST

The next day, May 4, Agnes Lamont was again allowed through the Federal blockade. She brought news that the Government again said it would allow only eight to ten members of her immediate family to attend the funeral, and that they would not be allowed to bring food for the traditional wake. The chiefs were also allowed through that day, along with Ramon Roubideaux. This was the first time a member of the legal defense committee had been permitted into the village since April 17, when the Government let in Ramon to arrange a cease-fire after they learned that Frank Clearwater had been wounded.

That night, with the advice of Agnes, the chiefs, and Ramon, the people in Wounded Knee agreed to a compromise offer: if a letter came from the White House assuring the treaty meetings, they would settle for the rest of the April 5 agreement. A compromise was reached on the funeral as well – that it wouldn't be open to everyone who wanted to come, and the roadblocks wouldn't go down, but that all relatives could attend. They would have to enter through Government checkpoints, give their names, and be checked out as soon as it was over. Ramon relayed these proposals to the U.S. officials in Pine Ridge, who were no longer willing to come to Wounded Knee to negotiate directly.

The talks went in circles, with the Government side repeatedly moving the discussion away from the political questions of treaty rights, and back to their military concerns – "dispossession" of arms, a "sweep" of the village, and arrest of the Indians. Then, in the last few minutes of the four-hour session, a tentative scheme for a settlement was outlined. It sketched a progression of events as follows: 1. A letter would be delivered from the White House to the chiefs promising later meetings on a treaty commission. 2. Then there would be a laying down of arms. 3. The roadblocks would be lifted to permit Buddy Lamont's wake and funeral to take place in Wounded Knee. 4. Seventy-two hours after the funeral, those with outstanding warrants would be arrested. 5. The treaty commission meetings would be held at Chief Fools Crow's land in the third week of May. Though this plan was a verbal one, and clearly yet to be finalized, it looked to people in the village that the battle was soon to be over.

The next morning, ION representatives went to meet with Government officials, thinking that they would work out a more detailed plan for the standing down of arms. Like the similar meeting following the April 5th agreement, it turned out that the two sides had greatly varying understandings of what had been reached the day before. The ION had understood that "dispossession of arms" before the funeral would involve a "pullback" – with the APCs and Federal personnel retreating from their positions, and the Indians giving up their illegal weapons, evacuating their bunkers and "laying down" – but retaining – their legal arms within the village. But Hellstern's idea was that the ION would turn all its weaponry over to the Government, and that Federal forces would then enter Wounded Knee and remain there to oversee the "open" funeral. "We can not guarantee the security of the funeral," he said, "if we are not in absolute control of the situation." The meeting ended with nothing resolved.

On May 5, Hank Adams, the Assiniboine-Sioux treaty expert who had participated in the April negotiations, and had been working since then on the outside to help arrange a settlement, delivered a letter from Leonard Garment, Special Counsel to the President of the United States, guaranteeing the meeting with the chiefs later in May. Adams was one of the non-Oglalas who had been ordered off the reservation by Richard Wilson, so he had to hand the letter to Chief Fools Crow over a fence at the reservation line. Fools Crow brought the letter to Wounded Knee, and along with other leaders of the Independent Oglala Nation, signed the document they had agreed to the night before.

BUDDY LAMONT'S FUNERAL

Part of the agreement signed on May 5 allowed for the burial of Buddy Lamont in Wounded Knee. So, after days of waiting for the negotiations to be completed, Buddy's family finally brought his body back on Sunday, May 6. The Government limited attendance to Buddy's relatives, letting them through the roadblock only if they signed in and checked out, and left their cars at the border. The Government said they were worried about guns being smuggled in, and hinted that the Oglalas might use the funeral to prolong the confrontation. But despite the restrictions, over 100 people came into the village — relatives, and many friends in strong support of the ION. The people inside greeted them warmly, knowing that in many cases they had experienced worse terror out on the reservation than had the people in the village.

Barbara, the reporter from the underground press who kept a journal, wrote:

Mid-afternoon. Cold and grey outside. We gathered in the little round Church of God around the coffin. Crow Dog with the sacred pipe speaking in Lakota, Buddy lying in his army uniform from Viet Nam, but wearing his Indian bead-work, moccasins, and holding a pipe. Agnes, his mother, and his sisters, all there. We filed past Buddy and then his family, tried to express our feelings — they most of all have to live with this sacrifice.

Followed the coffin down the road, then around the gully and up the hill to the tipi at the old massacre site. Buddy's close friends, other Oglalas from Last Stand bunker, carried the coffin. At Agnes' request it was draped with an American flag and a Wounded Knee flag — the four colors, red, yellow, black and white, for the four races and the four directions of the earth. On it was written, "Wounded Knee, 1890-1973."

Dennis, who knew Buddy well, spoke of him as a warrior who died a warrior's death, for his people. I think everyone feels the truth of that, and knowing that it could have been any of us instead, a special closeness in our sadness. With a 100-gun salute, he was buried next to the grave of Big Foot and his Minneconjou. A lot of strong feelings — this death is a beginning, not an ending.

Afterwards, we went to eat. Agnes brought in a feast. They butchered two cows and three sheep in Porcupine last night to feed us here — pot after pot of beef stew, boxes of fry-bread and pies and cakes. So many friends came in today — everyone is talking, exchanging stories, the isolation of many weeks suddenly broken. Started thinking about how said it will be to leave this place and everyone here.

Agnes Lamont spoke at her son's funeral:

This is the only son I have. I have nothing but girls, only this. He didn't have to go and fight [in Viet Nam]. They told me he didn't have to go. And I told him he didn't have to go, I need him at home. "No, mom, what should I do at home when the rest of them are going?" I prayed nothing will happen, I will see my son alive. And God must have answered my prayers — he came home alive.

And again, when he joined this, when the roadblocks were open, I met him right out here. He's a big eater, he loves to eat. I brought him food for two days. I asked him to go home. "I need you at home," I said. "Well, mom, maybe you need me, but," he said, "I'm here for a good cause." He said, "Watch now, we're going to win. We're going to come to the top. And you're going to be happy. All the people will be happy. So in the end we will win — you remember that," he said . . .

And that's the last time I saw him.

Wallace Black Elk later spoke at a meeting in the trading post, about
Buddy Lamont and Frank Clearwater:

. . . This boy was murdered by the United States Government. He served in Viet Nam, he fought for them. Then when he came home to ask for his rights from the United States Government, "You shut up — or else!" And then they shot him, right through his heart. Clearwater was thinking about his Indians, and they shot him in the head, in his brain. So talking about thinking for the future, thinking for Indians, and for love of the Indians, one got shot in the head and the other one got shot in the heart. It was sealed with their own book in the eyes of the Great Spirit. So this is a total judgement: they'll have to face those two boys when the time comes. Before the Spirit, these two boys will be standing there.

"Downtown" Wounded Knee on May 2 — as seen through a telephoto lens from RB-2. This is the same field-of-fire the marshals had with their telescopic rifles and rapid-fire weapons. At the top is the burnt-out trading post and at bottom is the little white church kitchen with reinforced walls. To the left of the kitchen people are washing clothes.

PREPARING TO MOVE ON

The Independent Oglala Nation had entered into negotiations again reluctantly. People in the village felt the Government was not more serious in its promises of investigations, audits, and prosecutions at Pine Ridge than they had been in April. Still, the Oglala chiefs were optimistic that something might come from the meeting later in the month with the White House representatives. For 50 years their organization, the Black Hills Treaty Council, had been seeking unsuccessfully to have such a meeting with the White House, to talk about the broken treaties and the stolen Black Hills. Matthew King expressed their view the night the May agreement was signed: "In the past, the Indians have exhausted all means of negotiations with the Government . . . The different departments we consult will not listen to us. Now, tonight, we are recognized." Although the U.S. still did not acknowledge Oglala sovereignty, the chiefs felt there had been some movement in that direction and that maybe it was time to concentrate on other methods.

The Wounded Knee community was tired. The only food left now was a few bags of rice and beans. The beef had been eaten, the coffee was gone, and even the peanut butter supply had been eaten. Yet, people were still confident of their defenses, and their ability to hold off the Government. Work crews were building extra walls around more of the housing, and the bunkers were undergoing another stage of enlargement and reinforcement.

In the days after Buddy's death, the Government again attempted to increase the isolation of the Independent Oglala Nation. The Federal army had created a state of martial law on the reservation, particularly in the communities surrounding Wounded Knee. It was practically impossible to move along the roads without being watched by helicopters, APCs, or police patrols. Homes of known sympathizers were under constant surveillance. Supporters coming onto the reservation to deliver food and ammunition to the village often had to turn back. As the containment grew, the only method of resupply left was by an air drop, and none ever came in the critical days of early May.

The ION community had debated openly for days whether to open up a front behind the Government's lines to take pressure off the village, to try and hold out longer by negotiations, or to take the fight elsewhere. But finally, at the direction of the chiefs who had asked the people to come to Wounded Knee two months earlier, they agreed to the negotiated settlement and the date for the stand-down was set for May 9. The community envisioned a stand-down, rather than a surrender, in which both sides were to pull back from their bunkers and lay down their weapons.

TALKING WITH GRACE BLACK ELK

When dark fell the night of Buddy's funeral, many of the people in the village hiked out, taking their weapons with them. Some were caught by the ever-tightening circle of marshals, but many managed to slip past the ambushes and disappear into the countryside.

The next day, Monday, the sun shone warm and people did laundry by the white church kitchen, and rested in the sun. In her house, converted from an old storage building behind the trading post, Grace Black Elk talked with some friends, including two members of the underground media, as she packed her belongings, preparing to leave Wounded Knee. (Everyone except Grace is typed in italics.)

It's sort of funny, isn't it. It's like the end of something, like a ghost town here, almost.

Well, you haven't really noticed because a whole bunch of different people come here together, but it's probably always been a ghost town here before this museum came, and the trading post. I remember when I was a little girl, I came here in this area, my uncle used to live here, and my auntie. I heard of Wounded Knee. I heard of the store, trading post, and my sisters, my uncles, my stepmother, they come here to sell drums, way from Denver, bring all that stuff down there. Sell drums to them, and tipis. Yeah, that's a long way to bring it, spending gas money coming down here. Really, I don't think they made very much.

What are you going to do after Wounded Knee, Grace? Are you going to the AIM convention?

Probably. Because that's what we've been doing, going to help Indian people. Like on the reservation, we each have presidents, but they don't help their people. Like Dickie Wilson, he's not helping us at all. See, I'm from here. I'm enrolled from this Pine Ridge Indian Reservation. I'm enrolled, and I have lands here. Like my step-son told us, the minute the American Indian Movement shows their face around Pine Ridge BIA office, Wilson was going to shoot their heads off, shoot them on sight. But what if I went there. I'm an Oglala Sioux. He's supposed to represent me. Is he going to shoot me on sight? I wanted to come that time. Right the minute he said that, I said, "I want to go to that office."

I hear Dickie Wilson might come arresting people — those that stay.

This Dick Wilson, he hates AIM people because they are doing what he should have been doing. So he's jealous of them, more jealous than anything else. That's how come he calls them outsiders. But when you take that word "AIM" — an open "A" and put down "I" and then "M" down, it turns into an arrow, and that arrow will go back — all the words that the white people taught us, will go back to them and they will have to listen to them words this time. So those people are not outsiders, they are red men, they are a red nation. The AIM people are Indians — they are not outsiders like Dick Wilson said. I think *he's* an outsider — maybe he's from Mars.

[another man enters the house]

Didn't make it out last night. Tried. I don't know, might try again tonight if it rains. I think that's about the best time.

The FBI said they might come in here with gas masks tomorrow, said they might use gas if they have any resistance. Maybe they're gonna use it anyway. I don't know.

Resistance from what?

From the "militant Indians."

Ooh, that's the one word I *really* hate — *militant*. I'm not militant. I'm a member of the American Indian Movement, but we're not militant — unless we're forced to be. And what do they call themselves up there, the FBIs? I think they're more militant — they're military. They call us militants, but, like Dickie Wilson said, we're renegades and hoodlums and clowns — I said if he thinks I'm a clown, he must be a bigger clown to represent me. *[laughing]*

The Grand Jury met in Sioux Falls today, and they were supposed to hand down some indictments against Wilson and his goons. I wonder if they did.

This would be the first time they charge the goons instead of the people inside here, if it happens.

They should have charged them before *us* — before we came down here.

. . .

We're supposed to be savages because we carry a dangerous weapon like a little tiny bow and arrow. Compared to [the Government's] APCs, boy, that's a toy, to me. And the difference between arms — like a bow and arrow, we carry that, and we have tomahawks. They're not so big. We have to get close to a person, you know, to maybe whack them on the head. But them, they can stand way up there and kill us. This tomahawk is more like a hand-to-hand fight, go close to each other and then fight like that. But they were scared of that. So they make them lay down that bow and arrow, that tomahawk, and if we carry that, we're called savages.

So they want to convert us to Catholic, Episcopal, all that trash, and believe in the Bible and go to a place where they call heaven, and if we don't we go to hell, and so on. So the Indian's supposed to lay down his weapons and be converted into Christian way. No more savage, he's gonna be a Christian. I guess he'll grow some wings right away, so he can be equal to the white men. But I don't see no wings on white people. All I see is horns on them. They are actually the devil.

Especially when I go out at night here, and all those spotlights. Like, for instance, if you was sleeping, and you lay down, and I come in here with a flashlight and put it in your face, and everytime you move, I put a flashlight in your face, I bet you really get sick and tired of me doing that. I'll be just like a devil trying to torment you mentally. And that's just what they're doing. That's mental cruelty. Boy, if I had my way I'd charge them with mental cruelty, trying to tear us apart, and not feeding us, not sending us groceries, even though people have it in their hearts to pity the Indian people for their grievances. They understand.

You know, I was thinking of these young schoolkids who were bringing groceries down here. And they crossed the Nebraska state line, so they arrested them — because they were bringing food to some people that are hungry. I don't think taking food across a state line is a crime. But I think it's a crime for the United States to take guns and go over across the ocean and kill people over there. And so there's a big difference between these schoolkids and this government.

You see, these people that come here on foot, they were thinking about us Indians and they know that we're hungry. I think they're good Samaritans, these people that have it in their hearts to crawl all over these hills to reach us and help us. They must have love in their heart for their fellow man. But as far as many white people go — they're pig-headed, they don't care if you white people stay here, they don't care whether you get killed or not. They don't care whether even the CRS gets killed. They were shooting at us when the CRS was here. That's how much they care for their own people.

I don't think the white people really care for each other. Like if you're hungry, you can't go into a cafe and get a free meal. You have to pay for it. Like these people, for an example, yesterday there was a woman that lost her boy here. Her only son — she lost him. And she bought a lot of groceries to come and feed us here. She has it in her heart for Indian people. That's the way Indian people are. They'd rather give than be greedy and take everything away from other people.

. . .

I think the Government knows it. He knows we're here because of — he calls it grievances, but we call it treaties — that he promised and never fulfilled. And he just calls it grievances — "Well, after they lay down their arms, we'll listen to their grievances and probably forget about it.

Do you think they ever will do anything about it?

Well, if they call themselves Christians and they really believe in that Bible, put their religion ahead of their APCs and all their guns. But they're just using that Bible as a mask. Every Sunday they go to church, and then Monday morning they stand in line making machine guns and tanks and H-bombs and nuclear heads and all that.

Do you think what happened here at Wounded Knee is going to change any of that?

That's what we're trying to do, change his mind, about

a lot of things that he don't know himself. He don't even know his own mind. He don't even know if he's going to heaven or hell. But I think he's going to hell, or wherever he calls hell. See, man makes his own hell. I don't think our creator, the Great Spirit, created any hell. He created everything — all these green vegetations, trees, water, four-legged animals, flying creatures, and us two-legged creatures. He made everything. The moon and the stars in the sky. Snow. Rain. Hail.

Like some people came to our place one time and asked us if we know God. And before we even answered, they asked, "Do you know God, do you know this, do you go to church?" They throw questions at us like they think we're pagans or something. We don't know beans from buckshot, the way they talk. You know, they think they know everything. Some of them call themselves "the Awake." They should wake up — right now! I think they should be wide awake by now if they hear from us.

So they say, "Don't you ever go to church? What religion do you belong to?" I say we don't belong to no white religion, we have our own religion. Indian religion. Indian ceremonials. And they say, "Well, you should at least go to church once a year, because you don't know what's gonna happen today or tomorrow. Tomorrow the world might end." And they keep saying in their prayers, they say, "As it was in the beginning, it is now and ever shall be, world without end. Aaaamen. Halleluuujah." And so on. And they don't really believe it, because they told us the world might end tomorrow.

And I was working my fingers to the bone, trying to make some miniature tipis, and so on, drums to sell to the wholesale companies, so we can pay our gas and lights. I was really working in the next room, and my husband Wallace, he was talking to them in the living room, and they were telling him the world might end tomorrow. So after they left I said, "Wallace, let's not pay the gas bill. World might end tomorrow." That's how far they believe in their religion. Yes, I think *they* might end because of the way they live. They're not going very far with APCs and guns. I don't think St. Peter will allow them packing guns in there in that heaven, whatever they call it, because a child could go to that heaven, but not these people.

Especially now. Like some nights I go out there, and they stand out [on those hills] like sore thumbs. And I just stand there and look at them. I wave to them too, every time they put their lights on me [*laughing*], although I hate their guts worse than they hate me.

Grace Black Elk.

. . . Sometimes I think he's the devil himself. Especially these FBIs, Federal Bureau of Investigation. I used to think they investigated things before they go in there. But he hasn't. Between us and the Government we're talking about treaties, but he hasn't even investigated 1868 Treaty. That's the reason we're here, but he hasn't even looked into it. And if he's going to call himself Federal Bureau of Investigation and if he really is an investigator, he better go to Washington, D.C., and investigate those treaties that the United States didn't fulfill.

. . .

When that 1868 goes through we'll give those arms back to who it belongs, because it really belongs to the white people. We don't manufacture things to kill people with. A long time ago my ancestors had a bow and arrow that they used to kill animals to eat. Nowadays you see white people making ammunitions, but they're not doing that to kill buffalo and kill meat and eat it. All they think of is trophies, and leave the carcass out there to rot. Whereas the Indians used to use every bit of it. God didn't put that animal here to throw his meat away and hang it on the wall to see how sharpshooter he is. So people can come in — "Is that a trophy, did you get that?" — and throw the meat away. It goes to spoil. They're just playing. Whereas an Indian is hungry so he goes out and shoots a deer to eat it, and they don't even want him to do that — he has to get a permit first.

You know, everything's white man's law. *Everything.* What if it was the other way around? Like I asked one policeman over in Scottsbluff. I said, "Do we have to go under white man's law all the time? You're not the only race here on earth. There's the black race, there's yellow race, there's red race and there's white race. But it seems like we always have to bend to your will, bend to white people and their laws, man-made laws."

And he looks down on the rest of the colors. But the Great Spirit made those colors. And he had in his mind beautiful colors. Like the sky is blue, the mother earth is real green, and the animals are all colors, even the snake is real pretty. Different colors, different shades. And even them shells, them seashells under the sea, are beautiful pink. The way you go down deep in them waters, get them shells out and look at them. They're real pretty. Just like hand-carved. And that's the way he carved everything, that's the way he made everything. And the white people don't really care about anything like that at all.

He don't think anything's beautiful. Specially probably when he sees the night, he thinks the black is evil, so he thinks the black people are evil. Probably thinks the yellow race is so yellow he don't like them, or slanted eyes, so he don't like them. And us red people especially.

Like, for instance, we have beans and rice here, and just today I was thinking about the yellow race. All they eat is fish and rice, but boy, they grow, they have a big population. So if they keep feeding us rice we might get as many as the Chinese! *[she laughs]*

[another man comes in the door]

Hi, Francis, what's going on out there?

Everybody's gone.

Are the searchlights on yet?

Yeah.

Grace, what do you think is going to happen in the American Indian Movement after people leave Wounded Knee tomorrow?

As long as Indians are alive there will be an American Indian Movement.

Do you think it will keep on getting stronger and stronger?

Yes, that's what the Great Spirit said and that's the way it's gonna be. Whether the white people like it or not, us American Indians are gonna move all the time, to help any people that we can across the country, until we get to a place that we're free from this Government. This BIA, this Bureau of Indian Affairs, is not doing any good for any reservation in this country. All across the country, all red men are having troubles over this BIA, and people like Dick Wilson. Like if Dick Wilson is Indian, and like he says, he represents 12,000 of his people, like for instance, myself, if he was representing me, he'd be here right now, working for that 1868 Treaty that the white people promised us long time ago, which they never fulfilled at all. And they don't want to, cause it covers a lot of territory. They don't want to give up what they stole. But actually, when it comes down to everything, this earth belongs to the Great Spirit. So, actually, he planted us here and they're trying to take it away from him too.

Do you think the Government will have to give it up eventually?

239

Yes, if he means peace on earth like he's been saying, he has to recognize the red man as a nation. That's the only way he'll gain peace. Because the Great Spirit created four divisions, that's the white, black, yellow, and red race, and he cannot bar the red man anymore. He'd like to keep us down, kick us down, keep us under his thumb and keep us on reservations, but he cannot do that anymore.

Like I said, our ancestors used to go to Washington, D.C., going to talk to the president, whoever happens to be president. They go up there with what they call grievances, they go up there to accomplish something, which they never do. They just go up there and take pictures with them and come back, they pat them on their back and "The Congress will look into it and in two years you'll get what you want" — and that's all bullshit. Because after the chief leaves they tear it up and throw it in the wastebasket. And they forget about it and they think we forget about it. But we're not going to.

I saw a sign on the door, it says, "The Indians would rather die standing up than be on their knees forever." And that's where they've been keeping us, on our knees. All the time. Keeping us in poverty.

They always think that we should do what they say most of the time, but this time they got to do what we want. We came here because of what we want, not what they want, not what the marshals or FBIs want. And they even stopped the food and they even stopped our fuel, but now the Great Spirit's gonna punish them by stopping most of the fuel, so they're running short on fuel. And pretty soon, since they've been stopping the food from coming in, there's gonna be starvation coming to the white people. And since we've already been in poverty, we know what to do to get by. They can't — they're used to sugar, salt, coffee, and all that business. You know, they're used to a lot of things that we don't really need in our world.

And then the electricity, that's where our sacred eagle comes in, he controls the weather, and he's gonna see to it that pretty soon there won't be any electricity for the white people. They have electric stoves and electric everything. And one of these days they're gonna realize how they hurted us. They're gonna be hurt by it too. And they're gonna starve. They're just gonna have to be satisfied with horsemeat. The meat is so high, they can't buy that, too much money. The Government, that Nixon cabinet, keep raising and raising and raising. There's not enough jobs for people, so they don't know what to eat, so they're starting to eat horsemeat. It's

gonna be worse. They're gonna get a taste of their own medicine.

But we've been starving all our lives, so it won't be nothing new to us. They're gonna have the hardest time. You read in the paper to save fuel, not to drive so fast, but they've been driving real fast all their lives, they run a fast world. But it's gonna be a dead end for them — for what they done to us.

. . . We don't want to be like them. They make bullets and they take our boys and send them to wars when in the first place they disarmed us, and they shouldn't even send us to the war as long as they are the ones that are making it. The United States sticks its nose every place, and on account of them doing that most of our good boys, our healthy boys, are killed down there. And we don't want that no more. If they want to disarm us, well, we want them disarmed too. I hope that someday this will be accomplished, that peace could be attained here in the United States. And they'll have to lay down their arms. The Indians are the only ones they want to disarm, but I think the Great Spirit wants everybody to be disarmed.

MAY 8 / STAND—DOWN

With half of the community gone and most of the defense forces dis-
mantled, the ION requested that the stand-down be moved up a day to
May 8. Monday night, May 7, those that were left were up all night,
manning the bunkers against the vigilantes who were out in force in the
hills, shooting into the village.

The next morning, everyone sat down to a big breakfast of pancakes in
the little white church kitchen. The food came from the emergency food
supply, still being saved in the last days since no one really knew for
sure how long they would be in Wounded Knee. Then, everyone gathered
outside around the drum to sing the AIM song. Wallace Black Elk spoke:

We have come to understanding, all of us,
white, black, yellow, and us red people.
I thank the powers of the four winds,
and to the Grandfather, Great Spirit,
and I thank the sacred Mother Earth, Grandmother.
Thank you.
I ask you and bless all people here,
from the powers of the four winds,
and Grandfather, Great Spirit, we thank you this day
that we are alive.
Grandmother we thank you for keeping us alive.
Grandmother we stand here on your lap and once again
you cradle us in your arms, and feed us, and comfort us,
and heal us and forgive us.

Metakuyeayasi – all my relations.

The processing took all day. About 150 people were still in the village on
the last day, approximately one-third of them local residents, one-third of the
them Oglalas from other towns on the reservation, and one-third supporters
from around the country. All spent the day on the hillside in the hot sun by
Roadblock 1, surrounded by a circle of armed marshals. One by one, people
were taken out of the group to be searched, questioned, fingerprinted, and
photographed. Nobody knew until they were questioned whether they would
be arrested or not.

At 7 a.m., according to a timetable agreed upon with the Government
negotiators, the Community Relations Service of the Justice Department
came into Wounded Knee. They collected all remaining weapons and
drove everyone, including all permanent residents, to the Government's
Roadblock 1 for processing. The first to go were two men who had outstanding warrants on them, but when one of them, Al Cooper, a white
warrior, learned with surprise that Defense Committee lawyers were being
kept away from the roadblock, he locked himself in the CRS car and refused
to move until the lawyers arrived. Finally, Government officials allowed the
lawyers to witness the processing and advise their clients, as had been guaranteed in the May 5 agreement. The lawyers later said that if it hadn't been
for Al's insistence, they would not have been allowed at the roadblock. The
Government was to break the agreement in many other ways during the last
day at Wounded Knee and the weeks following.

While the people were being processed at RB-1, the "mutual pull-back" of
arms proceeded. According to the May 5 agreement, all APCs were to be

out of the area before any weapons were taken from the ION warriors. The marshals were to search the village for arms after the people had left to be processed. ION and Government bunkers were to be covered over simultaneously — Government bunkers because the people in the village still did not trust the Government to end the siege peacefully — ION bunkers because the Government did not want the public to see photographs of the impressively fortified defenses on the recent battlefield in South Dakota.

Four warriors were assigned by the Independent Oglala Nation to monitor the marshals' sweep of the village. One of them, Arvin Wells, a warrior from Oklahoma, described what happened:

We waited for the people inside of Wounded Knee to be brought up to be processed, and once they were all outside the village, we went in. They made Onco and Spang sit on the front of a jeep going down Pine Ridge Road inside of Wounded Knee, in case of land mines or anything like that — they would be the first ones to get it. And me and Richard were in the back of a truck.

They had two skirmish lines go on down into Wounded

Arvin Wells.

Marshals at RB-1 on the last day.

Knee with automatic weapons and high-powered rifles with telescopic sights. And they got to the Pine Ridge roadblock, and one man jumped out with a mine detector and about five to eight people got out and they were all probing around there with bayonets and stuff like that. And we told them ahead of time that there were no mines and that there were no booby-traps, you know, in the place at all — that we had taken them all out. And they didn't believe us and they went through the whole thing. After that, they drove us on the other side of Pine Ridge roadblock and two bulldozers came in and they bulldozed down the place.

All this time, they were supposed to be bulldozing down their bunkers. They weren't. Their APCs weren't even moved out of the area. They drove into Wounded Knee and drove around inside of Wounded Knee. And anyone that says they didn't is lying. They were just driving around, playing around, as usual.

Maybe I shouldn't say this, but to me, it was really a pitiful sight. Man, I don't think we should have ever surrendered. I don't give a damn whether they'd have come in there and killed us, man, because it was really humiliating the way they treated us all through that whole day.

After we searched the church for weapons we came down and all these marshals had grouped around in front of the church. They told one of their marshals to get up on top of the steeple and take down the AIM flag that we had up there. And this other marshal was holding the United States flag, and they said that they were going to have a little ceremony there, a victory ceremony.

I was standing on the steps, and it really kind of pissed me off. I got tired of all this bullshit. And I was told to cooperate with the marshals and be cool — and I had cooperated with the marshals. But to me, this was adding insult to injury, and they didn't win no victory there as far as I'm concerned. But they proclaimed that they did.

And I said, "You mean we have to stand here and listen to this bullshit about raising the goddamn flag?" And the guy that was head of the marshals came up there — he was an ex-Green Beret, and he come up there and said, "Boy, don't you *ever* say anything against that flag again. Or else I'll knock your fucking head off." And I told him, I said, "All right." And he said, "Do you hear me?" And I turned around and told him, "All right." And he said, "Do you hear me?" And he told me that about three fucking times. And I told him the same damn thing. And then after he got his little satisfaction of trying to ridicule me in front of my people, he said, "All right, you guys get over there by the vehicle. You get over there before I kick your ass over there."

So we all trucked over there and jumped in the little vehicle and they raised up the flag and he went down there and gave his little speech and they all fired off their weapons and all this bullshit. It was really sickening. They fired, and the Green Beret officer, he had an automatic weapon and he pulled the bolt back and he had a full clip in it, and everybody fired their weapons. He fired his until the clip was empty. Those people are supposed to be professional soldiers, but to me, that day they acted like little kids.

You know, the people — soldiers in the group — they were cool about it, but the heads, like the squad leaders and the captains — they were all-American boys, Stars and Stripes forever. And they treated us like secondary-class people. We were treated like animals. And they said that we was prisoners of war. We were POWs. That was their exact statement.

There was not supposed to be any BIA pigs down there. But there were six units down there, that I saw. They had free access to the place. Their units were up around the church, and there was a unit up in the graveyard and their peo-

Those who were not arrested being bused off to Rapid City.

ple were picking flowers off the grave. That kind of pissed me off too.

And the way they treated Black Elk was really pitiful, man. He got out of the car, and they grabbed him like they would grab some young dude and threw him up against the car. They took his headband away from him, they took his medicine bag, everything that he had on him they took away

Wounded Knee residents Rachel White Dress and her daughter Helen — two of the fifteen people arrested.

from him. And as far as I'm concerned, those people have made an enemy for the rest of their lives.

Because even in war, the so-called Americans, when they go into war, they're supposed to respect the Red Cross and the enemy's side of the medical personnel. They do all that, and here in their own country, they won't even respect the Indian medicine man. And that's really pitiful.

As Arvin described, BIA police accompanied the marshals down into Wounded Knee. They proceeded to break into the cars that people had left there, and into the homes of the original residents who were still at the roadblock. They also accompanied the trading post operators to people's homes, looking for objects which they claimed had been stolen from the trading post.

Later, the Government allowed the press to enter the village, and told them that AIM was responsible for the destruction. But resident Eddie White Dress described how he had seen BIA police destroying their homes and cars from the window of the Government bus which was taking the people from the processing point at RB-1 out to Rapid City via Wounded Knee.

Off-duty Federal personnel watching the processing.

Two shackled warriors.

We found our car trunks busted open. The BIA police been rummaging through there and searching through the pockets of the clothing that was just scattered all over the ground. I saw one of them. He just hammered away on this trunk, and they busted the lock and they opened it. The bus pulled up alongside them and I had the window down, so I could see everything. And when we pulled up alongside of them, we asked the BIA police what they were doing, and they didn't say anything -- they just jumped in the car and drove off.

Grace Black Elk also commented on the Government's accusation of the American Indian Movement for the destruction in Wounded Knee:

We were all held up on the hill while they let the police and Dick Wilson's goons down there. So they went down and wrecked the place and blamed the American Indian Movement. But that's not so at all. We saw that old lady, her picture was shown in the paper with all her things thrown on the floor, but I know Sally Hat was living with that old lady and they left that place in good condition before they went up on the hill. And while they were up there — see, they let the goon squads in so they wrecked the place, shot up our cars, and wrecked most of the local people's cars too — and that wasn't in the agreement either.

As the Independent Oglala Nation POWs arrived in Pine Ridge, they were greeted by a crowd of supporters singing the AIM song. Here, Agnes Lamont (center), is speaking to the marshals guarding the prisoners on the bus.

Those who were not permanent residents were not permitted back into the village to collect their belongings and their cars. Instead, at the end of the day, everyone was driven by bus out to Rapid City.

At the end of the processing, people sat on the hill waiting for the buses. The Federal perimeter of several miles that had surrounded them for two months had finally shrunk to a small circle. But inside that circle, tired and hungry from the long day, people expressed anything but defeat. Gladys Bissonette, who had stayed in Wounded Knee throughout the 71 days, commented:

Well, for myself, I think this was one of the greatest things that ever happened in my life. And although today is our last day here, I still feel like I'll always be here because this is part of my home. And I do know that we have accomplished quite a bit. Ever since I was a child I thought someday we would reach a goal like this. Although we haven't gone through negotiations yet, I'm pretty positive that everything will turn out all right for the Oglalas and the Indians throughout the nation.

I do think that people are beginning to realize — and I do know we have a lot of support on our own reservation. They have finally opened their eyes to what corrupt governing bodies we have on the reservation and they have finally realized that they should stand up to intimidation and stand up for their rights, now. I do really think that we have brought a lot of people to sanity instead of letting everybody push them around. I hope that the Indians, at least throughout the Pine Ridge Reservation, unite and stand up together, hold hands, and never forget Wounded Knee.

. . . Well, we didn't have anything here, we didn't have nothing to eat. But we had one thing — that was unity and friendship amongst 64 different tribes and that's more than I could say that the Pine Ridge Reservation has ever had in my life. I have never seen anything like this and although we were half-starved here, we didn't mind it. We were all happy together and it is kind of sad to see everyone leave but we know we'll all be together again, soon. ■

12. LOOKING AHEAD

"Our people believe in the paths of life. We talk about the path of peace — and how sometimes you have to go the path of war because there's nowhere else to go and still remain as an Indian. Our people have wanted to do that for a long time."

246

Not long after the end of the siege of Wounded Knee, one of the American Indian Movement leaders spoke about his ideas for the future of the Indian struggle in North America:

Our people are sovereign, each tribe unto itself, and have been like that for thousands of years. We fought against white people and were conquered. And we've had to try a system of government that's foreign to us. We've tried this government and it's failed. It's degraded our people and caused the ills that have fallen upon us. So we can see that the only way to regain what we've lost, regain our relationship with the Mother Earth, is to go back to the system of government that's done so well for us for so long.

Sovereignty means the ability to guide our own lives, the ability to even make mistakes if that's what it takes. We know the way we want to live, and how we want to survive. We know how to live with the world, instead of on it, or off it, or against it. What it all boils down to is how we can make things better for our people.

Standard of living and economic conditions are a problem for Indian people only in so far as we are related to the white economic system. Once we're divorced from that, our problem won't be to upgrade our standard of living. We want to have, of course, enough food to eat, and we want our tribes to be able to live without starving.

We're concerned with having our people free to live on their land and not have a constant pressure from the U.S. Government to move them off it. We see this as the Government's main aim in Indian relations — to finally take all our land and have Indian people become homogenized into American society and not have any identity of our own. That is our greatest danger, and that is the real genocide against our people. They kill off the dissident ones — what they used to call "hostile" ones, now the "militant" ones — get rid of them physically. And then they get rid of the rest of our people by trying to get them to become brown white people.

The U.S. Government has pretty well kept us as a race of paupers by making us dependent on their economic system. The BIA has complete control of the economy of the reservation, and the monies generated by the reservation go into white hands. The Government in return gives Indian people welfare, and commodities — surplus food — to keep them alive.

That's *their* plan. *Our* plan is to take the white ranchers and leasers off of all our land and then tell the Government we don't need their welfare and we don't need any of their services.

At first, when we close a reservation, we're going to have to live like we lived at Wounded Knee. We're going to have to be killing them cattle to eat, and live on beans and stuff for a while. And we're just going to have to toughen up until we can get all our shit straight. We drive the white ranchers out, and our people no longer get those lease payments that they depend on. But those lease payments are the very things that's held them in bondage for so damned long. Now they might get $1000 a year for a family of 20 people. That's not enough to live on, but it's been enough to subsist on if they also get those rations from the Government. They'll just have to do without that $1000 and those rations. But eventually, we'll have control of our economy. On Pine Ridge Reservation, the white ranchers generate over $12 million a year. If that money were controlled by Indian people, it would far exceed the welfare roll for this reservation.

We also have to make it where no person owns the land any more. We don't believe in ownership of land because the land is part of us — you can't own each other and you can't own land. Once we have control of a reservation and its borders, you can live anywhere you want. The land that isn't lived on will belong to all the people and the benefits derived from that will be given to all the people on the reservation.

. . . You know, our people believe very much in the paths of life, that there are different paths to follow. We talk about the path of peace — and how sometimes you have to go the path of war because there's nowhere else to go and still remain as an Indian. Our people have wanted to do that for a long time.

Our revolution never ended. A lot of the old people on the reservations remember the time when they bore arms against white people. This has been passed right down to their children and now their grandchildren. Wherever the American Indian Movement has gone we've found our widest support amongst the old people and people who live traditional lives on the reservations. Where we don't have support is among those who got over-educated in white schools, living in the cities,

working for the BIA — but that's a minority of Indian people. So I don't have to make revolution. The revolution is going on in the minds of the people.

Our people have to get organized, particularly our young people — and then they have to be taught exactly how it is. Because many of them are growing up in a white society, white education, and you know, their outlook is a white outlook. They have to be taught by our traditional people and our medicine men what it is to be Indian, and then all Indian people have to gather in that kind of unity and that kind of force before we can have other people with us.

We did have some really aware white people, Chicano people, and black people come into Wounded Knee — and a small number can be absorbed. We took seven white people as citizens into the Independent Oglala Nation. But our movement couldn't take a large body of white people coming in until we learn to stand on our own two feet first. I think that white people who support our way should do that from the outside, because we would run the risk of destroying it by too much white input.

The difference between us and black revolutionaries or white revolutionaries is that we're not searching for something. We already have that. We're just trying to re-establish it. I think that eventually Indian people can guide the people in this nation that are dissatisfied with the way that the American Government handles itself. Although small in numbers, the Indian people have the ability to give an American revolution its soul.

Indian people know how to fight and live, to fight and take care of their people, all at the same time. Indian warriors know that they can't be like an army — where you are just a hired killer, taken care of in all your needs, except that you go out and kill every day and you're fed and clothed and housed. They have to accept the duties of being a husband and father and man of their tribe, and also a warrior. As a matter of fact, being a warrior has to be secondary to all the other things. They'll begin to teach other revolutionary people that this is a part, and a very big part, of the total revolution. When people learn that, they can move their whole life away from that city and away from that very social structure that they're trying to destroy. They can change their own lives into something that's meaningful, move into the land and fight from there. All people can do that.

So far, the revolutionary movements in America haven't been able to rally forces with the type of dedication that you must have to win. People must be so dedicated to the movement that they're perfectly willing to die and perfectly willing to fight against overwhelming odds, willing to go without the comforts of home, willing to starve and be out in the cold and do things that are generally considered impossible. Those kind of people can be developed and motivated by having a very strong spiritual center. That's what Indian people have to offer. We don't have the numbers, we don't have the cadres to go out and teach and train. All we have is a very close relationship to our mother earth.

We believe in the sacredness of a circle where everything has its place, from the lowliest insect to the sun. When I have a brother he is actually part of me because we believe we're part of that same earth, and my power goes through that to him, and his to me. And if you can realize that, it don't matter what culture you used to be from. You accept all people as being part of you, and you're able to extend that not only to the people but to everything. These things are part of the nature of Indian people and our cultural heritage. We never think that we have to conquer anything. We don't have to build a big dam to divert a river that would eventually end up harming the balance of nature. We don't have to send something to the moon — which is our sister — and take away a part of her flesh and bring it down here for no reason whatsoever. Those things are not to be done and the great circle is not to be tampered with. And the American people are learning that finally.

Our prophecies predicted when the white people would come here and start destroying our mother earth. But they also talk about how Indian people, after being conquered and subjected to the degradation that we have been subjected to, would eventually come back and show everybody in the whole world the way that they could live on this earth. One of our prophecies says that there's going to be someone coming from the east who will have a face like death. It will be all white and he will be all-powerful. He can make things disappear before your very eyes, and he'll come here and do much harm to Indian people — and if Indian people don't hold tight to their religion and tight to their circle of life, he will completely destroy them. It goes on to say that in the seventh generation after the second coming of the white people, our young will begin to rise up against this type of oppression and they will start waging a war that will eventually free the people.

Of course, you can't go back to the old Indian way of life at this point. We have to deal with the mother earth in its present condition, which is pretty bad. Right now the United States has to be constantly building — they call

building, we call destroying — or else it begins to degenerate. We would allow that physical and economic degeneration to begin taking place. It would be a transition where we didn't explore new modes of destroying our mother earth or increasing our technology, but at the same time we wouldn't take it all away and stop industry. But we wouldn't pave over the whole United States the way they're doing now. We'd stop that. You know, just to stop building roads would slowly bring about the cessation of industrialization. Because as roads over the years degenerated, things would have to slow down, and by slowing things down America could begin to get a grip on itself.

It's my belief that America is still not overpopulated. We're just all trying to live in the same place, and by trying to live in the same place we've created cities and ghettos and everybody is pushing each other around. This land has the ability to sustain all the people here and it's not necessary for us to build great industries to do that . . . I think the very basic thing that you have to realize is that Indian people, Indian religion, and Indian society are readily adaptable. Our society and our peoples have changed with various things that have come into our lives over ten thousand years. But we never lost sight or focus of one thing — that we don't have to take away from the mother earth.

Everything will have to be a slow and on-going process. And it's going to be a process that most of us won't even be around to see. We will be gone before we're able to live like we want to live, but our children will be able to, or maybe our grandchildren or great-grandchildren, and that's what we're going to be building for.

What we have to do is to set the guidelines for revolution, and to begin the physical fighting. And then as it is carried on and is closer and closer to reality, the very small details like, "Do we leave the McNary Dam standing or do we blow it up and let the river go back the way it was," you know, all those kinds of details will come along after people, masses of people, are involved.

The American Indian revolution is right now pointed towards showing the people that they can struggle against the U.S. Government, and that they can win. That's why it's important that the leadership of the American Indian Movement not be sent to prison — not because any of us are vital to the movement, but because we're symbolic of resistance. As long as we are out, going around and talking to our people, they can see that, "this man led the people against the U.S. Government in a fight, and he's still here and he's going to fight some more pretty quick and maybe I should join him." They see that they have a chance to win, where before there was despair.

Wounded Knee was an educational process for all Indians. Right there you had Indians from Los Angeles and San Francisco, New York and Chicago, Minneapolis and Oklahoma City — big cities where Indians live and become urbanized. They went into Wounded Knee and met there Indians who had never been off the reservations, who live in the traditional way. The two of them met together and found out that they were still one people, still one race, and that they can be together again. The urban Indians found out what it was to be able to worship their mother earth the way they want. They'll go back to their cities but they'll always have that religion in their hearts. They'll look at the city streets and buildings and cars and they're going to hate it. They're really going to hate it. So they're going to go back home to their people more and more. They're going home in droves now, the Indians to their homes, their land, and this will accelerate the process.

Then of course, our people on the reservation, where the oppression has been so tremendous, have learned that there's a lot of Indian people off of the reservation that are perfectly willing to come home and fight with them — young men and women that have been to school will come home and help them figure out how to deal with the Bureau of Indian Affairs. They're not standing alone.

13.
TREATY
MEETINGS
AT KYLE

"The chief would like to ask one question with a simple answer, yes or no . . . 'Can we be reinstated back to the 1868 Treaty?' "

Chief Red Cloud, Bradley Patterson, and Chief Fools Crow.

put into a cage, and that our freedom of spirit can never be contained or taken away.

We are able to touch each other in song, in conversation, in love and respect for our race, and for one another. We realize that as the sacrifice in battle is necessary . . . other types of sacrifices must be made. And until the day that the Great Spirit takes us by the hand to free us of the Gun and the Whiteman's way, as he did Frank Clearwater, Buddy Lamont, Richard Oakes, and Raymond Yellow Thunder, we must sacrifice in any way we can . . . Let Indian people, and enslaved people all over the world, see freedom and dignity through our example. But let them see that this is an old example set by Crazy Horse, Chief Joseph, Cochise, Osceola, Gall, Satank, and other warriors and chiefs in our past. Let Indian people see that our way to freedom is in our culture, our spiritual ways, and our strength to uphold these . . .

from the Pennington County Concentration Camp,
Larry Tennecour
Vaughn Baker
Al Cooper (held on $25,000 bond)
Walter Ten Fingers
Eugene Heavy Runner
Pedro Bissonette ($150,000 bond)
James War Bonnet
Stan Holder ($32,000 bond)

At the end of the siege, the Oglalas were looking forward to the May treaty meetings to settle some of the issues which had brought them to Wounded Knee. But the hopefulness was hard to hang on to. Federal violations of the agreement continued in the days following the stand-down. One clause in the agreement specified that, "The Government will make no bond or terms of release recommendations" to the courts when those arrested were arraigned. This was held to in many cases, and arrestees were bonded out of jail on their own recognizance. But others, considered leaders, even when charged with the same "interfering with a Federal officer," were held on high bonds at the instigation of Government prosecutors. One group of prisoners who were still in the County Jail in Rapid City two weeks after the stand-down, held on bails ranging up to $150,000, issued this statement:

. . . One thing this Government better realize is that what came down at Wounded Knee was real in every aspect, and as far as calling it an occupation . . . they are completely wrong in every way. It was a war where people died and people got shot, where any second you had the chance of being shot by the Government forces, with all their nice shiny weapons . . .

You people should have seen the looks on their faces, of disbelief, when we came out. What was before their eyes was old men and women, kids, babies — a handful of tired, happy people. It was as if they were expecting monsters in tanks, or a completely equipped army. Then they go down to Wounded Knee, finally, after 71 days, acting like they won a big victory. The Government should realize . . . there was no victory for them . . .

So now we are POWs . . . but for a young Indian warrior who for 71 days felt the true meaning of being free, and being Indian, the term means very little. The only meaningful possession is the pride that the Great Spirit reinstilled into our traditional people . . . [We] realize that only the flesh has been

Wounded Knee itself, since the end of the siege, had become a virtual ghost town. The Government's use of heavy weaponry, and their eventual takeover of the village, had caused a great deal of destruction there. Only some ten families were still living in their original homes. Many of the residents had no place to stay other than a fenced-off compound of trailers in Pine Ridge provided by the Tribal Government.

Ninety-year-old Stella Bear Shield, who stayed in Wounded Knee during the siege, talked about the village to some people who visited her in mid-May. She spoke in Lakota, and Ellen Moves Camp translated her words:

She said they lived in Wounded Knee all their lives. They have land there. Ever since Wounded Knee happened, the pigs — — the goons, marshals — came in and burned down all the grass on their land, burned their home down, even throwed her boy in jail. And *afterwards* — what more do they want? She said they were in there without eating, because they wanted something. Now that her boy's out and he's at home, the goons have been after him. They been hitting him, beating him up and they even took shots at their home.

The arbor at Fools Crow's camp.

She said before 1934 their living was good. They didn't have relief, but they always had something to eat. Nobody fought each other — everybody was good to each other. Ever since 1934, the BIA buildings and Tribal office went up in Pine Ridge, and from there on everybody was fighting each other and nothing's good. And they're still living on rice and beans and that's all they have.

These are the things that are happening on our Pine Ridge Indian Reservation. These are the things that caused Wounded Knee. It's because our Indian people here — the ones that live way out in the country — they do have a hard time. They don't have no income — what little income they do have, maybe it's $19 a month.

I know Stella. I went to her home a good many times [as a Community Health Representative] — made home visits to her. There was times she didn't have sugar, salt, or bread. If we had an extra dollar in our pocket we'd give it to her. If we could, we'd buy them what they needed and take it out to them.

And it's getting worse. Our people on the reservation — it's time that we have to fight for them. We can't quit — we got to keep fighting in order to get what we want. Because these people — our Indian people — are not going to be left out any more. If I have anything to do with it, they're not going to be left out.

On May 17, several hundred people gathered at Chief Fools Crow's camp in Kyle for the long-awaited treaty meetings with the White House representatives. Present were many Oglalas, as well as traditional spokespeople from the seven other Teton Sioux reservations, and the other Indian nations that signed the treaty — the Cheyenne and Arapaho — and other guests, including a delegation from the Iroquois Six Nations Confederacy. In an attempt to intimidate local supporters, Dick Wilson's "goon squad" and BIA police established a roadblock on the road to Fools Crow's and required people to identify themselves before being allowed through. Despite this, a crowd had gathered by early on the morning of the 17th. Also present at Fools Crow's camp were several dozen U. S. Marshals, there presumably to protect the Federal visitors.

It was early afternoon before the White House emissaries landed in their helicopter. They came hours late because they had stopped first in Pine Ridge to meet with Dick Wilson, apparently to reaffirm Washington's support for the "duly elected government of the reservation."

Most of those in the Federal team were middle-level functionaries from the Justice and Interior Departments, including Charles Soller, acting Associate Solicitor of Interior's Division of Indian Affairs; Craig Decker, a trial attorney with the Land and Natural Resources Division of the Justice Department; Leslie Gay, chief of the Tribal Government section of the BIA; and Bobbie Greene Kilberg, attorney and former White House consultant. They were led by Bradley Patterson, an assistant to White House counsel Leonard Garment.

The May 5 agreement had guaranteed that "representatives of the White House" would be sent to Kyle — as a recognition of Oglala Sioux sovereign status. The chiefs were concerned that the delegation sent had neither the knowledge to discuss the 1868 Treaty and its violations nor the authority to make any commitments for the Government. So at first they refused entrance to four of the delegation, while they questioned Patterson, the delegation's head, and the only one actually working on the White House staff.

Patterson: At this time, Mr. Chief, I would appreciate it if my associates could join me here.

Matthew King: Before we start our negotiations, Mr. Fools Crow would like to ask one question with a simple answer, yes or no.

Chief Fools Crow speaks in Lakota, and Matthew King translates his words:

"Today I met one of the good representatives of the Government. I want him to take a good look at me and my mother earth. This is my country. I want to ask him a simple question: Can we be reinstated back to the 1868 Treaty? We're going to prevent all the time we could waste with that simple question. I want Mr. Patterson to say yes or no on this matter. Can we be reinstated back to the 1868 Treaty?"

Patterson: That's right, this is the letter which Mr. Garment gave on May 4, and as you remember, it said we will come here to meet with you for the purpose of examining the problems concerning the 1868 Treaty. Now, what is your specific question? Is your question, "Can we, can the five of us, rewrite the treaty?"

Matthew King: No. We want to be reinstated. The treaty-making period was cut off by introducing the Indian Bureau in its place. We want to be reinstated back to the 1868 government.

Patterson: When you say the Indian Bureau, what you mean is that in 1934 you had the Indian Reorgan —

"We are not asking for the negotiation of new treaties. We are merely asking that the treaties that already exist be enforced . . . Unilateral action by the Congress and the States cannot destroy the natural elements of sovereignty . . ."

U. S. Government representatives at Kyle; Bradley Patterson is at left.

Matthew King: — No, 1871. 1871.

Patterson: Well, the 1871 — which are you talking about, the —

Matthew King: Before that we was a nation.

Patterson: Yes —

Matthew King: — making treaties with the United States.

Patterson: Right. Act of Congress —

Matthew King: — and we were a self-sustaining people.

Patterson: Right.

Matthew King: And we got along with that period of time. And after 1871 the Bureau was introduced and the Government says, "Well, you're not supposed to make any more treaties with the Government," and they practically forced in the Indian Bureau. Now, we want to be reinstated back to that period of time, and be a self-governing nation.

Chief Fools Crow, holding a peace pipe, opens the meeting with a prayer.

Patterson: I understand. Well, I'll give you the answer. In 1871, the Congress passed this law which said as you described. No one in the Executive Branch, even the President if he were standing here personally, can change that law. The only way that law can be changed is if the Congress changes it itself.

Matthew King: If the Government could change the law in '71, when our treaties were the supreme law of the land, he could change it again.

Patterson: The Congress can change it. Now the chief should understand that a committee from the Congress is planning to come here to hold hearings in a few weeks. And since only the Congress can change the law, you may well want to present your case to the Congressional committee at that time.

Now there are questions which I am sure you may have about the treaty, about the agreement of April 5, about the things that are taking place here pursuant to that agreement. And I would at this time like to invite my colleagues here, who

can answer to some of those questions in detail. Since they are the other White House representatives, I would appreciate if they could join me.

Vern Long, President of the Oglala Sioux Civil Rights Organization: Our chief just asked you a simple question, yes or no, on the 1868 Treaty.

Patterson: I think I gave you an answer.

Vern: Yes or no answer —

Patterson: Only Congress can change the law of 1871.

Vern: In other words, you're just here — and then promises, promises, and you'll go back and that's the end of it!

Patterson: I'm here precisely as the agreement of April 5 said I would be here, to listen to your concerns about the 1868 Treaty. So I'm anxious to do that and my colleagues are anxious to listen with me, and we are able to answer some of your questions also. I would like them to join me —

Vern: In the past 100 years, the same thing you're doing to our ancestors, you're doing it today. You listen, listen — promises, promises! What do we get?

Patterson: I said the Congress is another branch of the Government besides the President, and some of these things —

Vern: All we want is a simple answer — yes or no.

Patterson: I think I have answered it, I really do. Now if you're talking about other things, for instance civil rights, you remember the April 5 agreement said that there is an investigation about civil rights practices —

Vern: That's not the question. We just asked you a simple question.

Patterson: I *would* like to bring my colleagues in. They have come all the way from Washington . . .

Although the Oglalas were angry at what appeared to be a deliberate snub to their claims of sovereign status, the chiefs finally decided to admit the other representatives to the meeting, and hear what they had to say. Throughout that afternoon, the U.S. delegation gave speeches on their fields of expertise, ignoring the fact that the Sioux were challenging the entire framework of U.S.-Indian relations.

Using a brightly colored map, Carl Decker lectured about the loss of Indian lands since 1868; Leslie Gay explained the Howard-Wheeler Indian Reorganization Act and reminded the people that, "in the eyes of our Government, the Oglalas are under this law." He also said that the petition to call a referendum on a new form of government for the Oglalas, on which supporters of the Wounded Knee occupation had gathered 1400

Mrs. Fools Crow encounters several of the marshals at the water pump.

*signatures, had been rejected by Interior Department Solicitor General --
and former negotiator -- Kent Frizzell, despite the fact that that figure
was more than the required one-third of the voters in the Oglala Sioux
Tribe. Frizzell's office ruled that for such a referendum the people
would have to acquire the signatures of one-third of the eligible voters,
rather than those registered to vote, and also questioned the submitting
of signatures of those between the ages of 18 and 21, even though they
are permitted to vote now in Federal elections. [In 1968, a referendum
was approved by the Secretary of Interior after called for by a petition
with 800 signatures.]*

*The next morning, May 18, the U.S. delegation and the several hundred
Sioux returned to the meeting site under the arbor. Matthew King, a
long-time treaty rights leader and Chief Fools Crow's interpreter, opened
the meeting.*

We believe that nature is god, and god is nature.
We have to live by nature.
Before the coming of the white man
we were alone in this vast country.
No one to depend on,
we found our way in life.
There was no known crime, there was no "Indian problem."

When the white man first came into our country
we welcomed him.
We helped them —
in fact, they wrote back,

"We have met some people here who have
a wonderful country, and they're easy targets,
and we will take it from them.
We will take everything they have away from them."
So right from the beginning they showed their gratitude
in that way.

We gave them food, we gave them medicine,
we gave them everything we have —
corn, potatoes, beans.
We gave them clothing — buffalo robes and bear robes —
made them comfortable.
But as they grew in power they cut us down,
little at a time.
That was their gratitude.

This is the first time in the history of our Oglala Sioux
since 100 years ago
that we get together and demand what is rightfully ours.
We waited for the white man to take action
as he has promised. He never did.
And I'm very sorry that we used violence to be recognized.
That was the only thing the white man recognized.
We are not that kind of people.

We made treaties since 1789,
over 180 years ago.
We waited all that time for the Government.
So today we are here, to present our case —
a hearing at least.

I want to tell you a few words of that great chief, Red Cloud,
during the Fort Laramie treaty.
Red Cloud walked out, he didn't want to have
nothing to do with the treaty. He didn't want to sign.
They caught him, they brought him back to the tent,
and they asked him why.

He said,
"You are a white man —
I am an Indian.
You want me to change my ways to that of yours.
But you have to give me a long, long time to do that.
Because first I'll have to learn to lie.
Then I'll have to learn to be greedy.
Then I will go to other people's homes just like
it belonged to me, and take things away from them."
These are some of the words that Red Cloud spoke
to the delegation at Fort Laramie.

Throughout the day, Indian people spoke to the Government representatives about their many concerns relating to the 1868 Treaty. Foremost was their demand for the establishment of a treaty commission composed of representatives of both the President and the concerned Indian nations —instead of, as Patterson had suggested, taking their "grievances" to Congress.

The people at Kyle also demanded protection of Indian water and mineral rights guaranteed in the treaty; for a referendum vote by which the Sioux could choose whether they wished to remain under the BIA Tribal Governments or return to the independent, traditional forms; and for the U.S. to live up to its responsibility under the treaty to prosecute whites who harmed Indian people on treaty lands — such as the murderers of Wesley Bad Heart Bull and Raymond Yellow Thunder. They also made clear that Wilson's administration was continuing its reign of terror.

Bob Burnette, a former Tribal Chairman of the Rosebud Tribe, and an AIM supporter, told the officials, "We have to have these changes or there will be Wounded Knees after Wounded Knees after Wounded Knees in various ways." At the end of the day, the Indians asked to hear from the Government representatives what they felt they had learned in the meetings.

Patterson: The White House representatives are not themselves a treaty commission. They have come to listen to your views. We've had an earful. Some of it has been humorous, some of it has been insulting, some of it has been tragic — all of it I think has been serious and sincere.

I've heard you speak about the problems of the 1868 Treaty, but I have heard you so much more speak about more immediate problems, about what I would call "fairness" in Tribal Government. Fairness in the government under which you exist. And for while I hear you tell me certainly about the 1868 Treaty and about fairly and thoroughly enforcing that treaty, what I hear you telling me even more clearly is, "Why can't we have a fair and just Tribal Government here?" Now this seems to be a question that Indian people throughout the country would raise — "Are Tribal Governments fair?" Now you are perfectly well aware that this is raised about the Government in Washington all the time. But that's what you're telling me, that you've got to have here, as we have in the rest of the United States, a political process.

Mr. Patterson's associates answered the question, too.

Bobbie Kilberg: I think when you're talking about fairness in government, you're also talking about form of government, and I think part of what I've understood in the past two days is what you're saying is that as long as the form gives you a highly centralized power in a tribal chairman, be it Mr. Wilson

or anybody else, you come to despair of having that fairness which that form cannot give you . . .

Onondaga Chief Oren Lyons stands by some of the U.S. Marshals who came to "protect" the Federal representatives.

"Now we've got Dickie Wilson's goon squad running up and down the street — they don't do anything to them because they're Dickie's goons. That includes my nephews, and two of my sons. And all these things, where can we go? I go to the FBI and the Superintendent. They say, 'Those are internal affairs.' So does Mr. Abourezk. 'Those are things you've got to straighten out yourself.'

Two of my granddaughters were abducted night before last by two of these goon squad — and they're so scared, they're afraid to tell. Now that's a shame, and I'm embarrassed in telling it. But you've got to know these things from the grassroots, from the people it happened to."

— Ethel Merrival

Ethel Merrival, an attorney who practices in the tribal court at Pine Ridge.

Patterson: I'd like to ask my colleagues Mr. Decker or Mr. Soller if they'd like to respond in any way in response to your questions to them.

Craig Decker: My friends, I have listened to you for two days now also, and I think I have learned a lot, and been touched by many of your thoughts. I don't agree with all of them, but some of them I do agree with. One of the things I agree with is the fairness situation. Now if it's unfair now, it should be changed. It should be fair and a representation of the people. Now that's what our Government's supposed to be based on. Our great President Abraham Lincoln said so. That this is a Government of the people, by the people, and for the people. We do not have that here presently. It's got to change. It's got to change by a lawful way.

Patterson: I suppose you are going to boo me for this, but if you want me to speak with a forked tongue, I'll speak differently, but I do not think you do. I could not speak to you honestly from the White House if I were to tell you that the

President would look on the prospect of more Wounded Knees with any equanimity. That is not the way the Indian people or any other people in our society are really in the long run going to get any real progress. It raises enmity. It gets the President mad, it gets Congress mad. It gets the American public mad, in the long run. And I could not be here among you and near that place with any implication that we are here because of that, or that we in any way condone that . . .

Many of the Indians were angered by these comments. Oglala attorney Ramon Roubideaux and Irma Rooks, an Oglala from the reservation community of Wanblee, spoke back.

Ramon: I think I really should rise to point out an instance or two where I don't think you've been listening. In the first place, I don't see how you could keep from arriving at the conclusion that we have a dangerous, explosive situation here on the Pine Ridge Reservation, a situation that demands *immediate* action. Between now and November when the primary

"It's not a father and son agreement, in a treaty. He calls you his children — you're not his children. A father has the right to reprimand his son, but a brother doesn't have the right to reprimand his brother. A brother doesn't have to have his brother's permission to do something in his own territory.

"I have a wampum belt with me that is part of our understanding, the Iroquois people. This wampum belt is called the sentok, the two row wampum. It represents the white man's government, as one row. It represents the Indian government — the way the creator gave to us, our way of life — as the other row. They never come together. The creator didn't mean us to come together. He gave us our way, and when we deviate from that, we become weak."

— Lloyd Elm

Onondaga Chief Lloyd Elm, one of the visiting Iroquois delegation, speaks to the meeting.

election [for Tribal offices] is held, I guarantee you that if nothing is done, you're going to have on your hands the deaths of several people on this reservation. I don't think there should be any doubt in your mind that there's been a total breakdown of Tribal Government on this reservation. The abuse of Indian people is continuing. It's an *emergency* situation, and if you didn't get that out of this meeting, then I don't think you've been listening.

Irma: Mr. Patterson, yesterday I talked about, you know, the BIA and the Tribal Council and how it was affecting us. They didn't help us, they didn't solve our problems, they didn't even help us educate our children — everything concerning the BIA and the Tribal Council *doesn't show me shit!* What took place in Wounded Knee is that *we don't want* Tribal Council, we don't *want* BIA. We want our 1868 Treaty!

Ramon: Let me tell you something, Mr. Patterson, to explain this a little better. Right now, we have pending a divorce action between the Indian people and the Bureau of Indian Affairs. The grounds are extreme cruelty. And what bothers me is that *we* know the marraige has ended, but you don't know it. And those of your colleagues who are in the Interior Department have talked continuously for two days about changes you're going to make in Tribal Government — in other words — to patch up the marriage. But we want you to know the marriage is dead.

Patterson and his colleagues left for Washington with a promise to return to Kyle in two weeks. So on May 30, several hundred traditional people of the Teton Sioux again met at Fools Crow's. But instead of a personal delegation, a U.S. Marshal delivered a written statement from White House Counsel Leonard Garment. In response to the Oglala's primary concern, a Presidential Commission to review the 1868 Treaty, he wrote, "The days of treaty making with the American Indians ended in 1871, 102 years ago . . . Only Congress can rescind or change in any way statutes enacted since 1871, such as the Indian Reorganization Act . . .

Insofar as you wish to propose any specific changes in existing treaties or statutes, the Congress is, in effect, a Treaty Commission."

So now the White House was saying that creating a Treaty Commission was not within the power of the President — as Chief Executive — even though the Justice and Interior Department spokesmen, themselves part of the Executive Branch, had negotiated on that very demand in trying to settle the confrontation at Wounded Knee. Kent Frizzell's words in the earlier negotiations rang hollow now — "We'll get you that treaty meeting with the White House . . ."

The Sioux at Fools Crow's wrote back to Leonard Garment:

Dear Mr. Garment:

We have received your letter dated May 29, 1973, and it has caused great anger and dismay among the members of the Teton Sioux Nation . . . Evidently, those who represented you during the May 17-18 meeting must have thought they were dealing with ignorant Indians who knew nothing about the facts of law as they exist between the United States and Indian Nations . . .

We are well aware of Title 25, Section 71, of the United States Code [the 1871 Act Garment had referred to]. But let us remind you that we are nevertheless a treaty-making nation. We have made many treaties with the United States. The language in the section which states, "but no obligations or any treaty lawfully made and ratified with any Indian nation prior to March 3, 1871, shall be hereby invalidated or impaired," is still in full force . . .

We are not asking for the negotiation of new treaties. We are merely asking for the treaties that already exist to be enforced. . .

"Between now and November when the primary election is held, I guarantee you that if nothing is done, you're going to have on your hands the deaths of several people on this reservation."
— Ramon Roubideaux

Unilateral action by the Congress and the States can not destroy the natural elements of sovereignty which include but are not limited to self government, minerals, water, hunting and fishing rights in the western half of South Dakota . . .

In the coming years you will find greater resistance to the Government's unresponsive rules, regulations, and its so-called "policies." Our forefathers died protecting this land, and we would be cowards if we continue to allow the federal, state and local governments to continue racial and cultural genocide against us and our Indian brothers and sisters across this continent . . .

Ellen Moves Camp.

"I will stand with my brothers and sisters. I will tell the truth about them and about why we went to Wounded Knee. I will fight for my people. I will live for them, and if it is necessary to stop the terrible things that happen to Indians on the Pine Ridge Reservation, I am ready to die for them. But the judge and his lawyers must know by now I will never lie against my people, crawl for a better deal for myself. I stand with Russell Means, Gladys Bissonette, Carter Camp, Ellen Moves Camp, Clyde Bellecourt . . ."

— an affidavit presented to the court on June 27, 1973
by Pedro Bissonette

AFTERWORD

May, 1975

Ramon Roubideaux's words at Kyle proved to be prophetic. By the winter of 1973, 6 Wounded Knee sympathizers on the reservation had been killed. In the winter of 1974, people began to talk about "the murder of the week." By spring, 1975, there were two a week in a reign of terror — bad before the occupation, but worse now.

Immediately after the occupation, Federal Marshals and FBI agents remained on the reservation for months. Their "law enforcement" seemed selective — AIM complaints went unnoticed; AIM members were the first to be arrested. Finally, in March, 1975, things had become so bad that the U.S. was forced to act — BIA personnel were "reassigned" and a special task force was sent to take over. A grand jury was convened. A series of murders and the beating, allegedly by Dick Wilson and the goon squad, of a group of white lawyers, had finally been too much.

On October 17, 1973, BIA police shot and killed Oglala civil rights leader Pedro Bissonette. Pedro was to have been one of the key defense witnesses in the Wounded Knee trials. Shortly after the end of the siege, while still in jail on $150,000 bond the highest in the Wounded Knee cases — Pedro came to trial on a charge predating the occupation. He was offered probation on his own case if he would turn state's evidence and testify against the American Indian Movement leaders indicted for Wounded Knee. He was threatened with a 90-year jail sentence if he refused. Shortly thereafter Pedro's case was dropped, on grounds of Government misconduct. Pedro's testimony was

to be used by the defense to prove gross Government misconduct in its own courts. But he never lived long enough.

In the agreement to end the siege, the Government promised to investigate the Tribal Government, to curb the terror on the reservation, and to reexamine the 1868 Treaty. But no action has been taken. Criminal and civil investigations may have been undertaken by the U.S. Government, but only misdemeanor charges have been lodged against seven members of the tribal government or its supporters as a result, and that in early 1975, two years after the occupation. The Senate's Indian Affairs Subcommittee held hearings in June, 1973, in Pine Ridge, but took no action. As for the promised Treaty Commission, the meetings to which the traditional Teton Sioux leadership came so hopefully in May, degenerated into a meaningless exchange of correspondence from Washington, D.C.

But the Government has not been sitting back quietly. It is still on the offensive against the American Indian Movement and its supporters. According to a conversation with one of the marshals a few weeks after the stand-down, the elite Special Operations Group [SOG], which had surrounded the village, was slated to be expanded in size by more than half again. Since then, a squad of BIA policemen drawn from reservations all over the country has been trained in riot control at the so-called U.S. Border Patrol Academy, in Los Fresnos, Texas, where the U.S. Agency for International Development trains Latin American police officers in "counter-terror techniques." This BIA group will be called together at the scene of any future confrontations between Indian people and the U.S. Government.

Meanwhile, the Justice Department launched a judicial attack on the Wounded Knee participants. Court actions were brought against more than 300 people on charges stemming from Wounded Knee and the Custer demonstrations which preceded it. Fewer than half this number were brought to trial. Most of these cases ended in either dismissal or acquital. There have been only ten or so convictions to date — and most trials revealed that it was the U.S. which had acted illegally, not the native people. Still, there are some trials still in process, and it may be a year or more until the final box-score is known. It was the largest and most complex mass trials in the history of the U.S., but like the occupation itself, little was said in the media, and readers of this one book now know more about Wounded Knee than 99% of the U.S. population.

26

Yet, the court became a forum for the same issues that were brought out at Wounded Knee. The defense challenged the U.S. Government's jurisdiction over Indian people, and showed how the situation at Wounded Knee was caused by U.S. violation of Sioux treaties. The defense also exposed illegal activities on the part of the Government both at Wounded Knee and in prosecuting the trials — false arrest, illegal wire-tapping, lying by FBI agents, paid informers, illegal use of the military. The charges against Russell Means and Dennis Banks were dismissed for these reasons.

With the dismal showing of the U.S. in court, it is clear that the U.S. will not be able to defeat the growing movement for native American self-determination, which Wounded Knee helped to spur.

The Oglalas, like Indian people all over this continent, have a history of resistance to oppression that leads from Crazy Horse to Pedro Bissonette. They have a strength that the Government cannot wish away, or destroy.

People say the Indian movement will not end at Wounded Knee — that it will go to New Mexico, or Montana, or Oklahoma, or any of the many, many places in North America where Indian people live. And these issues affect everyone, not just Indians, because they deal with the misuse of the land and of the people, and the dictatorial methods of government that have been placed over them. There was a prophecy quoted in Wounded Knee, that "when the red man will begin to unite, all other races will join with him."

Now that the native people have found something they believe in so strongly they are willing to commit their lives to bringing it about, they ask the question of other residents on this Mother Earth who are concerned about future generations of children. What do you believe in so strongly that you are willing to commit your life to bringing it about?

WOUNDED KNEE CHRONOLOGY 1868-1973

1868	The U.S. sues for peace after losing war with the Sioux. Fort Laramie Treaty signed. "Great Sioux Reservation" established, with hunting grounds covering seven states.
1871	Congress declares Indians to be "wards" of the U.S., to be administered by the Bureau of Indian Affairs.
1875	Dept. of War orders all Sioux to come into the reservation centers. Declares all others to be "hostiles."
1876	General Custer sent to bring in the Sioux bands hunting in the Big Horn mountains. Battle of the Little Big Horn — Custer's defeat. U.S. illegally seizes Black Hills from the Sioux.
1888	Congress passes Dawes Allotment Act to divide up Indian lands.
1889	Remaining Sioux lands divided into five reservations. Pine Ridge allocated to the Oglalas.
1890	Ghost Dance at Pine Ridge. Sitting Bull murdered. Wounded Knee massacre.
1934	Congress passes Indian Reorganization Act, creating "tribal councils" responsible to the BIA.
1950s	Federal policy of termination of Indian tribes and relocation of Indian people to the cities.
1968	American Indian Movement founded.
1970-71	Occupation of Alcatraz Island by "Indians of all tribes."
April 1972	Richard Wilson takes office as Tribal Chairman at Pine Ridge. (see chronology page 15)
Nov. 1972	Occupation of Bureau of Indian Affairs building, Washington, D.C.
Nov.-Feb. 1972-1973	Oglalas organize to impeach Wilson. Wilson calls on U.S. Marshals and FBI for support.
Feb. 1973	Oglalas call on American Indian Movement for support.
Feb. 27	Oglalas and AIM supporters liberate Wounded Knee.
Feb. 28	Marshals and FBI surround the village with armored personnel carriers. Wounded Knee begins setting up a defense.
March 1	Oglalas in Pine Ridge demonstrate in support of the people in WK. Larry Casuse killed in New Mexico. Shooting between marshals and occupiers of WK.
March 2	Senators McGovern and Abourezk visit WK. More marshals and FBI agents arrive.
March 3	Armored personnel carrier overruns Oglala bunker. AIM member DeSersa's home firebombed in Pine Ridge.
March 4	Ralph Erickson of the Justice Dept. arrives for negotiations. Makes offer.
March 5	Press allowed into WK for the first time. First volunteer medical team arrives.
March 6	WK rejects Erickson's offer. First air-drop made to WK.
March 7	Tribal Chairman Wilson threatens to attack with "900" men. Erickson issues ultimatum. 40 people hike in at night. Sporadic firing all night.
March 8	More APCs brought in. Govt lifts deadline. Firefight — two people wounded in WK.
March 9	20 people arrested hiking into WK. (89 arrested so far.) Gunfire in evening.
March 10	Govt lifts blockade of WK. Victory ceremony held. More supporters come into the village, including Oglala chiefs.
March 11	Independent Oglala Nation declared by chiefs. Four Govt. agents caught inside Wounded Knee. FBI agent wounded.
March 12	Govt roadblocks go back up. Grand Jury convenes in Sioux Falls to investigate WK. Provisional govt formed in WK.
March 13	Govt negotiator Harlington Wood begins negotiations. Tribal Council passes resolution banning all non-Oglalas from reservation. Graciano Juaraqui, WK supporter, killed in Rapid City.
March 14	Blizzard. APCs move in closer. More firing. Grand Jury hands down 31 indictments for conspiracy, burglary, civil disorder, etc.
March 15	Blizzard continues.
March 16	5000 people march in support of WK in Denver. Porcupine community center raided by U.S. Marshals.
March 17	Louis Martinez killed in Denver. Wood presents surrender plan to WK. Govt positions fire on WK for three hours. Medic wounded.
March 18	Oglalas reject and burn Wood's proposal.

March 19 Independent Oglala Nation citizenships given out. In Pine Ridge, Oglalas present Interior Dept with petition calling for referendum on tribal constitution, signed by 1400 Oglalas. Iroquois Six Nation delegation arrives.

March 20 Sporadic shooting at WK in morning and evening. Trading post meeting reports on demonstrations around country. Yuwipi (peace pipe) ceremony at night. BIA police arrive from other reservations to support marshals.

March 21 Another firefight. Another snowstorm.

March 22 Ghost Dance. Wounded Knee Legal Defense/Offense Committee formed. Another firefight at night.

March 23 Iroquois delegation leaves through roadblock.

March 24 Sporadic night shooting. Fuel in Catholic church runs out. APCs move closer.

March 25 More firing throughout the night. WKLDOC members obtain court order allowing them to bring in food and medicine.

March 26 Remaining network press forced to leave WK. Wilson sets up roadblocks. Govt initiates most intense firefight to date. Marshal Grimm wounded. Banks and Means go to Rosebud Reservation to find support.

March 27 All-morning firefight, heaviest yet.

March 28 Rapid City negotiations fall through.

March 29 Wounded Knee general clean-up. Night barbecue.

March 30 Govt agrees to negotiate on the 1868 Treaty.

March 31 Six-day series of negotiations begin in WK.

April 1 New volunteer medical team refused entrance by Govt.

April 2 Evening meeting — 70 new telegrams of support read. Kitchens serving one meal a day.

April 3 Nine-man pack team arrested hiking out. People are leaving in expectation of an agreement.

April 4 APC moves in on Wounded Knee's Manderson roadblock.

April 5 Independent Oglala Nation and U.S. negotiators sign agreement. Firing breaks out at night.

April 6 Snowstorm. Means, Bad Cob, and Crow Dog in Washington.

April 7 April 5 agreement breaks down.

April 8 Govt calls off preliminary treaty meeting in Washington.

April 9 APCs near WK again. Vigilante roadblock up again, supported by FBI. Traditional chiefs, just returned from United Nations, come into WK.

April 10 Some shooting into WK.

April 11 First child born to the Independent Oglala Nation.

April 12 Wedding in WK.

April 13 John Hussman manning the vigilante roadblock. Gives press conference claiming to be "Wounded Knee resident."

April 14 Justice Department's Community Relations Service blocked at Hussman's roadblock.

April 15 Govt. refuses ION request for discussions. Snipers fire into the village.

April 16 First large group of people hike into WK since signing of April 5 agreement.

April 17 Air drop. Day-long firefight. Clearwater fatally wounded and three others shot.

April 18 Fourteen local Oglalas run Federal roadblock.

April 19 Snowstorm.

April 20 ION medicine man and negotiator Leonard Crow Dog returns from from Washington and hikes back into WK. Govt stalls on ION requests for negotiations.

April 21 U.S. Marshals move their Manderson roadblock 300 yards closer to Wounded Knee.

April 22 Rosebud support march begins.

April 23 Shooting into WK. WK bunkers fortified. Vigilante (Tribal) roadblock arrested by U.S. Marshals.

April 24 Vigilante roadblock goes back up. Vigilantes and marshals engage in a firefight.

April 25 Frank Clearwater dies in Rapid City.

April 26 Vigilantes provoke most serious and last firefight of siege, lasting late into the night.

April 27 Firefight resumes early morning and continues until mid-afternoon. Buddy Lamont is killed.

April 28 Negotiations begin in WK.

April 29 Trading post burns.

April 30 Oglala chiefs meet with people in WK to discuss negotiations.

May 1 Agnes Lamont enters WK to discuss her son's funeral. More Govt personnel and helicopters arrive in Pine Ridge. Clearwater buried at Crow Dog's on Rosebud Reservation.

May 2 Chiefs and ION meet with Govt negotiators.

May 3 Negotiations.

May 4 Buddy Lamont's wake in Porcupine.

May 5 Agreement signed.

May 6 Buddy Lamont's funeral in WK.

May 7 Half the people have left at night. Approximately 150 still in WK.

May 8 Stand-down of arms. Evacuation of WK. 146 people bused out to Rapid City by U.S. Marshals, after "processing" at RB-1.

May 9-10 Arraignments in Rapid City.

May 17-18 Meetings with "White House representatives" in Kyle.

May 30 Meeting planned between Oglalas and Govt. White House sends letter instead.